Knowledge Work and
Knowledge-Intensive Firms

ONE WEEK LOAN

Knowledge Work and Knowledge-Intensive Firms

Mats Alvesson

OXFORD
UNIVERSITY PRESS

OXFORD
UNIVERSITY PRESS

Great Clarendon Street. Oxford OX2 6DP

Oxford University Press is a department of the University of Oxford.
It furthers the University's objective of excellence in research, scholarship,
and education by publishing worldwide in

Oxford New York

Auckland Bangkok Buenos Aires Cape Town Chennai
Dar es Salaam Delhi Hong Kong Istanbul Karachi Kolkata
Kuala Lumpur Madrid Melbourne Mexico City Mumbai Nairobi
São Paulo Shanghai Taipei Tokyo Toronto

Oxford is a registered trade mark of Oxford University Press
in the UK and in certain other countries

Published in the United States
by Oxford University Press Inc., New York

© Mats Alvesson 2004

The moral rights of the author have been asserted
Database right Oxford University Press (maker)

First published 2004

All rights reserved. No part of this publication may be reproduced,
stored in a retrieval system, or transmitted, in any form or by any means,
without the prior permission in writing of Oxford University Press,
or as expressly permitted by law, or under terms agreed with the appropriate
reprographics rights organization. Enquiries concerning reproduction
outside the scope of the above should be sent to the Rights Department,
Oxford University Press, at the address above

You must not circulate this book in any other binding or cover
and you must impose this same condition on any acquirer

British Library Cataloging in Publication Data
Data available

Library of Congress Cataloging in Publication Data
Data available
ISBN 0–19–925934–8
ISBN 0–19–926886–X (pbk.)

1 3 5 7 9 10 8 6 4 2

Typeset by Kolam Information Services Pvt. Ltd, Pondicherry
Printed in Great Britain on acid-free paper by
Biddles Ltd., King's Lynn Norfolk

Preface

I HAVE worked in the field of what can loosely be termed know-ledge-intensive organizations for over fifteen years. I started with an ambitious case study of a medium-sized IT consultancy company. It was more or less chance that I studied this organization: my major interest at the time was to develop cultural understand-ing of organizations, and I at first treated the case study primarily as a means of developing theoretical ideas. Later on I decided that the broad set of organizations doing mainly 'knowledge-intensive work' and/or dominated by professionals seemed to be an appropriate empirical and theoretical category to con-centrate on. It raises interesting and timely questions about a variety of important issues such as management versus autonomy, and is considered to be of great and increasing social and economic importance. There seems to be a good mix of variation and similarity among firms in the field, giving scope both for in-depth case studies exploring unique features of different organizations and also for making comparisons and developing synergy effects through comparing and confronting cases.

Having studied the IT consultancy firm, I became involved, with co-researchers, in very intensive case study research on advertising agencies, followed by work on a large management consultancy firm and a large science-based company. This book draws upon and to some extent reports findings and ideas de-rived from these studies. However, I also draw substantially on other research, so that the book is primarily a broad review of some key themes in the fields of knowledge-intensive firms and knowledge in organizations, introducing and developing a par-ticular theoretical perspective.

The ambition is to break with some of the conventional wisdoms of the fields. Many readers are likely to find the text provocative. For me, a major research ambition is to investigate critically and to problematize prevailing ideas and lines of reasoning.

Parts of the book draw upon articles previously published. Chapter 3 is to some extent based on 'Organization as Rhetoric: Ambiguity in Knowledge-Intensive Companies', *Journal of Management Studies*, 30/6 (1993), 997–1015. Some ideas from 'Knowledge Work: Ambiguity, Image and Identity', *Human Relations*, 54/7 (2001), 863–86, surface in Chapters 5 and 9. Minor parts of Chapter 6 have appeared in 'Social Identity and the Problem of Loyalty in Knowledge-Intensive Companies', *Journal of Management Studies*, 37/7 (2000), 1101–23. Some parts of the paper 'Up-or-Out vs. Fun-and-Profit: A Study of Two Management/IT Consultancy Companies', Lund Institute of Economic Research, 2002, are summarized in Chapter 7. Chapter 8 varies themes addressed in 'Odd Couple: Coming to Terms with Knowledge Management', *Journal of Management Studies*, 38/7 (2001), 995–1018 (with Dan Kärreman). I am grateful to Blackwell's for permission to use the text from my *Journal of Management Studies* articles and to Sage for using the Human Relations piece.

This book has been possible through grants from the Research Council for Working Life Research (now Vinnova) and Jan Wallander and Tom Hedelius Research Foundations. Completion of some parts of the book took place during a period as a visiting researcher at the Said School of Business, Oxford University, in January to March 2003. I am grateful for this financial and institutional support.

I am also grateful to my co-researchers Dan Kärreman and Stefan Sveningsson for their excellent cooperation and for permission to reuse material from our joint publications.

I should also like to thank a number of colleagues who have read and commented upon the whole or parts of a draft of the book: Laura Empson, Royston Greenwood, Dan Kärreman, Ray Loveridge, Bente Löwendahl, and Tim Morris. In particular, Royston offered a detailed set of sharp and constructive comments and also pointed me towards North American publications that I had missed.

Mats Alvesson

Lund, Sweden
July 2003

Contents

Abbreviations

HRM	human resource management	KIF	knowledge-intensive firm
IT	information technology	KM	knowledge management
		PSF	professional service firm

Chapter 1 Introduction

THIS book aims to contribute to the understanding of two seminal themes: knowledge-intensive work and knowledge-intensive firms; and knowledge—in particular, social processes around knowledge—more generally in an organizational context. What these rather difficult concepts may mean will be explored in depth in the next chapter. For the moment I will just say that work and organizations that are knowledge-intensive revolve around the use of intellectual and analytical tasks, and are typically seen as requiring an extensive theoretical education and experience to be carried out successfully. Jobs are not highly routine and call for some degree of creativity and adaptation to specific circumstances. Examples of knowledge-intensive firms include management and IT consultancies, and high tech and R&D based companies. Lawyers, accountants, consultants, engineers, and scientists belong to occupations involved in knowledge-intensive work. 'Knowledge' is very difficult to define and delimit: like many other common terms, it covers everything and nothing. In a sense we need knowledge to make an appropriate handshake—at the right time and with the right pressure—as well as to send people to the moon. Over the course of this book my own view on the subject will become clear, but for now I will summarize it as an interest in the use of judgement backed up to a high degree by theoretical, intellectual knowledge—the kind of knowledge that professionals and other well-educated people are expected to rely on. Later I will delineate some complications around this conventional—some would say conservative—view.

The two themes of knowledge-intensive firms and knowledge are very timely—some might say opportunistic—and elicit great interest among practitioners as well as academics. Knowledge-intensive firms (KIFs) are expanding and are widely viewed as important. Of course, the term itself is not unproblematic, but broadly it relates to large firms employing substantial numbers of people working with complex tasks that call for autonomy and the use of judgement, possibly rendering traditional forms of control inadequate or only partly relevant. 'Knowledge' and 'knowledge management' are very popular terms at present. Are we facing yet another fashion, one in an endless line of attempts by pop-management and academic writers to convince their readers that we have now got it right—that knowledge is the key to excellent business practice and a satisfying working life? Given the title and the theories of this book, you may conclude that I too am an advocate of this view—but I have doubts. This book expresses these doubts and avoids the self-conviction of those who have seen the light.

The two themes of the book overlap and the idea is that explorations of one should support the study of the second. Knowledge in organizational contexts can be studied productively in the domain of KIFs, where we ought to find many good examples of it. And one good entrée to KIFs is through themes such as knowledge and knowledge management.

However, the two themes cannot be reduced to one other and the book does not confine itself to knowledge in KIFs. The KIF theme goes well beyond a focus on knowledge: there are many other interesting features of knowledge-intensive work and organizations than those captured by the term 'knowledge'. Complex social and political processes, human resource management (HRM) themes such as motivation and retention, the problems of marketing and identity, are all issues that need to be considered outside the knowledge theme. We also need to consider and incorporate other vocabularies such as ambiguity, persuasion, image, and identity. The idea is to provide an understanding of the management, organization, HRM, identity work, and client relations of KIFs, and relate these to the theme of knowledge.

Knowledge also demands a review of ideas and insights more broadly than through studies within the KIF sector alone. Much of the literature on knowledge and knowledge management is, of course, general and theoretical, and not exclusively relevant to KIFs or professional work. Most empirical illustrations—and indeed the focus of this book—tend, however, to relate to KIFs and knowledge-intensive work, with some emphasis on professional service work such as management consultancy.

Some of challenging questions that I shall address are as follows:

- How can we describe the developments and the current significance of knowledge in the economy? Do we, in the most developed parts of the world, live in a knowledge economy, or is this hype? I shall address this question in this chapter.

- What are the characteristics of KIFs? How can we understand this type of organization and the role of management in them? Do standard dimensions and models work, or are KIFs so special that we need moderately or radically different ideas and vocabularies? Can we really make clear distinctions between KIFs and non-KIFs? Perhaps all companies are knowledge-based. Perhaps it is a mistake to assume that there is a point in addressing KIFs? I shall deal with this in Chapter 2.

- In the best of worlds, knowledge is based on truth and its application is a rational process leading to positive outcomes, problems being solved. But is it always or even typically so? We may even consider the opposite possibility: Can professionals create confusion? Perhaps knowledge can create problems? Chapter 3 will discuss the ambiguities of knowledge work, in terms of inputs, process, and outputs.

- It is frequently said that we live in an age characterized by the importance of images and brands more or less disconnected from 'objective qualities'. Can businesses and work based on specialist knowledge concentrate on delivering substantive results, carefully assessed by rational and knowledgeable customers? More on this in Chapter 4.

- It is often said that networks and networking are crucial. In KIFs this is probably truer than in most other organizations, but how should we understand the nature of social links in this sector? Knowledge work, in particular in the service sector, is intangible, and it is hard for a client to know what he or she will get in return for often very high fees. Purchasing knowledge is a risky business, and it is not easy for KIFs to market and sell it. Issues of trust, relationships, and networks then enter the picture. Chapter 5 will elaborate on this theme.

- What are the characteristics and challenges of management of KIFs? Can qualified people working autonomously and dealing with complex issues be managed? If so, in what sense? Do qualified professionals really 'need' management? Or is management mainly a service and coordination function? These and many other issues will be targeted in Chapter 6.

- It is often said that employees are the key resource in KIFs, so a crucial issue is to recruit, retain, develop, and motivate personnel. Are there common ways of solving this problem, or do organizations vary in how they approach HRM? Do they use the same or different models of 'human resources'? I shall address this theme in Chapter 7.

- The very idea of knowledge management promises the rational use and reuse of knowledge, but can knowledge really be managed? This is a key question of Chapter 8.

- It is often said that we live in a turbulent and complex social world, where identities of people are no longer given, but have to be achieved. Is this valid also for people in KIFs or other organizations doing knowledge work? Extended education, high status, and membership of a profession would automatically produce a solid identity, one might assume. Or are there threats and challenges to these identities? Chapter 9 will address the possible shakiness of identities in contemporary business and working life as well as managerial efforts to regulate the identities of their employees.

Many other themes will also be treated, but these are the dominant themes of this book. Before moving on, I will briefly address the first, as it forms much of the background to the issues discussed here.

The Claimed Significance of Knowledge in Companies and in the Economy

Few people seem to doubt that knowledge is of the utmost significance for contemporary business and working life. Organizational practitioners, consultants, business journalists, and academics all highlight knowledge and competence as a key dimension in management and organization. The expansion of higher education in most wealthy countries—many of which have set a goal where half the population will take a university degree—is in line with this emphasis on knowledge (or alternatively, with the desire to give the impression of taking knowledge seriously).

Authors report that the locus of organizational exemplars has shifted from capital-intensive industries, such as steel and automobiles, to information-intensive industries, such as financial services and logistics, and now towards innovation-driven industries, such as computer software and pharmaceutical companies. In the last, knowledge, and the ability to apply it, i.e. competence, are seen as vital. Many researchers take it for granted that 'the foundation of industrial economies has shifted from natural resources to intellectual assets' (Hansen *et al*. 1999: 106) and that the 'knowledge factor becomes increasingly important...and will gradually take over the influential position previously enjoyed by real capital' (Ekstedt 1990: 21). Teece (1998) says that 'many sectors are animated by new economics, where the payoff to managing knowledge astutely has been dramatically amplified' (p. 55).

A similar development is portrayed by Clegg *et al*. (1996), according to whom the 'new paradigm' of management means that core competence drives product development and that the 'tacit and local knowledge of all members of the organization is the most important factor in success, and creativity creates its own prerogative' (p. 205). Other authors talk about the need constantly to fuel employees with new knowledge (Wikström *et al*. 1993). Business has simply become more knowledge-intensive. It is claimed that, in order to generate, bring in, apply, and exploit knowledge in production processes, goods, and services, new forms of organizing and new relationships with suppliers and customers are needed. These authors suggest that we see the company as a 'knowledge system'.

Many people thus want to single out knowledge as the key to current and future business. Davenport and Prusak (1998) are in no doubt that 'the powers of knowledge...are precisely those needed in a rapidly changing, increasingly competitive global economy' (p. 14). Knowledge built into an organization's culture and into people's ways of thinking and doing things in a company cannot be easily copied and is thus the resource that potentially provides real competitive advantage, we are repeatedly told. The 'knowledge-intensive or knowledge-based firm', the 'knowledge economy', and 'knowledge management' are key terms for understanding contemporary business and working life, it is claimed.

This interest in knowledge is related to ideas on novel organizational forms or modes of organizing that involve 'post-bureaucratic' features. Management and organization literature is full of claims about radical breaks with earlier organizational principles and logics. These overlap and fuel a strong interest among organizational practitioners and academics in highlighting knowledge as a key dimension in management and organization (e.g. Davenport and Prusak 1998; Spender 1996). Large, integrated, machine-like organizations emphasizing mainly productivity have given way to more mixed, flexible organizational virtues, it is claimed. 'Modernist' organizational principles—division of labour, hierarchy, mass production, large size—have lost ground. As summarized by Lee and Hassard (1999) 'the coherent bulk of the large organization, once a source of pride, now appears one of strategic, operational and frequently financial embarrassment. This is the era of organizational networks, strategic alliances, "factories within factories", outsourcing and business process reengineering' (p. 394).

It is argued that society has entered a new era, where the epochal shift lies in the turn from stable to turbulent markets and rapid technological change, particularly in information technology, and to a focus on uncontrollability, chaos, flexibility, and disorganization. As Parker summarizes this view: 'The structures that we have been used to since the industrial revolution are fragmenting into diverse networks held together with information technology' (Parker 1992: 9).

All this means, it is argued, that organizations are transformed into more flexible, ad hoc forms, greatly reducing hierarchy and allowing more space for the initiative and discretion of knowledge-able employees so that these 'intellectual assets' can be used effectively. A large body of authors claim that the entrepreneurial orientation of highly qualified personnel is more and more central to the operation of companies. According to Miles et al. (1997), for example, certain trends have characterized organizational evolution for quite some time. First, more and more organizational members are expected to develop the ability to self-organize around operational marketing and partnering tasks. Secondly, there has been an increase in the number

of personnel expected to perform entrepreneurial tasks—
identifying customer needs and then finding and focusing resources on them. Thirdly, opportunities have increased for
members to experience psychological ownership of particular
clients, markets, customized products and services, and so on.
This trend has reached its peak in what Miles *et al.* refer to as 'the
cellular organization'. This differs from the network organization
in that it lends itself to sharing not only explicit know-how that
cells have accumulated and articulated, 'but also tacit know-how
that emerges when cells combine to design new customer solutions' (1997: 16).

Cellular organizations are said to call for 'a bold managerial
vision and, even more importantly . . . a unique managerial philosophy' (Miles *et al.* 1997: 17), including an emphasis on investment in human capabilities and a willingness to take substantial
risks to maximize their utilization. Risks arise because returns on
investment are difficult to predict and not everyone whose skills
are enhanced will remain with the firm. The biggest challenge 'is
not just the investment required to build key competencies; it is
the willingness to allow the levels of self-governance necessary to
fully utilize that competence' (p. 18).

Of course, a lot of this discussion concerns knowledge and
competence in very general and vague ways, and is somewhat
outside the knowledge concept of primary interest in this book,
but it is still relevant to note the broad emphasis on knowledge as
a key factor in the economy and working life.

That a large majority of academics, consultants, and business
journalists make claims of this kind does not mean that we must
necessarily accept them, at least not without reservation. While it
is tempting to join the chorus of people confidently portraying a
clear economic development, in my view much of this talk is
exaggerated and ill founded. There is probably an equally strong
case for the continuing expansion and economic significance of
less grandiose occupations and organizations than those associated with the concept of the knowledge-intensive. As Thompson
et al. (2001) argue, it is likely that key growth areas will be in low-
level service occupations such as waiter, security guard, cleaner,
and health or care assistant, as much as or more than in the
knowledge-intensive sector. The transport industry is also huge
and hardly diminishing. In many service occupations, and in

significant parts of the manufacturing sector formal education and intellectual skills are of less interest to employers than the social competences and aesthetic qualities (appearance) of employees (Thompson *et al.* 2001). The rationalization of large parts of the economy, organizations, and work tasks leads Ritzer (1996) to talk about the 'McDonaldization of society'. The competence of personnel is perhaps one of the most vital sources of competition, but companies are busy reducing this resource through rationalization, outsourcing, and temporary employment: 'taking employees out of the organization or diminishing their attachment to it is a growing trend' (Pfeffer 1994: 22). If this is correct, there are perhaps limits to the presumed significance of knowledge. Companies at least do not wholeheartedly emphasize it over factors such as training, development, and experience for large groups of people. Knowledge and competence are important, but so are rationalization and cheap labour. It may be misleading to say that knowledge has simply become more important than labour.

A sign of the increasing significance of knowledge may be the expansion of consultancy businesses. This is a strong trend, but it is not necessarily a sign of a general increase in the number of qualified jobs. This expansion and the increasing size of consultancy firms in many fields, in particular management and IT, may partly be an effect of rationalization and downsizing affecting middle management in client companies. Getting rid of large numbers of middle managers means that relatively well-qualified employees and competence are lost, and that consequently the need for consultancy services to add managerial power becomes strong. To some extent we may say that jobs for qualified employees move from regular employment to employment in consultancy firms. That the latter category is visible does not mean that it is representative of a broader trend in terms of increased need for qualified labour ('knowledge workers'), but only that these are organized differently in the contemporary economy.

It is important that an interest in knowledge-intensive work and organizations does not reinforce the myth of a general increase in knowledge-intensiveness among (post-)industrial societies and organizations. Powerful groups including corporate managers, occupational representatives, pop-management writers, and politicians, are eager to promote this myth of companies, workers, and societies as increasingly advanced and knowledgeable, and it is seen as not far from being politically incorrect to question a bright future in which the knowledge society creates the good working life for a very large part of the workforce and motivates the uptake of university courses for up to half the population. Some years ago I wrote a letter to a Swedish newspaper referring to US forecasts predicting the growth of jobs in the mass service sector. The Minister of Education responded, saying that my 'thesis belonged to the ideological junkyard'. The idea of knowledge workers employed in KIFs in a knowledge economy is certainly appealing for most people, but one must be careful about regurgitating ideologically seductive ideas. Unfortunately, many publications, including academic ones, do so.

Despite this reservation, there are good reasons for taking knowledge-intensive work and firms seriously. One can do so without exaggerating their scope, significance, or future expansion. Perhaps 10–15 per cent of the entire workforce in western Europe and North America work in knowledge-intensive fields and this may increase to 15–20 per cent in a decade or two (Thompson *et al.* 2001). Knowledge-intensive work is a substantial part of all organizations and its economic significance may be greater than these figures suggest, as they frequently influence the practices of other organizations through the development and diffusion of ideas, technologies, and standards for operating (Greenwood *et al.* 2003). Certainly this very large sector is more than enough subject matter for a single book and there is no need to emphasize that knowledge-intensive organizations are, or soon will be, dominating the economy and working life in terms of absolute numbers.

The possibly 'real' trends within work and organizations, as well as the frequency with which ideologically appealing but questionable truths are spread, motivate an interest in the phenomenon. The rationale of this book thus includes

- frequent testimony of the rise and expansion of knowledge work and KIFs as an important and increasingly significant phenomenon calling for improved theoretical understanding;
- the need to critically assess testimonies and ideologically loaded accounts of the trends and characteristics of this kind of work and organizations.

Knowledge issues sound 'good' and are rhetorically appealing, but there are traps involved in much thought and writing on these issues. The frequent discussion of the knowledge economy, the centrality of knowledge work, and the highly positive contributions of KIFs express not so much important facts as a set of popular ideas and/or a dominating ideology. Taking a close look at these ideas and claims made by the various actors who refer to them is an important task for research. However, while a fair dose of scepticism is surely desirable, one should not throw the baby out with the bathwater.

The Recent Interest in Knowledge-Intensive Firms

The increasing interest in knowledge-intensive firms (KIFs) reflects at least to a reasonable degree the growth and significance of this sector of the economy. This interest overlaps the general interest in knowledge in organizations. Although knowledge is said to be universally significant for companies, its role clearly varies between companies. When authors deal with knowledge at work or knowledge management, they very commonly pay particular attention to, and take examples from, KIFs. One reason for the increased attention paid to KIFs as organizations is the rapid expansions of management and IT consultancy firms and the increased size of many KIFs. Many firms have expanded from being based in a specific profession to broaden their range of services to include a variety of occupations such as auditors, IT people, tax specialists, and consultants (Suddaby and Greenwood 2001). Today a number of international firms have more than 100,000 employees, such as the accounting (etc.) firm Price Waterhouse Coopers and the management (etc.) firm Accenture. This increase in size is partly a matter of expansion, e.g. in management and IT consultancy, partly an outcome of mergers and acquisitions, e.g. in the accountancy field. While professional and consultancy work has historically involved liberal kinds of activities carried out by individuals or rather small, loosely connected organizations—perhaps a few people sharing office and administrative support—the organizational dimension of much knowledge work has become increasingly significant. This is also the case for groups such as university teachers and doctors, who increasingly work in and are subordinated to large bureaucracies (Reed 1996).

The idea of the KIF as a specific, increasingly significant category differs to some extent from the idea of a general increase in the significance of knowledge in organizations. The idea of singling out the former as a key category is based on the assumption of a clear difference between knowledge-intensive and other firms, thus downplaying the idea of a more universal significance of (advanced) knowledge in the corporate world. The point of talking about something as knowledge-intensive is that there are a lot of organizations and work that are not, so that the KIF as a fruitful category presupposes that many companies are not usefully considered as 'knowledge-intensive'. (All categories are valuable to the extent that they make productive distinctions possible, i.e. do not cover everything.) This of course does not mean that knowledge is not important in these companies, but there may be other and better ways and vocabularies for understanding key aspects of these not so knowledge-intensive jobs and organizations. Management and other employees may not devote a lot of interest in developing, sharing, and utilizing knowledge among broad groups of employees or see the intellectual skills or theory-based knowledge of candidates as key criteria for employment. There are a very large number of jobs where the employer would benefit little from employing bright students from top universities.

Of course, there is no contradiction between claiming the distinctiveness of the KIF group of organizations and assuming a general increase in the relevance and level of knowledge, as long as there is a distinction (significant difference) between the knowledge-intensive and the rest of ('average') organizations. Even if a substantial number of this larger population of organizations should become less dissimilar to knowledge-intensive firms—and this is certainly debatable, as discussed above—it may still make sense to take an interest in this particular group, although care should be taken not to exaggerate its exclusiveness. As we shall see, part of what is distinct for KIFs revolves around features other than the degree of knowledge-intensiveness. In this book I shall examine many such features, a key one being a high degree of ambiguity, addressed at some length in Chapter 3.

The Purpose, Thesis, and Style of the Book

This book sceptically, sometimes even critically, addresses some aspects of the claimed significance of knowledge in contemporary organizations. It is easy, however, to be caught in abstract and superficial discussions if the object of inquiry is not sufficiently delimited. Through concentrating on so-called knowledge-intensive firms we pick up on organizations that can most strongly be said to be exponents of the trend.[1] Of course, this category is still fairly broad and one must be careful not to over-generalize from it. Arguably, taking a closer look at some cases within this loose category offers a good entry into investigating some key dimensions of knowledge work and the management of it. Also in regard to high tech, R&D based, or professional service firms (PSFs), knowledge is said to be the key issue—to a much greater degree than in most manufacturing and (mass) service work. It is not very meaningful to try to address knowledge on a general level covering all sectors of business or working life: understanding knowledge calls for a focus on a particular version of knowledge and careful appreciation of context. In order not to spread myself too thinly I concentrate on business organizations and, in the main, refrain from addressing public sector work and organizations such as health care and universities, and professions, such as medicine, the clergy, and dentistry.

KIFs may be seen as exemplary and a good vehicle for understanding some key aspects of knowledge in organizations and for exploring its significance and meaning. Arguably, knowledge themes are more salient in the work in these settings. This is not to neglect the fact that knowledge may be said to be a key part of any job and organization and that without it only the simplest of

---

[1] The term 'intensity' is used in this book to refer to the significance of a particular dimension for the actors involved and/or the analytical relevance and power of a concept for the researcher in her effort to understand the specific setting addressed. Knowledge-intensity, ambiguity-intensity, image-intensity, etc. thus indicate the salience of a particular phenomenon (set of qualities or characteristics), the productiveness of addressing that phenomenon in a nuanced way or of ambitiously exploring it, in order to manage and cope with, or study, business, organization, and work.

As with all terminology, mine is neither precise nor innocent. It constructs reality in a particular way, illuminating certain aspects and preventing others from being considered.

activities can be carried out. Similarly, fairly repetitive jobs employing people with little formal schooling undoubtedly call for skills and the exercise of judgement (Tsoukas and Vladimirou 2001). These requirements can frequently be understood without necessarily invoking the concept of knowledge. My idea in this book is to use the concept of knowledge to draw attention to analytic, intellectual, theory-guided activities. I am not trying to argue that this is the true or superior form of knowledge, but am focusing on knowledge in this sense and the firms in which it can be assumed to be vital. Practical skills, the ability to use the body, and creative talents—crucial in art, crafts, and sport, for example—are not necessarily best understood in terms of knowledge, and particularly not as the term is used here. Perhaps this might be referred to as 'talent-intensive' work.

Of course, a precise treatment of a subject matter calls for even more specificity and focus than provided by the rather vague category of knowledge-intensive work and firms, but there is a point in working with this category. Arguably, taking a somewhat closer look at such organizations might give us the impetus to rethink claims about knowledge and perhaps identify alternative conceptualizations of knowledge and knowledge-intensity in management and organization studies.

- This book then aims to address the issue of knowledge in an organizational context and highlight some crucial aspects that tend to be obscured by the predominant literature on the subject, briefly reviewed above.
- In order to do so, but also as an objective in itself, a new theoretical understanding of knowledge-intensive work and KIFs is suggested. It takes ambiguity seriously, and explores the consequences of this quality for management, organization, and identity.
- This interest in ambiguity and the ways in which people in organizations relate to it—or deny it—is so significant that it merits the status of a third ambition of the book. And that is to contribute to an ambiguity-focused understanding of organizational life. Although this approach is particularly relevant to knowledge issues, it is in no way limited to this field and also is important to understanding management and organizations more generally.

This book thus takes a somewhat sceptical view on the dominant understanding of the nature and significance of 'knowledge' in contemporary companies, and in particular in KIFs. The text aims to be self-critical—to be aware of the problems and limitations of its own argument and vocabularies, confronting the favoured approach with alternative viewpoints and vocabularies, and realizing that there is more than one way of understanding the social and economic world. It is important to be modest and careful with claims that any particular way of grasping the issues addressed is definitive (Alvesson and Sköldberg 2000; Rorty 1989).

Having said that, I must add that my key point is relatively forceful. The overall argument looks like this: Knowledge is best used to refer to cognitive issues that are fairly complex, and often slippery and ambiguous, as is its role in what is constructed as knowledge work and the evaluation of work outcomes. Knowledge is of most interest considered in a situation of complexity calling for the exercise of informed judgement. Given this ambiguity, the management of rhetoric, image, and social processes appears crucial in organizations of this kind. We must look carefully at the claims of KIFs and professionals about knowledge, its use, and outcomes, and not take them as read. Difficulties in demonstrating and assessing competence and performance and the great dependence on giving the right impression make work identity difficult to establish at the same time as it becomes a key element in selling and doing knowledge work. Successful rhetoric, image production, and orchestrating social interaction then call for regulation of the identities of employees, as people need to have the 'right' subjectivity in order to convey credibly the impression they seek to convey. Of course, as with all arguments in social science, this view is more productive in certain situations and as applied to certain issues than others. No theories or ideas are useful or relevant in all instances. My view is that it says something sufficiently important about a substantial amount of knowledge work and KIFs.

This book is intended for academics and for students with a basic grounding in management or other social sciences related to employment, work, and organizations. It should be of interest to those specifically interested in knowledge in organizations and in

KIFs, but it may also be read as a more general text on management and organizations, addressing broadly relevant themes and using this business and organizational sector as illustrative. Knowledge, identity, image, client relations, and ambiguity are as important as those themes covered in conventional books giving a broad view of management and organization studies.

The Structure of the Book

The book is divided into ten chapters reflecting a particular argumentation. Some hints of the questions addressed in the various chapters have already been provided, but I will give here a more straightforward account of the evolution of the argument in the book. Having dealt with how we can understand knowledge-intensive work and firms in Chapter 2, I discuss in Chapter 3 sceptically dominant views on knowledge. The reliability, objectivity, and functionality of knowledge are questioned. So is the role of knowledge in the work of those supposed to be knowledge workers. The chapter also tackles difficulties in assessing the work results of knowledge workers and knowledge-intensive organizations. Because what knowledge work more precisely is about and how work results can be assessed are seldom obvious, image and reputation become very important as themes of concern and conscious acts, and this is the focus of Chapter 4. The current interest in brand names and images is an illustration of this point. Related to it is an interest in the significance of rhetoric in many, though not all, KIFs. Some standard forms of rhetoric in the consultancy industry receive attention. Chapter 5 looks at social relations and coping with social and political processes, and also touches on the marketing of professional services. Thereafter I address more conventional organizational themes such as the role of management and organizational control (Chapter 6) and HRM (Chapter 7). Chapter 8 concentrates on knowledge management, and in particular the problems of managing knowledge. Chapter 9 focuses on identity—to some extent organizational identity but especially the identities of personnel in KIFs. In particular the chapter examines how organizations try to regulate the identities of employees. The final chapter summarizes the book and develops a framework for understanding KIFs. Overlapping these objects of inquiry, but also taking a more general direction, is a proposed approach for an ambiguity-sensitive organization theory.

Chapter 2 On Knowledge-Intensive Firms

IN this chapter I aim to do three things: to define the characteristics of knowledge-intensive firms (KIFs), to review critically some key ideas on what are being institutionalized as professions and professional organizations, and to compare the category of KIFs with that of the profession (professional workers and organizations). This is necessary as the terms cover similar terrain, and are sometimes used in more or less the same way, but represent a somewhat different focus. I also discuss the virtues and problems of both categories, emphasizing that self-criticism and doubt about the major concepts one is working with are important.

Types of Knowledge-Intensive Firm: Professional Service Firms and R&D Companies

KIFs can be loosely and preliminarily defined as organizations that offer to the market the use of fairly sophisticated knowledge or knowledge-based products. The products may be plans, prototypes, blueprints, or mass-produced products where the R&D cost outweighs manufacturing expenditure. The core of activities in these companies is based on the intellectual skills of a very large proportion of the labour force deployed in development, and often also in the sale of products and in service work. A large section of the employees typically have an academic education and relevant experience. The significance of education is not self-evident. There are other routes to jobs in KIFs than a university degree, but there is a strong tendency for this type of organization to employ a large number of graduates. Formal education is seen as very useful as facilitating theoretical and analytical abilities essential to such organizations. Education may also be seen as something of an indicator of competence and as legitimizing expert status and high fees. Symbolic work—using ideas and concepts—is crucial, while the transformation of material objects or the carrying out of tangible services are typically not very significant. Theory-guided cognitive activity is important—or at least makes a difference—in more situations and for more people in a KIF than in other organizations.

People in KIFs are typically paid far above average salaries and have high status. They are sometimes referred to as gold-collar workers. In some companies there may be great disparities between different parts of the organization in terms of knowledge-intensiveness. A bank may, for example, have specialized units with several experts, while, at the same time, most of the organization deals mainly with routine tasks and here workers are typically less educated and less well paid. A pharmaceutical company may have a large R&D department with many employees with a doctorate, but also sales and manufacturing units of considerable size, making it important to realize that the idea of knowledge-intensiveness cannot be applied sweepingly to all parts of the company. Sometimes organizations are more than willing to emphasize or exaggerate their 'knowledge-intensiveness'. Pharmaceutical companies, for example, prefer to stress their science and R&D rather than their frequently very large sales and marketing units and costs. In order to make the term 'knowledge-intensive' applicable to a firm, the significance as well as relative size of its knowledge-intensive units must be substantial. In many corporate contexts, it makes more sense to talk about knowledge-intensive units than companies. In this book the term 'KIF' refers to organizations with large such units, and then mainly to those parts of the firms that are knowledge-intensive. Most of the ideas in this book are also relevant to understanding knowledge-intensive sections in companies that on an aggregated level are hardly seen as knowledge-intensive. These may be professional departments and work groups, e.g. a corporate law unit or a strategic planning group. Sometimes these units have organizational characteristics more similar to those of organizations dominated by their profession than to those of their employing organization as a whole (Wallace 1995).

There are two major groups of firms in this category: professional service and R&D firms. Typical examples of the former are law and accountancy firms, management, engineering, and computer consultancy firms, advertising agencies, and investment bankers. Examples of the latter include science-based companies such as pharmaceutical and biotech companies, and high tech companies based on engineering knowledge.[1] The trend is that large firms include several professions or areas of expertise, which means that it is sometimes misleading to describe these firms by way of a particular profession or function. Firms may, for example, combine auditing, tax advising, and management consultancy, although they often have one dominant area of work.

An important difference between the professional service and most of the R&D firms is that the former deal very much in intangibles and most of its professionals interact directly with the market (clients), while R&D companies typically produce a (tangible) product and the interface between its employees and customers is often narrower as contacts go through marketing units. Most R&D companies thus have division of labour between functions, which means that R&D sometimes becomes separated from marketing and/or manufacturing. However, sometimes technologically sophisticated projects involve close collaboration with clients, and here the division of labour is not so pronounced. Sometimes the product is not highly tangible, with knowledge expressed rather in the form of a design or a blueprint to be used or (mass-)produced by the client. The distinction between 'pure' professional service and R&D is not always so clear, since R&D work can be carried out on a consultancy basis. In professional service firms (PSFs), marketing, production, and development are often carried out by the same people. This calls for certain types of combination of skills and a tendency to be strongly client-oriented, sometimes at the expense of internal activities and long-term development.

The category of knowledge-intensive workers and firms overlaps with, and includes, the notion of professionals and professional organizations, but is broader and does not emphasize the features ascribed to a typical profession, such as a code

---

[1] Other companies may also be seen as belonging to the overall category of KIFs, e.g. health care and mass media companies. As most larger health care organizations in most countries belong to the public sector, I refrain from treating these. Mass media companies—newspapers, film production companies, publishers—are sometimes more talent- than knowledge-based, so they differ a bit from organizations in which formal, theoretical knowledge is central. I therefore address these only marginally and concentrate on the more typical sets of KIFs.

of ethics, standardized education, criteria for certification, etc. Many KIFs such as management and IT consultancies, pharmaceutical companies, and high tech companies are not necessarily best described as professional firms, at least not if one uses the litmus test that all or most of the traditional criteria of a profession should be fulfilled. (These criteria will be addressed in the next section.)

PSFs tend to be characterized by the relative homogeneity of the profession, the common knowledge base, and the strong significance of the profession for identification.[2] These features typically reduce variation between organizations within a particular industry dominated by the profession. Other knowledge-intensive organizations may have a more organizationally specific knowledge base and be more idiosyncratic (Morris and Empson 1998). In some examples of KIFs the characteristics of professions may be significant for the functioning of the organizations, but frequently some of the dimensions emphasized by the literature on professionals—e.g. code of ethics, restricted access or monopolization of work, emphasis on formal association and certification, and homogeneous education—are not very salient.

For example, in management consultancy work there is no regulated entry, standardized educational and further training, certification, or homogeneity. There are often elements that deviate even more sharply from what is typically considered as characterizing professions associated with the work carried out and the marketing of it. Almost all claims to professionalism rely on the assumption that the professional knows better than the client, and actions of professionals then supposedly typically involve a client moving, through the act of problem-solving, from a state of uncertainty and being riddled by a problem to one of harmony and security. But certain forms of management consultancy involve the creation of a problem—the perception of suboptimal, obsolete functioning—not as 'objective' or spontaneously discovered, but as actively and perhaps sometimes arbitrarily constructed by consultants. 'Consultancy is fuelled by their provision of a sense of reassurance to management and at the same time reinforcing or creating insecurities' (Sturdy 1997: 397).

---

[2] As I have said, sometimes they include more than one profession. Different parts can be characterized by different professions as sources of knowledge and identification.

An even more profound deviation from the more frequently proposed criteria for professionalism is the nature of management trends and fashions, which have little to do with science and validated practice. The premium on novelty, exaggeration, persuasiveness, and crude commercial and grand claims runs directly against the somewhat conservative, supposedly rational and sober practice of the recognized professions, relying on science and solid experience. The idea is to discredit established wisdom, and this is not a good ground on which to build a traditional case for professionalism. It would probably be misleading to accuse most management consultancy of creating insecurity as part of strong marketing involving selling new concepts, but there are clear deviations from conventional ideas of professionalism in, for example, sectors of management consultancy.

Characteristics of Knowledge-Intensive Firms

There seem to be a number of circumstances specific to KIFs as against other organizations in terms of the nature of the work and how it is managed and organized (e.g. Alvesson 1995; Deetz 1997; Løwendahl 1997). These include:

1. highly qualified individuals doing knowledge-based work, using intellectual and symbolic skills in work;
2. a fairly high degree of autonomy and the downplaying of organizational hierarchy;
3. the use of adaptable, ad hoc organizational forms;
4. the need for extensive communication for coordination and problem-solving;
5. idiosyncratic client services;
6. information and power asymmetry (often favouring the professional over the client);
7. subjective and uncertain quality assessment.

While the fifth and sixth characteristics are relevant mainly to knowledge-intensive and professional service firms, the others are equally valid for product-oriented knowledge work and organizations. Some of the characteristics overlap.

Knowledge Base

In terms of what type of knowledge is significant, many organizations emphasize knowledge embedded in techniques, rules, and procedures. KIFs to a greater extent revolve around knowledge based in the cognitive skills of personnel and rooted in the work culture as shared collective understandings (Blackler 1995).[3] Some commentators say that for 'knowledge workers, knowledge is simultaneously an input, medium and output for their work' (Newell *et al.* 2002: 14). Knowledge work—analysis, the exercise of judgement, and problem-solving—is thus carried out by the majority of the personnel and not centralized on a managerial or technocratic elite, designing systems and procedures for others to follow. In KIFs the division between conceptualization and execution of work is limited. There is not much space for management to establish a monopoly of intellectual work—in opposition to classic organizational forms, which build upon an extensive hierarchical division of labour.

As the very label 'knowledge-intensive' suggests, issues of competence are broadly viewed as the most significant dimension in this category of organizations. In KIFs, in particular, competitive advantage lies mostly in the effective use of human resources, it is argued.

The distinctive competence of a professional services firm is the skill of its staff and if those people can be obtained just as readily elsewhere, and if they have no attachment to a particular firm, then the competitive position is diminished. This is why many well-managed professional services firms emphasize recruitment, selection, and building strong cultures to retain the skilled employees who constitute the basis of their success. (Pfeffer 1994: 21–2)

A strong knowledge base and emphasis on competence development are thus key features of KIFs.

---

[3] Blackler, based on Collins, addresses five forms of knowledge: embrained knowledge is dependent on conceptual skills and cognitive abilities; embodied knowledge is action oriented towards and dependent on practical, intimate knowledge of a situation rather than abstract principles; encultured knowledge refers to knowledge about cultural meaning systems and is about reaching shared understanding; embedded knowledge is knowledge which resides in systemic routines and is related to technical and institutional arrangements; encoded knowledge is information conveyed by signs and symbols.

Autonomy

Knowledge work includes the exercise of professional judgement in the effort to solve complex, frequently unique problems. The individual knowledge worker (or team) is often in the situation of having the best general insights into the problem area as well as being the person (or team) with most familiarity with the specifics of the actual problem. Superiors may have more general experience and overview but have less understanding of what can and should be done in specific situations. Owing to the uncertainty and complexity of the work, means of 'distance control' such as rules or output measurements are often not so relevant. This means that the knowledge worker (or team) must have considerable discretion. Situationally relevant expertise may often carry more authority than formal position, so that knowledge work often makes an organizational hierarchical structure flexible and sidestepped by knowledge-based authority. Løwendahl (1997) says that 'expertise is multidimensional, is frequently not linked to seniority and administrative experience, and operational authority may be unrelated to hierarchical position' (p. 95).

The codes and expectations of the professional communities carrying out knowledge work also involve a high degree of self-determination and collegial relationships across hierarchical positions.

Organizational Forms

From an organizational and management point of view, a heavy reliance on self-determination, downplaying of a single, one-dimensional hierarchy, and the comparatively weak position of top management may lead to quite unconventional organizational relations (Alvesson 1995; Deetz 1998; Hinings *et al.* 1991; Kunda 1992).

Many knowledge-intensive organizations deviate more or less sharply from bureaucratic principles, although there are, as will be addressed later, important exceptions. The high degree of customization in PSFs and innovation in other KIFs make traditional management principles such as standardization, routinization, and supervision difficult to apply. This is not to say that these principles are absent in KIFs, but they typically play a less prominent role than in most other organizations: they are typically used more flexibly.

A move away from bureaucracy towards companies that are flatter, more networking, innovative, ad hoc, etc. is sometimes said to characterize organizations in general, but this does not rule out the fact that many KIFs may, to a much greater degree than many other companies, be organized around self-motivated and highly qualified individuals. From another, more sceptical position, one might say that the perhaps debatable claims of a universal development in the directions mentioned appear to be more relevant—or less irrelevant—in the case of the group of organizations discussed here. In other words, if one is looking for non-hierarchical, ad hoc organizations, then the category of KIFs should offer relevant examples.

Extensive Communication

These organizational forms and in particular their more or less unique, complex, and ambiguous tasks imply the need for extensive communication for the purpose of coordination and problem-solving. Of course, there are some areas and organizations where much work is carried out on an individual basis; for example, many lawyers work only with an assistant, and some consultancy work involving advice-giving and building on esoteric expertise is carried out by single individuals, but here also the need to create shared understandings and expectations with clients calls for a fair amount of communication. More generally, complex group work is common in KIFs. In project work the identities of those involved, in terms of how they place themselves or how they are placed in the division of labour, are often fairly open during initial stages. Work in ad hoc settings calls for mutual adjustment. Planning, rules, and methodologies that in detail prescribe how things should be done always play a role in work organizations, but to a lesser extent in many KIFs, which means that organic, short-term planning and replanning following gradual problem-solving and problem-encountering become salient. Deetz (1997) stresses that agreement on problem definitions and solutions requires active communication and negotiation. Even though there are constraints, 'employees frequently engage in role creation and negotiation to determine what needs to be done, how to do it, and their personal responsibilities' (p. 185).

Client Relations

In PSFs client relations are highly complex and call for a high degree of customization. This of course fuels the need for extensive communication. Client-centred work means that technical problem-solving and 'substantive' matters cannot be separated from social relations. The strong component of face-to-face interaction with clients is, according to Maister (1993), a key feature of professional service work, quite different from 'ordinary' service work, where interaction is limited in terms of time and complexity. In many product-oriented KIFs working on a mass market, e.g. many high tech and pharmaceutical companies, there are no specific client relations, although of course large retailers may be key customers. Frequently the distance between the market and the knowledge workers is very long, and only marketing and sales people deal with customers. In some KIFs producing a tailor-made knowledge product for a particular customer, e.g. a prototype or a complicated piece of equipment, the client relations may be important, although the company–client interface seldom resembles that of a consultancy team working at the client's site in close collaboration with the client personnel for several months in a joint project. Of course, sometimes the distinctions between service and product work and consultants and co-workers become rather meaningless.

Quality Assessments

Dealing with complex, unique problems often brings difficulties in assessing quality. In much R&D work there are lengthy periods of work where it is difficult to anticipate the result. In the pharmaceutical industry it frequently takes years before it is possible to assess whether an idea and line of development may become successful or not. In professional service work the often intensive interaction with clients and shared responsibility for problem definition, and also work on problem-solving, make projects difficult, which leads to major challenges of quality assurance—in terms of both the output of the project and the contribution of the service provider. I shall address ambiguities around performances and results in Chapter 3 as well as in later chapters.

Asymmetrical Power Relations

Sometimes the power asymmetry in the relationship to the client favours the professional organization owing to its knowledge and/or status in a specific area (Løwendahl 1997; Sharma 1997); at least, the notion of the professional expert indicates such an asymmetry—the carrier of esoteric expertise has by definition a knowledge-based position of superiority to the client. The client then becomes dependent and vulnerable. In many situations of professional business services, however, clients may be knowledgeable and powerful and have very clear ideas of how a consultant should be used, and here information asymmetry and power positioning may be unfavourable to the service provider. As the client is paying, there is frequently a financial asymmetry favouring the client and placing the PSF in a subordinate position. There may thus be different power asymmetries in different professional–client relationships that are important to consider. More about the asymmetries of relations in professional service work appears in Chapter 5.

Knowledge-Intensive Firms: Problems with the Concept

As I indicated in the Introduction, the idea of KIFs and related concepts such as knowledge work are valuable, but also in many ways problematic. Rather than try to convince the reader and myself that the chosen vocabulary offers a superior road to insights, as is common, I think we must try to consider how language use can trick us into false certainties and fixed meanings. It is difficult to substantiate KIFs and knowledge workers as distinct, uniform categories. We are not talking about a precise category that corresponds to something unique and unitary. Knowledge workers and KIFs have, on many points, a lot in common with many other organizations, and there is a lot of difference between, for example, an advertising agency and a pharmaceutical company. If we take any one of the seven characteristics just discussed, one can hardly argue that there is a strict demarcation line between all KIFs and all other organizations. Many KIFs do not fit all characteristics very well and many other organizations can to some extent be understood through these characteristics. The world is simply not structured in ways that make it possible to use categories that order it in an unproblematic way.

The distinction between knowledge-intensive organization or knowledge worker and those that have less of this knowledge quality is not self-evident, as all organizations and work involve knowledge. The concept is indeed difficult, as will be explored in the following chapters. The distinction may create or reinforce additional asymmetries in terms of prestige and power, to the advantage of those that can most easily make a case for being highly knowledgeable (Knights *et al.* 1993). The concept of knowledge-intensiveness is vague, especially if one not only considers formal, science-based knowledge, but also defines it broadly and includes more 'embodied' and 'encultured' versions of it (Blackler 1993).

It is important to reflect upon how words do not merely mirror reality, but construct a particular version of it. 'Objective' business and work reality do not stand in an one-to-one relationship to words, concepts, and proposed images, and it is not self-evident that we have a need for a concept or category of the 'knowledge-intensive' in management and organization theory— at least, not a need associated with a desire to mirror the 'nature' of contemporary organizations. Other kinds of desire may originate in wishes to launch new selling concepts by consultants and academics (see Czarniawska-Joerges 1988) or in wishes of managers and other employees in particular kinds of organizations to adopt concepts that help them in their struggle with identity and image problems (but not necessarily with more 'substantial' problems). The label 'knowledge-intensive' portrays certain organizations in ways that draw attention to certain characteristics, and away from others. It has effects in terms of status and legitimacy. As with so many other examples of language use, it is political. It is thus similar to the term 'profession' and may be equally attractive as a label worth striving for—although a difference worth noting is that 'professional' is sometimes used to indicate official status and the formally supported privileges contingent on it.

In Sweden, as in many other countries, the label 'knowledge company' has been very popular. This was partly fuelled by a bestselling book with that very title (Sveiby and Risling 1986). It is my impression that some Swedish organizations with rather shaky foundations in terms of both substance and status have been quick to label themselves 'knowledge organizations'. One example is that of a public organization that, in response to questioning about the rationale for its existence, tried to convince itself and its environment of its mission as a knowledge developer and diffuser (Ramfelt 1993). In another public sector organization, a child psychiatric clinic, people referred to their clinic as a 'knowledge company'. Although this was a public sector institution and very different from a business, the label 'company' did not seem to disturb its personnel. It is prestigious to be seen as 'knowledge-intensive', and many people want to present their organization in this way. People sometimes appear to feel insulted if their organization is not included in this noble category. The strong symbolic value of knowledge easily creates biases in discussions and should thus prompt scepticism about it. Intuitive appeal may be counteracted by careful reflection and healthy suspicion.

Nevertheless, there are, in many crucial respects, differences between many professional service, high tech, and science-based firms on the one hand, and more routinized service and industry companies on the other. Although there are many firms and other organizations in the grey area between machine bureaucracies and KIFs, it makes sense to use the KIF as a vague but meaningful category, with sufficient heuristic value to be useful. The category does not lend itself to precise definition or delimitation; it includes organizations that are neither unitary nor unique. It is actually common for popular terms to be vague and used in different ways. As one author reviewing the field of leadership research concluded, the only thing that people agree upon in their definitions is that it is about influencing (Yukl 1989). What 'strategy' signifies varies widely and is often unclear (Whittington 2002). The word is frequently used to refer to very different phenomena with very little in common (Mintzberg and Waters 1985). As will be explored below, the meaning of 'profession' varies widely, and there is a retreat from the earlier position of defining what a profession really is, making most uses of the label contestable. Terms such as 'strategy', 'leadership' and 'profession' are used in highly varied, often vague, and typically ideologically loaded ways. This does not, of course, mean that they are meaningless or that we would necessarily be better without them. We have to accept some uncertainty in the terms we are using to direct the spotlight in a particular way.

As students of language have pointed out, language does not mirror reality, it constructs particular versions of it. We have to use language that is not neutral or self-evidently productive of understanding. Hopefully, the use of the concepts of KIFs and knowledge workers has more positive than negative effects: it may focus attention and contribute to a better understanding of an important part of business and working life, and not simply overemphasize arbitrary distinctions between the knowledge-intensive and something else, thus supporting certain economic and political interests over others. Awareness of the problematic nature of all language use is as crucial as it is neglected in research (Alvesson and Deetz 2000). This book struggles with the dilemma and will in different ways try to confirm and respond to the insight that any inquiry and use of a vocabulary constructs the theme in a particular, and to some extent arbitrary, way. The choice of the key term—'knowledge work', 'professional work', 'symbolic analytical work', or 'gold-collar work'—is, for example, not self-evident. The selectivity, even bias, of any understanding produced by a particular choice of language and reasoning must be born in mind. Taking this into account—a part of a reflexive approach (Alvesson and Sköldberg 2000)—may frustrate some readers, as the text will become less straightforward and streamlined. It may be of some comfort to the reader that this is also frustrating for the author since it calls for more work and possibly fewer readers as the less patient fall away.

One key element in my approach is that it is perhaps *the claim to knowledge-intensiveness* that is highly distinctive of KIFs compared with many other (average) companies. So also is the broad expectation of the KIFs environment that knowledge capital and knowledge use are central to the firm's operations; i.e. the claim is on the whole accepted, although frequently with some doubt. A KIF is an organization broadly recognized as creating value through the use of advanced knowledge. The expectation of clients, the informed public, and people working in the company is that education, training, problem-solving ability, creativity, and intelligence are crucial parts of the work. This may seem like a circular definition, but the key point is social recognition and social construction—not knowledge as an objective fact. This aspect will be emphasized in later chapters.

Despite problems in clearly defining KIFs, the term encourages an interest that goes beyond the single case of, say, a pharmaceutical, IT, or accountancy firm, without aspiring to talk about organizations in general, loosely pointing to an organizational category about which one may say something interesting. In this book I try to do so, but also and perhaps in particular frame this treatment so that broader ideas of the significance of knowledge in contemporary organizations and working life are highlighted.

The book includes a review of a number of studies, in particular case studies, of KIFs. I shall also go further and challenge some of the ideas of the characteristics of these firms as suggested in the literature review above. The significance of knowledge is critically addressed, and a number of other candidates for capturing what is really crucial in firms of this kind are suggested. Given that the KIF category covers PSFs, the challenges are also valid for the latter group of organizations.

Professions and Struggles for Professionalism

Given my ambivalence about the advantages and problems of the concept of KIFs, the reader may wonder why I am not referring to professions and professional organizations instead. These are established categories and some readers may perhaps think that they do not include the problems of vagueness that the category of knowledge-intensive does. But the concept of profession is contested and problematic, and calls for further discussion for a variety of reasons.

'Professional work or organization' is sometimes used in a broad sense, as a synonym for 'knowledge-intensive work or organization'. It is difficult to avoid using the term 'professional' as it is employed so frequently and in so many ways. Sometimes it refers to an occupation (in contrast to the term 'amateur', or the category of people not characterized by the same profession), and sometimes it refers to all groups of employees belonging to higher strata in business life, e.g. above blue- and lower-level white-collar workers but below or outside the rank of managers. Sometimes it refers to a limited and elite selection of occupations that enjoy particular privileges, sometimes to a broader set of occupations. There are many views about which occupations qualify for this exclusive label. As Abbott (1991) puts it: 'because the term "profession" is more an honorific than technical one, any apparently technical definition will be rejected by those who reject its implied judgments about their favorite professions and nonprofessions' (p. 18). The diversity of opinions and frequent confusion about what is to be counted as a profession parallels the discussions of what is meant by 'knowledge-intensive'.

There are a number of more or less accepted criteria for a 'real' or 'true' profession:

- The occupation is based on a systematic, scientifically based theory.
- There is a long and standardized formal education.
- A strong professional association regulates its members.
- Members have autonomy in the sense that professional knowledge rather than bureaucratic position governs decisions and work within the professional sphere.
- A code of ethics is established by the occupation.
- There is a distinct occupational culture.
- There is client-orientation.
- The occupation is socially sanctioned and authorized.
- There are criteria for certification.
- There is a monopoly of a particular labour market through self-regulation of entry to the occupation.

If we apply all these criteria, it is probably only doctors and perhaps dentists, vets, and psychologists who would qualify as true professionals, while, for example, priests, accountants, and lawyers do not base their work on systematic, science-based theory. (This is not to deny that the disciplines of their education are scientific in one sense or another: my only point is that their occupations are very much based on social rules, norms, and traditions.) Sometimes researchers emphasize certification as a major criterion, which would limit the category of PSFs to law and accountancy firms. (I do not include health care organizations, which in most countries belong to the public sector and are generally not firms.) In some other groups certification is part of membership of associations, e.g. some engineering specialities, but far from all potential members join these, and the absence of this formal recognition does not make much difference to clients. Scientists, of course, do base their work on scientific knowledge, but there are no government regulations for who can work as a scientist, and there is in most cases no powerful formal association that regulates professional conduct. Management consultants and engineers would also fail on most criteria.

It is arbitrary where to draw the line between a profession and a non-profession. Often unfounded weight is placed upon official recognition, a professional association, and a formal code of ethics. In work practice these elements may not matter very much, at least not in business. There are also changes in what is supposed to be central to a profession, which add to the arbitrariness of where to draw the lines: 'The attributes which sociologists of the professions used to identify as the hallmarks of a profession, such as education, vocation, esoteric knowledge, self-regulation, and civility, have been replaced, or at least augmented, by an interpretation that stresses punctuality, style, dynamism, financial success and entrepreneuralism' (Cooper *et al*. 1996: 631).

There are good reasons for breaking away from a very strict notion of profession as the key category in many cases. The term can, for example, be used to illuminate organizations in which a large proportion of the personnel belong to a well-paid, high-status occupation with a longer education and sharing an occupational community but who are not formally regulated and sanctioned. It does not seem reasonable to see law and accountancy firms—the most commonly recognized professional businesses—as distinct from architecture firms, management, engineering, or computer consultancy firms in terms of most management, organizational, and work aspects. Of course, one can use the concept of a professional organization more widely than a traditional or strict definition of profession allows. Many have done so. Sharma (1997), for example, suggests that 'much like doctors and lawyers, professionals in advertising, banking and consulting apply in their work a body of knowledge and techniques acquired through training and experience, have a service orientation and distinctive ethics, and have a great deal of autonomy and prestige in the modern economy' (p. 763). It is common to refer to engineering, marketing, and other consultancies as PSFs. I have no problem with that, and will also, to some extent, refer to this category in this somewhat loose way.

Rather than expand the category of profession, it may be better to sidestep the problem altogether and use concepts like knowledge-intensive work and KIFs instead. This would preserve some integrity around the term 'profession' so that it could be used to analyse, for example, the existence and significance of regulation and monopolization of labour markets, certification of official status as a profession, as well as standardization and control of professional institutions. Arguably, the distinctiveness of a profession is closely tied to these themes, processes, and struggles around professionalization—i.e. the efforts to attain official status and control entry within a particular work domain. All the new 'professions' mentioned by Sharma are 'open' for anybody to enter: workers may be very diverse in terms of educational background, and the controls exercised by occupational associations or public institutions are weak compared with those imposed upon lawyers or doctors. Many of the mentioned key features of a profession are thus not particularly relevant to understanding most knowledge-intensive occupations and organizations.

An appreciation of the problems that beset the notion of professions and professionals in organizations is helpful not only in seeing the merits of exploring the idea of knowledge-intensiveness, but also in pointing out difficulties that the latter must address. There are many lessons for people interested in knowledge work and KIFs from contemporary debates within the sociology of professions.

Older literature, in particular, but even more recent texts, describe the professions in such a way that one almost suspects that the public relations departments of the professions concerned had produced them. The central role of science and knowledge, autonomy, the solving of problems vital to society, affective neutrality, and altruistic service to clients are often emphasized, creating an 'image of a largely autonomous, self-regulating and self-perpetuating institution, the altruistic members of which are filled with a desire to work for the common good in the most effective way' (Brante 1988: 122). Great care should accompany

any reiteration or legitimization of, for example, a profession's claim to have a code of ethics, at least if the claim is presented as meaning something more than just the existence of a written document. Such a code is worth noting only if it plays a significant role for the professionals, and even then, critical scrutiny of how the code works in practice is called for. (One can also, of course, look at the rhetoric of ethics or ethical codes as legitimization, but this means that one disregards its significance for professional practice.) Current views in the sociology of professions are far more sceptical of the claim that professionals are bearers of a higher form of rationality and morality than other social groups (Collins 1990; Fores *et al.* 1991; Selander 1989). Some more modern idealizing expressions depart from the rational model and emphasize uncertainty and creativity. Howard (1991), for example, claims that 'true professional work is creative, complex and unique, involves more art than science'. The counter-position is, as Mintzberg's (1983) concept of the professional bureaucracy suggests, that qualified professional work is very much a matter of adopting relatively standard procedures. Much of the claimed creativity involved stands in an ambiguous relationship to a strict notion of professionalism and its drawing upon a recognized body of institutionalized knowledge.

These statements of professionals about themselves, as well as, to some extent, researchers' (uncritical) reiteration of such statements, can be understood as elements in their strategies for achieving, maintaining, and improving the status of a profession. In line with modern sociology of professions, it is, rather, *claims* to have these particular traits which are proposed to motivate a specific social position and certain privileges, including a monopoly on sections of the labour market, that are worth investigating (Collins 1990; Torstendahl 1989). 'Essentialist' ideas, stressing the universal qualities of professions, have become increasingly unpopular, while an emphasis on professionalization strategies and processes, i.e. efforts to gain recognition as a profession, have come more into focus (Collins 1990; Selander 1989). Self-interest and efforts to attain social closure—excluding other people from the right to certain jobs or tasks—is crucial for professions. Professionalization is very much about politics and the struggle for status, power, and material reward. It is not so much the characteristics of the work in themselves, or the knowledge base of a profession or a candidate profession, but the ability to organize and mobilize the powerful political project of getting acceptance for the claims to special status that is of significance (Collins 1990).

Instead of the 'essentialism' of a profession, i.e. its 'true characteristics' in terms of which side of the profession–non-profession (or possibly semi-profession) fence it belongs to, its politics and rhetoric are put in the spotlight. An ethical code, for example, is sometimes better seen as a symbolic vehicle supporting the political interests of the profession by promoting its image as highly respectable and credible than as a set of norms that in practice ensure morally superior behaviour on the part of the professionals. This is not to deny that the code may have regulatory effects, reduce opportunistic behaviour, and sanction cases of it if detected, although sanctions seem to be rare. The ideas (or myths?) of technocracy, solid knowledge, altruism, rationality, and neutrality are seen as ideologies for justificatory purposes (Brante 1988). This kind of changing focus is relevant also for the broader study of KIFs and knowledge workers.

Having said all this, my point is not to argue against all the good work done under the label 'professional', nor to say that the concept of knowledge-intensiveness offers radically different insights, nor to celebrate 'knowledge-intensive' as a superior term. 'Knowledge-intensive' and 'professional' are overlapping terms, in many contexts synonymous, and I shall mainly treat them as such in this book, although 'knowledge-intensive' covers broader ground. I shall primarily use the term 'professional' when I am referring to PSFs or issues around the struggles or effects of official status as a profession. Except in the latter case (i.e. discussing official status and certification), I refer to professionals rather liberally and broadly, as a synonym for knowledge workers.

Some Specifics of Some Professional Service Firms

PSFs are generally distinguished by the fact that they provide intangible products encoded with complex knowledge and that these products are customized to each client's circumstances (Greenwood *et al.* 2003). If we take PSFs that score high on the professional scale—mainly law and accountancy firms—there are two distinct aspects where it is important to single these out as different from most other companies, including other professional knowledge-intensive service firms with a less coherent and distinct profession as a basis. One is in those cases where there is an occupational group that dominates the organization that has a very distinct professional identity and standardized ways of certification and of belonging to the profession, e.g. many law and accountancy firms. The profession may be a stronger source of identification and standard-setting than the employing firm. The professionals may encounter conflicts between profession and organization regarding loyalty and identity, although it is important not to exaggerate the inevitability or significance of such conflicts (Wallace 1995). The strong significance of the profession and profession-based forms of knowledge and standards for working may also reduce the scope for distinct organization-based knowledge and work methods. Organizations then become arenas for the professions to carry out their work rather than significant institutions developing and shaping specific, more or less unique practices.

The second important theme is relevant to professional firms based on the partnership principle. Greenwood *et al.* (1990) refer to these professional partnerships as p^2 firms. In these some employees, after a lengthy period of work in the firms, are promoted to partners, e.g. shareholders in the firm. Partners blur the traditional distinction between ownership, management, and productive work by simultaneously owning, managing, and being operational in client relations and project work. The options are typically restricted, the more so in a prestigious firm. Those who are not promoted are often expected to leave the firm. To become a partner is often a crucial issue for the individual as well as for the company. Much is at stake—to a very different extent than in promotion situations in companies where ownership and the symbolic meaning of becoming a partner and the distinction between partners and others do not enter the picture. Maister (1982) views this specific career and promotion situation within PSFs as something that perhaps more than anything else distinguishes the PSF from other types of organization.

The partnership issue is not as closely tied to the degree of professionalism of an occupation as its certification of organizations. Any kind of organization can, in principle, be based on a system of partnership, as many management and engineering consultancies are. Many professional firms—in particular those that are not certified—are not organized as partnerships. Partnership and the degree of institutionalized professionalization go together, however. Of the 100 largest firms in each sector 100 per cent of law firms, 56 per cent of accounting firms, 18 per cent of architecture firms, 17 per cent of management consulting firms, and no advertising firms were partnerships (Greenwood and Empson 2003). This distribution reflects the degree to which these occupations are supported by institutions and their broad recognition of professionalism.

With the increasing size of many partnership-based PSFs, the meaning of being a partner and the role of partner group vary compared to the traditional situation of all partners jointly making important decisions. When the numbers of partners can be counted in thousands, a high degree of centralization and a strong hierarchy among partners become necessary. Partners may then no longer be equals; more senior partners may stand well above junior partners, and the relationship becomes more similar to an ordinary organization. In large partnerships the pressure of performance targets and control mechanisms put some partners in a position of subordination and lack of autonomy and influence (Covaleski *et al*. 1998). Still, the differences remain. Partners in senior positions are dependent on the compliance of the other partners and need a majority to support them. They cannot get rid of the subordinate partners, who may typically insist on recognition of their own views. Partnership involves a strong element of colleagueship even in situations where the size of the organization and the large number of partners produce a hierarchy within the partner category. I shall address the topic of partnership further in Chapter 6.

Summary

In this chapter I have discussed the concept and characteristics of KIFs. It makes sense to talk about two broad sets of KIFs: R&D based companies and PSFs. Between, but also within, the sets there is variation, but also sufficient common themes to make the broad concept of KIFs useful. Complementary terms are 'knowledge work' and 'knowledge worker', which parallel—but are a bit broader than—those of 'professional work' and 'professional'. An advantage with the former terms is that they allow the term 'professional' to be used in a more distinct sense, including primarily occupations that score high on characteristics of professionalism.

I have compared the terms 'knowledge-intensive' and 'professional'. Recent literature on professions and professionalism has been reviewed, in particular the more sociological and sceptical literature emphasizing the struggles to attain the privileged position of profession rather than the essence of a 'true' profession. This literature differs from most organization studies, which tend to take the notion of a profession as given and reflecting some 'essential' characteristics. I have some preferences for the more sceptical view, although one should avoid a cynical position emphasizing mainly power, self-interest, and smokescreens. Scepticism includes taking seriously the political element in efforts to establish an occupation as a profession. This point is, of course, also relevant to firms that lay claim to superior knowledge or expertise: this is politically neutral neither in intent nor in effect. It is therefore vital to study critically these claims and not, as a large part of the literature does, take them at face value.

The category of KIF includes what is referred to as PSFs, and I shall use the PSF literature extensively, but the former category covers a broader field and is not so focused on whether a group or an organization is 'professional' (i.e. belongs to the 'true' or acknowledged professions). Of course, some of the specifics of the category of PSF receive less attention in this book owing to its broader aspirations.

In the chapter a number of characteristics that tend to be typical of KIFs (and of knowledge work) have been identified:

- the centrality of intellectual and symbolic skills in work, motivating the term 'knowledge work';
- that self-organization and dispersed authority are typically salient;
- a tendency to downplay bureaucracy in favour of ad hoc organizational forms;

- a high level of uncertainty and problem-awareness in team-work calling for extensive communication for coordination and problem-solving;
- that in professional service work client services need to be client-centred and situationally fine-tuned;
- complex problems and solutions involving considerable elements of intangibility calling for subjective and uncertain quality assessment;
- that the expert position (or claim to or belief in such a position) creates a particular power asymmetry between professional firm and client (often favouring the professional over the client).

Problems with the concepts of knowledge work and KIFs have also been addressed in this chapter. The category of KIFs is loose and vague, and it is difficult to find strict criteria separating it from that of non-KIFs. The seven mentioned characteristics tend to be more relevant for understanding KIFs than other firms, but this type of firm has no monopoly on, for example, autonomy at work or subjective quality assessment and far from all work in KIFs is autonomous, while there are of course cases where quality assessments are viewed as clear and straightforward. These claimed characteristics can't be taken as given but call for critical investigation before being applied to specific instances. Still, there are fairly strong tendencies for KIFs to be characterized by these characteristics. In the final chapter I shall come back to the list and see what can, perhaps, be added to it.

I have also emphasized that key terms in social science—and in other areas—do not stand in a one-to-one relationship to something 'out there'. This is perhaps obvious when we use slippery words like 'knowledge', but upon reflection we may realize that the use of other popular terms does not score better. Our efforts to capture and represent what we are interested in are always problematic. This stems partly from the nature of social reality—it is not patterned and ordered as neatly as it may seem—and partly from language use, which cannot mirror reality but always constructs the world in a specific light. The appropriate response to this includes modesty, self-criticism, and tolerance of ambiguity. This does *not* imply the need for over-cautious and constrained research approaches that say very little about how complicated matters are and how vocabularies may conceal as much as they reveal. Theoretical boldness and strong statements are often to be preferred: they do not exclude self-criticism and doubt regarding the framework and line of interpretation used.

Chapter 3   Knowledge: Questioning the Functional View

TAKING ambiguity seriously into account encourages a slightly different understanding of knowledge than is promoted by conventional views. In this book this means a new theoretical framework for thinking about knowledge and knowledge work. Ambiguities are the central consideration when addressing knowledge, the significance of knowledge in relationship to other elements, and results claimed to be contingent upon knowledge work.

Knowledge—at least in the context of the business world and management studies—is normally treated as a functional resource, representing a 'truth' or at least something instrumentally useful on a particular subject, and/or a set of principles or techniques for dealing with material or social phenomena to produce the desired outcome. This view reflects somewhat dated ideas and calls for critical scrutiny. Important issues here concern the all-embracing and sometimes empty character of many conceptualizations of knowledge (and talk about it), the contestable nature of a large proportion of knowledge, and the question of the possible effects of knowledge.

Knowledge: Everything and Nothing?

Knowledge is celebrated as the clue to corporate performance in current and future business. The problem is that enthusiasts have great problems in theoretically defining knowledge or empirically describing it. Grant (1996), for example, in outlining a knowledge-based theory of the firm, modestly says that 'all I offer beyond the simple tautology of "that which is known" is the recognition that there are many types of knowledge relevant to the firm' (p. 110).

The influential resource-based view, which emphasizes the core competence of companies as central to their performance and strategic work (e.g. Prahalad and Hamel 1990), typically black-boxes knowledge and competence, confusing input, transformation, and output (for a critique, see Scarbrough 1998). People agree that core competence is important, but to actually identify it with any precision is very difficult.

In some ambitious empirical studies the black-boxing of knowledge and competence is avoided in favour of in-depth description. A problem here—at least in the context of the resource-based view and other efforts to capture broader organizational patterns and strategically important dimensions—is that the research often focuses on specific, localized examples of what particular workers do and how they think and interact (e.g. Cook and Yanow 1993; Sandberg 1994; Tsoukas and Vladimirou 2001). These studies illuminate what people carrying out a particular task do, but are informative about work tasks rather than broader organizational patterns. In very small and homogeneous organizations the work task and the whole organization go together (Cook and Yanow 1993), but in complex organizations taking seriously the knowledge in operation when carrying out work may lead to a focus on a limited part of the core competence of the organization. If the concept of knowledge is used to illuminate what people and work groups do, it becomes something completely different from what people in the strategy field have in mind when trying to capture the unique, overall competence of a company. The latter easily becomes very abstract and superficial. The word (signifier) may be the same ('knowledge' or 'competence'), but the meanings (signified) have very little in common.

Knowledge is a very broad and difficult concept. It is used to embrace information (the simple, fragmented kind of knowledge), knowing (how to do), explanation (knowledge answering the questions 'why?', 'what is behind?', 'what is the cause?'), and understanding (knowledge referring to patterns, connections, providing the gestalt of a phenomenon).

Two terms that are sometimes used in ways that overlap knowledge are 'competence' and 'information'. Some people use 'competence' in the same way as others talk about knowledge, but sometimes people use 'competence' to refer to practices more specifically oriented to a goal or demand, the ability to do something particular. 'Competence' is sometimes also used as a broader term, to include skills and talents.

'Knowledge' is often confused with, and reduced to, 'information'. There is broad agreement that the terms need to be separated. Sometimes the following set of distinctions is proposed: Data provide a record of signs supposedly indicating a chunk of reality. Information is data put into context: data with relevance given a particular purpose. 'Knowledge' means a framework and a capacity to reason and make sense of information (Davenport and Prusak 1998). Knowledge includes the exercise of judgement and the capacity to make interpretations. This means that we can hardly talk about knowledge as codified and stored in databases. This is then better seen as information, *not* knowledge, since knowledge calls for something including judgement, including the critical assessment of information and the ability to translate data into information. If one wants to distinguish between information and more complex stuff, e.g. research reports that call for special pre-understanding to be made sense of, one may talk about outputs and resources of knowledge work, rather than information or knowledge, preserving the latter term for something including the active use of judgement.

The definitions of knowledge offered by influential texts tend to follow this reasoning but are often rather all-embracing. Davenport and Prusak (1998), for example, define knowledge as follows: 'Knowledge is a fluid mix of framed experience, values, contextual information, and expert insight that provides a framework for evaluating and incorporating new experiences and information' (p. 5).

This is quite broad and may cover too much. The problem with the conceptualization of knowledge and the idea of knowledge-intensity is that it is very difficult to know where to stop including elements. Formalized, theoretical knowledge represents one pole; cultural, interpersonal, somatic, and other forms of experience-related, tacit, or half-conscious knowledge, together with creative skills and talents, represent the other. The first covers too little, the latter far too much, as a meaningful category.

If something is seen as important, it is often because the term signifying this important phenomenon has been used in a very broad way. Using a term to cover everything risks telling us next to nothing. Terms like 'knowledge'—such as 'quality', 'strategy', and 'leadership'—have strong rhetorical appeal. It is difficult to argue against claims such as 'the company's overall performance depends on the extent to which managers can mobilize all of the knowledge resources held by individuals and teams' (von Krogh 1998: 133). Given the broad view of knowledge that is often suggested, for example, by Davenport and Prusak above, not much is 'outside knowledge', and the mobilization of all of it becomes crucial to overall performance. Other authors are also quick to tie knowledge to performance: 'Although we may not be able to judge the knowledge itself, we can certainly see the results of the knowledge ... In any operation, different individuals using the exact same machinery may produce very different output, just as skiers or tennis players vary in performance using the same equipment' (Leonard and Sensiper 1998: 126).

Given a less all-embracing view on knowledge, one may allow space also for elements other than knowledge to make a difference, e.g. motivation, physical training, and muscles. A key factor behind performance in sport is presumably age: a coach is typically more 'knowledgeable' than the athlete being trained, but usually cannot compete with the athlete as ageing weakens physical ability. In business, knowledge can lead to thoughtful, reflective decisions arrived at in a rational manner, but in many cases rapid action may lead to better results than rational decision-making (Brunsson 1985).

Geertz (1973) recommends that concepts should be trimmed to 'cover less and reveal more'. As an anthropologist, he had students of culture in mind, but those who wish to say something useful about knowledge may be wise to follow his advice. Occupations (or organizations) that draw mainly upon talent-based and/or practical skills—such as designers, circus artists, chefs, and athletes—do not lack a 'knowledge component', but they can probably be better understood in terms other than the kind of knowledge concept most relevant to the people and organizations focused on in this book and most writings on knowledge work and KIFs, i.e. a more 'intellectual' or analytical idea of knowledge.

Problematic Distinctions: The Curse of the Four-Fielder

Distinctions in the literature between different forms of knowledge are proposed (e.g. by Blackler 1995; Scarbrough 1995; Spender 1996) typically based on a combination of two dimensions producing a four-fielder. The idea sometimes seems to be that we may not know what knowledge is or how to delimit it, but we can divide it into four versions.

It is common to distinguish between tacit and explicit knowledge, individual and social, ideational and materialized, etc. These distinctions are seldom unproblematic. 'Knowledge is a slippery and elusive concept, and every discipline has its own secret realization of it. Problems of interpretation haunt every attempt to use the concept effectively' (Scarbrough and Burrell 1996: 178).

The habit of slicing up the idea of knowledge into different forms is sometimes based on rather arbitrary and peculiar dichotomies. Hence knowledge is said to be either tacit or explicit, personal or codified, individual or organizational, procedural or substantive. There is some, but not much, variation in the four-fielder typologies produced (e.g. Blackler 1995; Nonaka 1994; Spender 1996). Whether this indicates that authors have got it right or that it is difficult to be original is hard to tell. (I should perhaps confess that I too have produced four-fielders in my day, although I have not divided knowledge into four versions.) Perhaps the most common distinction is between tacit and explicit knowledge, and here authors frequently refer to Polanyi (1975), who is credited with coining, or at least developing, the idea of tacit knowledge. However, while frequently (mis)used to justify it, Polanyi's approach undermines the logic of dividing knowledge into different forms. According to Polanyi, all knowledge includes a personal and a social–organizational element— there is nothing that is fully explicit and that works without involving meaning and judgement, and so tacitness is always vital: 'Even the most exact sciences must therefore rely on our personal confidence that we possess some degree of personal skill and personal judgment for establishing a valid correspondence with—or a real deviation from—the facts of experience' (Polanyi 1975: 31).

The distinction between tacit and explicit knowledge is valuable, but if it is used to refer to very different phenomena, it is misleading. As many commentators have pointed out, no knowledge is entirely tacit—even riding a bicycle can to some extent be described or instructed in words. And no knowledge is entirely explicit—even academic knowledge appearing in scientific

articles typically relies on pre-understanding and a feeling for
how to interpret the explicit that cannot easily be expressed. If
you don't master the cultural code you are lost. In a study of
consultancy firms that spend heavily on developing articulate
(explicit) knowledge and methods, the consultants described the
process of translation when working with specific projects not 'as
a conscious, analytical process, but rather as an intuitive process,
to a large extent based on tacit knowledge' (Werr and Stjernberg
2003: 896). Knowledge calls for the use of a theoretical framework
and active judgement—and this is not possible to make fully
explicit.

The tacit–explicit distinction is better seen as referring to different dimensions or aspects of knowledge that mutually constitute each other in a symbiotic relationship than as pointing up
different 'forms' of knowledge.

Distinctions between individual and social (or organizational)
forms of knowledge are also very common, but frequently also
problematic. Many authors divide knowledge into individual
and social–organizational. Others argue that knowledge is basically individual, but also that it is developed through social interaction and thus dependent on social context (e.g. Nonaka 1994).
Still others claim that knowledge is primarily social. A community perspective on knowledge is, for example, popular, viewing
social relationships and networks as crucial (e.g. Newell *et al.*
2002; Swan *et al.* 1999).

As with the tacit–explicit dichotomy, the individual and social
tend to go together. Newell *et al.* (2002) compare a structural
perspective with a processual one. In the former, knowledge is
assumed to exist on individual and collective levels, while a
processual perspective emphasizes how knowledge exists
through the interplay between the individual and the collective
level. In my view hardly any knowledge is developed in splendid
isolation from social context and culture, and knowledge shared
within a group (an organization or an occupational community)
is put into action fused with the individual experiences and
judgements of various practitioners. The individual is very
much a product of the social (i.e. culture, education, community
experiences, group work), but in most problem-solving and
knowledge-sharing situations the individual's unique experiences and abilities make a difference. Organizational knowledge

is thus carried by the ideas, reasoning, and storytelling of the collective of individuals and is not simply stored in formal routines, databases, and methodologies. At the same time the experiences and learning of individuals are contingent upon the frameworks and social practices of those individuals' occupational communities and work organizations. This does not mean that we cannot talk about individual and social–organizational knowledge—sometimes individuals make a real difference and may be very difficult to replace, and sometimes individuals in a company may be more or less replaceable—but one should not exaggerate the distinction.

Popular ways of making sense of knowledge by dividing it up into different forms are thus at best only partially helpful, and may exaggerate problematic distinctions. This reflects the tremendous difficulties in nailing down a workable concept of knowledge as well as in structuring it clearly and then comparing people, groups, and/or organizations within (or between) different knowledge form(s). This means that knowledge remains either rather vague and abstract or highly local and idiosyncratic. It also means that any understanding of knowledge must accept the looseness of the concept and thus appreciate the ambiguity of most uses of it. Acknowledging ambiguity means that empirical inquiry—including researching people's opinions—and researchers' analytical efforts must take seriously the non-distinctive, slippery nature of knowledge. We cannot directly observe or measure knowledge, and its partly tacit nature means that we can't expect people to produce highly precise accounts of their knowledge and knowledge use. Studying knowledge issues involves a fair amount of use of uncertain judgement; thus claims about knowledge are typically debatable. We can't avoid guesswork. The academic study of knowledge work is thus no different from the practice of knowledge work in other contexts: it is much about interpretation, use of judgement, and making informed guesses. The dominant tradition is to conceal this: the style of most authors gives the impression that they are referring to quite solid phenomena.

Against this, I suggest the need for a more reasoning, interpretative approach, one that is sensitive to uncertainty, incoherence, multiple meanings, contradiction, and confusion. In other words, ambiguity must be taken seriously. I am not suggesting that this is necessarily the best approach for understanding all kinds of

knowledge issues—there is so much variety that it would be
arrogant to claim to capture it all—but that there are a great
number of instances where this theoretical approach is productive and may offer new insights.

A brief review of the concept of ambiguity is therefore in order.

Ambiguity

In most social science as well as social life there is an interest in,
perhaps even a bias towards, finding and emphasizing clarity
and patterns. Disorder, messiness, confusion, and contradiction
should be avoided. Researchers and practitioners want to establish the 'correct' meaning of a phenomenon and proceed from this
insight. Knowledge, information, and data are the means capable
of accomplishing this. One might perhaps assume that knowledge and the actors—institutions, organizations, and individuals
—working competently based on it are a bastion against ambiguity. Where there is knowledge, there is at least reduced uncertainty. But one might argue that business, organizations, and
working life are very much made up of—or understood as—
highly ambiguous phenomena, and that the activities of those
seen as in knowledge-intensive fields are no exception. The high
level of complexity of many of the tasks and situations that people
in KIFs and professions face means that ambiguity may sometimes be a central feature of their work. The intangible nature of
much of the work also contributes to this.

I agree with Martin and Meyerson (1988), who say that it is vital
to acknowledge rather than deny ambiguity. This lesson is particularly fruitful for students of KIFs. Ambiguity involves uncertainty that cannot be resolved or reconciled—absence of
agreement on boundaries, clear principles, or solutions. Ambiguity means that a group of informed people are likely to hold
multiple meanings or that several plausible interpretations can
be made without more data or rigorous analysis making it possible to assess them. Ambiguity is different from uncertainty,
since it cannot be clarified just by gathering more facts.
Arguably, ambiguity is a crucial element in work and organization (Feldman 1991; Jackall 1988). In a study of social workers
Meyerson (1991), for example, found that

Individual social workers experience ambiguity in their structures, including their boundaries, technologies, goals, and evaluation criteria ...Thus insiders, as well as outsiders, hold diffuse ideas about what social work is and about who is and is not a social worker. In addition, technologies seem ambiguous because what one does as a social worker (e.g. talk to clients) seems only loosely related to what results (e.g. how clients behave). (p. 136)

Ambiguity is perhaps an even more central feature of most R&D work. Product innovation is 'inherently ambiguous', according to Dougherty (1996: 425). In a study of a science-based company that had failed to develop genuinely new products for an entire decade, we asked senior participants about the reasons for this. Interestingly they produced a great variety of explanations. Some blamed poor managers; others ascribed problems to errors in recruitment and wrong demography (recruitment of too many inexperienced individuals or too many old people); others spoke of organizational fragmentation and lack of integrative values; yet others thought there were indeed strong values, but the wrong ones, supporting a non-commercial, university attitude rather than a business focus. Another version was directed to a lack of strategic focus and directedness, etc. (Alvesson and Sveningsson 2002). Interviewees sometimes emphasized more than one explanation and not infrequently contradicted themselves. They did not express much doubt about their explanations, or mention qualifiers such as 'it is hard to say', 'I really don't know', or 'this is just a guess'. This case demonstrates both the fruitfulness of taking ambiguity seriously and an unawareness or unwillingness to acknowledge uncertainty on the part of organizational participants.

Ambiguity means that the possibility of rationality—clarifying means–ends relationship or exercising qualified judgement— becomes seriously reduced. Against conventional understandings, this book takes a number of issues seriously in terms of ambiguity and addresses some implications of and responses to this.

Knowledge: Objective and Robust?

Much knowledge talk in management and organization studies concerns its presumed objectivity and robustness. Most of the literature on knowledge seems to treat knowledge as expressing something 'true'. Nonaka (1994), for example, defines it as 'justified true beliefs'. Problems here involve the uncertainty of justifications and the difficulties of determining what is true. Something may be perceived as justified but not necessarily be true and something may be true but not (yet) be justified. There are frequently different perceptions of what is true and what should count as a sufficient justification.

The assumed thing-like nature of knowledge is clearly shown by some of the more popular metaphors embraced. These are typically brought in from the technical domain dealing with physical objects. One metaphor is construction work. For some, knowledge seems to be like demolition and house-building work, e.g. when they talk about the need to 'break down out-moded attitudes and practices... building up new, more appropriate competence' (Pettigrew and Whipp, cited by Clark 1995: 4). Knowledge is thus like a building block. The imagined robust-ness of knowledge is also expressed in the use of terms such as 'mass of knowledge' (Wikström *et al.* 1993). Also very popular is the warehouse metaphor: many authors talk about 'storing knowledge' (Bonora and Revang 1993; Starbuck 1992). All these understandings are problematic. They express a static, objectivistic, and reified view of knowledge—neglecting the active processes of knowing. It also tends to reduce knowledge to information.

Against objectivistic and reified understandings of knowledge, one can point to the uncertainties and controversies that charac-terize much of science (Brante 1988; Kuhn 1970) as well as to the fact that whatever the relative degree of rationality characterizing science and formal knowledge, people in their behaviour are much less rational (Fores *et al.* 1991). Few knowledge workers in business operate according to a handbook of scientific methodology, although in science-based fields this rationality may put a stronger imprint on activities. These two uncertaint-ies make the impact of the 'knowledge factor' or esoteric expertise much less clear-cut in practice. Knowledge is more often than not contestable and contested, and knowledge always has a subjective, personal dimension. It cannot be dissociated from the experiences and interpretations of those involved in know-ledge work.

In addition to such counterpoints to the robust, functionalist view on knowledge,[1] one can argue (*a*) that it is extremely difficult to isolate and point to knowledge as a particular factor that is, in itself, important; and (*b*) that KIFs and knowledge workers' success is contingent upon more or less loose *beliefs* about their being able to offer something specific to clients and customers. Against an objectivistic and functionalist understanding of knowledge and knowledge-intensity, social constructivism (Knorr-Cetina 1994; Steier 1991) and neo-institutionalism (Meyer and Rowan 1977; Scott 1995) offer valuable insights.

The main point of neo-institutionalism, which draws upon a (weak) version of social constructivism, is that 'institutionalised products, services, techniques, policies, and programs function as powerful myths' which many organizations adopt 'ceremonially' (Meyer and Rowan 1977). Meyer and Rowan argue that formal organizations 'are driven to incorporate the practices and procedures defined by prevailing rationalized concepts of organizational work and institutionalised in society'. Consequently, they 'dramatically reflect the myths of their institutional environments instead of the demands of their work activities' (p. 304). The myths of these environments have two key properties: they are rationalized and impersonal prescriptions that identify various social purposes as technical ones and they specify means to pursue these purposes; and they are highly institutionalized, i.e. it is taken for granted that they are legitimate. This appears to have a particular significance for understanding many workers and organizations that tend to be labelled 'knowledge-intensive'. Audits, HRM procedures, the use of consultants, the employment of new management ideas, the incorporation of specific professions, etc., all refer to important professional or knowledge work, and, according to neo-institutionalism, there need be no firm proof that this contributes to effectiveness and profits, but these experts, ideas, and arrangements are still seen as necessary and important to incorporate into organizations.

The process of institutionalization very briefly goes as follows. Certain kinds of knowledge (experts, practices) become, on loose

---

[1] Functionalism refers to an assumption that what exists typically does so for a socially or organizationally valuable purpose, serving the interest or the reproductive capacity of a social system. What is defined as 'knowledge' is assumed to be capable of accomplishing 'positive' outputs.

grounds, defined as true, valuable, etc. and are therefore adopted by some actors. Others tend to follow their example without necessarily having strong effectiveness-related reasons for doing so, apart from experienced uncertainty and a wish to imitate others. Then, at some point, it is very difficult not to follow common practice, for legitimacy as well as cognitive reasons. It may be perceived as deviating from what is normal and rational. Such perceived deviations might lead to legitimacy problems and sanctions, as people in the environment will think that this is odd or unprofessional, or in some other way diverges from the norm and the ideal. Following the established (institutionalized) way of thinking and acting is also experienced as the safest and most reasonable, even natural, thing for people to do, thus reducing their cognitive uncertainty. To think critically and independently and possibly deviate from tradition and what everybody else is doing is difficult and creates considerable anxiety.

In this book I am not drawing heavily on this approach, but it offers very interesting food for thought and I am inspired by a moderate rather than strong (relativistic) version of social constructivism.

Moving the focus in this way does not reject the idea that there are forms of knowledge that various people and organizations may possess or use in practice to different degrees, and that may vary in terms of support and ability to help people to accomplish desired outcomes. Social constructions that are, or may lead to, material constructions may occasionally break down—as is sometimes the case with bridges and space shuttles. In some forms of knowledge-intensive work and organizations dealing with material objects and natural laws, there may be more constraints and forces working against loose beliefs than in fields dealing with social phenomena, such as headhunting, market research, law, or organizational development, where the ambiguity of the phenomena may be strong and it is seldom possible to arrive at a final conclusion whether a proposal or a line of action was 'the best'. In other respects, too, there may be reasons to consider qualitative variation around social constructions. There are certainly good reasons to view Nazi 'science' about race as a social construction very differently from forms of knowledge backed up by empirical support and good arguments, produced and debated in a fairly free, at least non-totalitarian, environment. Social constructions may be produced in the context of open, qualified debate and careful reflection, or of group thinking and enthusiasm about fashion, or under authorization regimes.

In most KIFs, such as law firms, accounting firms, advertising agencies, and consultancy firms, 'raw' or 'naked' nature or material reality typically does not form a crucial input to beliefs and understandings concerning the 'objective' knowledge that these organizations 'possess'. Even when there is a clear material referent, as in engineering and science-based work, this calls for processes of knowledge construction in social contexts. Drawing attention to the socially constructed nature of knowledge does not necessarily imply embracing a radically relativist view—such a position is intellectually unproductive and politically dangerous—but it draws attention to the social processes as well as to the uncertainty of knowledge issues.

Against a reified view on knowledge—where knowledge can be put into products, organizational structures, information systems, manuals, etc.—what is counted as knowledge may be said to be closely related to social processes of interpretation and meaning creation. Polanyi (1975) says that 'all knowing is action', being about 'our urge to understand and control our experience' (p. 42). Judgement is a key element of knowledge, and is called for in the absence of certainty. Knowing is thus of more interest than knowledge (Blackler 1995). De-reifying knowledge means that it becomes unpacked and its ambiguous aspects become targets of inquiry. There are thus reasons to avoid treating knowledge as something 'robust' that produces good results. A significant quality is the ambiguity involved in meaning creation and negotiation of such an intangible phenomenon as knowledge. That social convention and common sense do not take this seriously is no reason why we should not.

Knowledge: A Functional Resource?

Many authors accept that knowledge is very difficult to define but treat it nevertheless as a valuable capacity that brings typically good results. The example of the machine operator, skier, and tennis player of Leonard and Sensiper (1998), cited earlier, illustrates this unfortunate tendency to trace the significance of knowledge through its effects, ascribing the effects to something that one knows little about. Similarly, a key characteristic of knowledge-intensive organizations is said to be the capacity to solve complex problems using creative and innovative solutions (e.g. Hedberg 1990; Sveiby and Risling 1986). A knowledge-intensive organization is thus a firm that can produce exceptionally good results with the help of outstanding expertise. Starbuck (1992) suggests, for example, that 'to make the KIF...a useful category, one has to require that exceptional expertise make important contributions' (p. 92). Ekstedt (1990: 21) claims that 'knowledge companies...supply the large corporations and the various public agencies and other institutions with the knowledge they need to solve problems of various kinds'. These statements are very much in line with an objective truth notion of knowledge, but the focus is shifted from this notion and knowledge per se in favour of the functional outcome of knowledge.

Authors who also emphasize the social nature of knowledge creation (e.g. Nonaka 1994) frequently stop short of acknowledging or taking seriously the socially constructed nature of knowledge itself as well as the outcomes of this knowledge put into use. Instead a more or less functional understanding of knowledge prevails, assuming that knowledge is something that leads to positive outcomes. This emphasis on what knowledge enables people to do, and the good outcomes it makes possible, is partly a response to increased awareness of the problems of talking about objective truth.

The reasoning goes as follows: Knowledge is something that solves problems and accomplishes good results. We do not know what knowledge is, but we know it accomplishes something good, e.g. solving problems or making important contributions. All sorts of objections can be raised here, of course, regarding what is a problem and for whom it is such; who is to tell whether it has been solved or not; what good results are in relationship to knowledge use; and whether it is possible to isolate knowledge as a specific factor.

So much of what we think we need for technical, instrumental reasons may be better understood through very different kinds of logics. Information, like many other elements in organizations related to knowledge, is not just valuable for its technical functions, but may frequently be seen as being a symbol: information symbolizes rationality, wisdom, intelligence, carefulness, etc. (Feldman and March 1981). By symbolizing these virtues, the impression is communicated that something rational, sensible, and valuable is being accomplished. If people report problems with lack of information, this may really mean something else: it may reflect a desire to express rationality, responsibility, or ambition by those reporting the shortfall of information, or it may indicate that people feel excluded from the inner circle.

Sometimes the emphasis on the functional quality of knowledge and knowledge use leads to more cautious, theoretically aware views, reflecting insights about problems with notions such as objective truth and distinguishing knowledge from the subject and her or his exercise of judgement. Spender (1996), for example, argues that 'Knowledge comprises theoretical statements whose meanings and practical implications depend on their use and on the framework in which they are deployed ... These days knowledge is less about truth and reason and more about the practice of intervening knowledgeably and purposefully in the world' (p. 64).

This statement is more philosophically up to date than much work on the specific subject matter. However, there is an implicit assumption about knowledge leading to intervention in a way that almost by definition produces good outcomes. Even if truth and reason cannot be guaranteed, there seems to be little reason to worry about somebody 'intervening knowledgeably and purposefully in the world'. It may seem self-evident that any talk of knowledge is about the ability to act in a way that makes it likely that intended positive outcomes are accomplished, at least most of the time.[2] However, it is possible to separate knowledge from the notion of positive outcomes in a more radical way. One may identify what is socially defined as knowledge, and then look at this as well as practices guided by it and try to find out what is happening, without assuming that 'good' outcomes prevail. As Suddaby and Greenwood (2001) remark, 'Management knowledge is valued not only for its contribution to achieving organizational efficiency, but also for its ability to enhance careers, give

---

[2] This is the case at least from the perspective and interest of the knowledge user; the outcomes for others may be seen in a different light, as all knowledge can be used in negative ways and lead to the manipulation of people or cause pollution.

status or to consolidate actors' positions within the organizational field' (p. 944).

There may actually be negative dimensions around knowledge, i.e. knowledge can be related to what is broadly seen as not so good. Often knowledge and professionals create problems by imprinting an idea of how things should be and indicating a gap between current imperfections and the ideal. This is not necessarily part of a process of improvement. As Collins (1990) remarks, juridical problems are one effect of the existence and rapid expansion of laws and lawyers. Without the dominance of institutions other problems would come to the fore, e.g. more salient ethical problems raised by the existence of other institutions. But it is not self-evident that the expansion of lawyers is only, or even chiefly, doing good things in society. Lasch (1978) suggests that the therapy industry creates psychic problems as much as they solve them by making people focus on themselves, leading to anxiety and exaggerated self-consciousness. Cosmetic surgery may make people even more aware of, sensitive about, or anxious about their blemishes and deviations from the ideal. The point is that problems emerge and are assessed within a specific context created by a particular domain of knowledge and professionals, not outside or independently of them. If we let an army of professionals loose on any organization or social setting, they are likely to find, or construct, a large, even endless, number of problems to work on: imperfect management, legal problems, health hazards, technical malfunctions, etc. The rich variety of perceived imperfections is often exploited by, for example, management consultants (Clark 1995, ch. 1; Sturdy 1997) and other 'professionals' merchandising new panaceas for business practices. Socially recognized forms of knowledge and knowledge-based practice are institutionalized, for better or worse, and people and companies respond to this in a sometimes conformist and uncritical way.

The issue of knowledge creating problems is not only a matter of the knowledgeable creating problems for others through social domination. People who propagate a form of knowledge may also themselves be subjugated to it, i.e. forced to adapt to the norms expressed by it. The most powerful and influential view of the fundamentally problematic nature of knowledge has been expressed by Foucault, who goes beyond a view of knowledge as an instrument in the hands of particular actors. For him, it is rather knowledge that is the actor. Modern power is actually closely related to and expressed through knowledge. According to Foucault (1976, 1980), a disciplinary or truth-inscribing quality is a characteristic of knowledge in general. Knowledge is neither innocent nor a neutral tool for accomplishing something socially valuable, but is closely related to power: knowledge creates the truth and imprints standards for being to which subjects subordinate themselves and others. This thesis has been supported by some work on management knowledge (e.g. Sveningsson 1999; Townley 1994). I am not here pushing for a distinctly Foucauldian view, since it can be criticized for overemphasizing the negative side of knowledge.[3] I would rather argue that thinking about knowledge calls for consideration of potentially negative or dangerous dimensions: the capacity of knowledge to locate reality, to produce the institutions and subjects that it simply claims to describe and explain. There are many examples of knowledge—models, recipes—that lead to the shaping of the social world in questionable ways. For example, strategic management knowledge suggests certain ways of understanding and acting in the corporate world that managers learn, identify with, and then reproduce in their actions. During one period the portfolio idea dominated, in which corporate conglomerates were seen as the normal way of managing companies. Based on this 'knowledge', corporate worlds were transformed. More recently, core competence has been viewed as the key feature of good management, encouraging concentration on a core business, and the selling out and outsourcing of peripheral activities and the use of alliances and networks in order to maintain speciality within the corporate umbrella. Corporate managers have acted accordingly. One can see this as a socially dominant and fashionable form of knowledge, defining the ideal corporate reality. This knowledge then expresses the normality of strategic management, and top managers are reduced to being agents defined by and defining themselves through these fashionable management knowledge discourses. Thus knowledge is the active force, with managers

[3] Foucault also talks about the productive side of power. Power disciplines and constrains, but also enables, making those targeted by power more likely to function in line with the imperatives of the form of power being activated. Still, his emphasis is on knowledge as expressing forms of power creating docile subjects and thus being dangerous.

only superficially in control, but mainly subordinated to the power regimes inherent in the forms of knowledge defining what is true and rational (Knights and Morgan 1991; Sveningsson 1999; see also Alvesson and Willmott 1995; Mintzberg 1990).

It is thus important not a priori to associate knowledge with positive outcomes. It is better to counteract functional assumptions and expectations and to postpone normative judgements of knowledge. Knowledge talk too easily leads to a positive bias as the term 'knowledge' carries a set of implicit meanings that have not necessary been subjected to critical reflection. It is important to be open about what is defined as knowledge in specific social sites and during particular periods as well as about the consequences and effects of the use of knowledge. Seeing knowledge as a simple resource in the hands of capable subjects may also be to lock the understanding prematurely: knowledge based upon, or fused with, myths, fashions, and power-potentials may control subjects and institutions as much as vice versa. As mentioned, the important work of Foucault can usefully be drawn upon here.

Knowledge as a Limited Element in the Work of 'Knowledge Workers'

The role of knowledge as such is also circumscribed by the work that many employees in knowledge-intensive organizations are doing. The assumption of knowledge being central in their work is common, but perhaps insufficiently studied and questioned. Freidson (quoted in Burris 1993) says that professionals are 'the agents of formal knowledge'. The significance of formal knowledge and formal education should not, however, be overestimated. Many professionals and other highly educated people acquire a large part of their qualifications after the termination of their formal education, and other knowledge workers are even less dependent on formal education. In addition to formal knowledge and work practice based upon a specific education, important criteria are, on the one hand, knowledge that is demanded by the market and is simultaneously relatively esoteric and hard to obtain for the common person; and, on the other hand, that these forms of knowledge and skills are associated with high prestige and comparatively high financial rewards (Brante 1989; Starbuck 1992 argues along similar lines).

It is probably important to consider both professional or intra-occupational criteria, recognition by prestigious institutions in society (e.g. universities), and market forces when assessing how groups and companies are located in terms of understood knowledge-intensiveness. It is important not to rely heavily on the market forces to assess knowledge issues. Knowledge-intensiveness cannot solely be measured against short-term commercial criteria. The market may respond to and reward effective marketing and those compliant with fashions and 'institutional myths' more than 'substantive' knowledge. A number of IT companies claiming to be knowledge-intensive and at the forefront of the 'new economy' had tremendous success during a short period late in the 1990s, but soon the bubble burst and their knowledge claims were largely discredited, indicating the difficulties of the market to produce reliable assessments. The rapid fall of Andersen after the Enron affair also illustrates the instability of market assessments in the field of KIFs, at least in the service areas.

It is rather idealized to say that the work content of KIFs is primarily to develop or apply advanced knowledge. In many cases this is a biased picture of what is really going on. Drawing attention to the legitimization aspect does not add very much to our understanding of what knowledge-intensive organizations and workers actually do, which is perhaps even more significant than what they know (Blackler 1993). Surprisingly few studies have looked more carefully at what professionals and knowledge-intensive organizations do at work. Frequently one has the impression that academics tend to see 'official' statements of these occupations and organizations as valid without much critical questioning or effort to produce an independent picture.

In a study of the work of psychologists and architects Svensson (1990) found a discrepancy between the rational model of knowledge and the uncertainty, complexity, instability, and uniqueness that characterize their work in everyday life. On questions concerning the knowledge tools they use in their work both the psychologists and the architects interviewed had difficulties in coming up with examples in which they rationally apply theoretical knowledge. They implicitly question the rational, technical model of knowledge which they espouse, in principle, in other situations, outside everyday work, and which their professions have historically been eager to put forward.

These findings support the argument of Fores *et al.* (1991: 97) that traditional understandings of professionals mean that

We are lulled into a sense of false scientificity: specialization, rationality, and scientific predictability allay the uncertainties of the human condition. But:

- applying knowledge is a highly incomplete account of what professionals do;
- there is no cut off point between professions jobs and other jobs; applying knowledge is an element in many occupations;
- the knowledge being applied does not for the most part partake of the Newtonian quality;
- close association with knowledge/science does not make human actors themselves scientific or rational;
- the focus on knowledge–rationality–predictability of outcomes distracts from the more important qualities of skill, creativity, judgement, and *savoir faire*, and the constructive response to the uncertain and unprogrammable.

In a case study of a computer consultancy firm it was found that managers and employees often downplayed the role of technical expertise in their work (Alvesson 1995). The work tasks varied a lot and often people were assigned to jobs for which they had very little formal education or relevant experience. Of course, this capacity to adapt to various contexts and tasks is an important part of consultants' skills, but it is a bit different from the application of a specialized set of knowledge. As one consultant expressed it, 'What I am selling is flexibility, the capacity to absorb knowledges and apply them. I can quickly see the context, make abstract evaluations, see the client's problem and do something about it.'

Clark suggests that the crucial skill is not so much the cognitive part of the knowledge base as the skill to give the right impression: 'In the absence of a clearly delineated and defended formal body of knowledge, consultants' success is determined by their ability to appear authoritative via their manipulation of a knowledge base that is ambiguous, tacit and constantly under threat' (Clark 1995: 91).

To say that the work of professionals and other knowledge-intensive organizations and workers are only or even mainly the direct or 'creative' application of a systematic, institutionalized body of formal knowledge or esoteric expertise may be misleading. Knowledge, in the sense of a body of information, theories, and methodologies that is broadly considered to have passed some tests of validity, and which is broadly shared by members of a profession or organization claimed to be based on a specific type of knowledge, is thus not necessarily very significant in the forms of work addressed in this book.

We can thus take seriously not only that knowledge in itself is ambiguous but also that it is often highly ambiguous what role this factor plays in most KIFs and professional work. This move is quite different from traditional views on professions and contemporary functionalist writings about KIFs in which ambiguity has been denied or downplayed while protagonists of the professions have stressed that these practitioners 'are applying knowledge, acting rationally, deploying trained and specialized competence. All this serves to take the sting out of the disorderly, threateningly ambiguous character of social experience' (Fores *et al.* 1991: 97). Professionals are certainly both more and less than agents of formal knowledge, adding other elements of work and only partially using the formal knowledge central to their education.

The claimed significance of the knowledge and talents of employees in at least some large KIFs can also be questioned in organizations offering relatively standard services. In some professional service firms (PSFs), for example, the quality of the services is mainly contingent upon the firm's ability to organize and run large, long-term projects, implying the coordination of a great number of personnel trained in the company's method to be able to put people to work quickly (Maister 1993). Individuals are put into work groups, receiving well-delimited and specified tasks. Space for special talents or esoteric forms of expertise is restricted (Bergström 1998: 80). Of course, this is contingent upon management ability (including knowledge), but the significance of sophisticated knowledge seems to be limited in most of the activities involved. As one person in a large management consultancy firm that we have studied said,

Customers see us as providers of competence but also as resources in pushing. They know that we go in there with high motivation, a willingness to work hard. They also expect us to contribute with new thoughts and ideas. But somehow it feels as though not many expect us to come as the real experts and contribute with fantastic, brilliant ideas that will revolutionize the world.... This is more a matter of hard work, producing sufficiently good ideas and drive to see that things are put in the right place. And it becomes increasingly a matter of getting things straight.

One consultant in a very large, global company said: 'we are the McDonalds of consulting, good in delivering but not very creative' (McGrath 2000). This is not fully in line with the idea of KIFs as populated by a large number of knowledge workers doing sophisticated intellectual work. To the extent that this is centralized around a senior figure supported by workers implementing systems and instructions, the situation is not very different from the many conventional companies where the workers follow the systems and procedures designed by top management or its techno-structure. We must be careful here neither to underestimate nor to overstress the distinctiveness of the category of firms we are addressing: they are certainly different from McDonalds, but may sometimes not be exclusive.

It seems common in the IT consultancy field that client companies need from the consultants additional labour to add quantitative capacity rather than something specific in terms of unique and additional knowledge. This does not mean that the consultants may not add something in terms of skills in project work, or feel pressure to, and perhaps actually, carry out intellectually demanding work. But it makes sense to hesitate somewhat before defining the majority of consultancy businesses and other PSFs as working in the area of esoteric expertise. An important contribution of consultancies is to add qualified labour, to make things happen by adding focus, commitment, and a project mentality.

Also in science-based work, such as in pharmaceutical companies, the degree to which very advanced intellectual work dominates is an open question. A lot of work is routine and adapted to new technologies testing various options, possibly reducing the scope of work involving a lot of creativity and sophisticated intellectual analysis (Kärreman *et al.* 2002).

One middle manager in a large company expressed the following opinion about the use of management consultants: 'You always feel cheated. You pay a lot of money for something that you could do yourself. You pay for the speed in carrying out the task. If you did it yourself you have to add the work to all your other tasks and then it takes time.'

Talking more specifically about a consultancy assignment that had just been completed he spoke positively about the consultant, 'who did a good job', but indicated that it was the CEO's wish to have it accomplished in short time rather than any need for a specific, unique competence that was the rationale behind the use of the consultant.

Of course, it is difficult to generalize around this and other examples. In cases where the client does not expect the consultant to make a unique contribution, the consultancy may be appreciated for providing qualified labour, temporarily adding to the capacity of the client's managerial or techno-structural functions. As we shall see in the next section, the exact relationship between the parties involved in terms of their contributions in a client–consultant project is difficult to sort out. Assessing the work of consultants is not easy. The client may underestimate the difficulties of the consultant and have too high expectations. It is an open question how frequently KIFs add esoteric expertise in comparison to what the client company can do. Frequently, however, the managers and others within PSFs try to portray what they are doing in more glamorous terms: they seldom say that they are in the field of renting (qualified) manpower, sometimes referred to as bodyshopping.

This may, of course, vary between projects and clients. It is also very much a relational matter. Knowledge-intensiveness is a relative issue: in the kingdom of the blind the one-eyed is king. With a client with a qualified workforce within a specific area, a consultancy company may simply add quantitative resources while the esoteric experience—and a more leading role—may be more central in a project of a similar kind but with a client lacking experience or expertise in the focal area.

To conclude, it is an open question to what extent knowledge—as an added quality, bringing superior expertise—is a particularly significant element in what KIFs do. It is frequently impossible to separate out knowledge and 'pure' intellectual skills (symbolic analytical work) from flexibility, organizing capacity, a high level of motivation, social skills, less esoteric technical skills, following methods and standardized ways of operating, and other elements in what is done in companies of this kind. Needless to say, some degree of knowledge and competence is a prerequisite for professional service workers to be used; we are still talking about typically highly paid people with a university degree and additional training and experience that clients find valuable. However, the exact relationship between added competence through (wo)man hours (more labour) during periods involving a peak in workload, and the engagement of esoteric expertise adding something qualitatively different from what the client company possesses, is sometimes hard to figure out. In science-based companies the distribution between routine and intellectually demanding and creative work is also often uncertain. My point is once again about ambiguity: I am *not* arguing that what is counted as knowledge-intensive work is consistently less demanding or difficult than is proposed in the literature; I am saying that there is a great deal of variation and uncertainty around the nature of this work in many organizations viewed as knowledge-intensive.

The Ambiguities of Results

A third vital aspect of *much* knowledge-intensive work—the ambiguity of knowledge and its significance were the first two—concerns the ambiguities of the results produced. Uncertainty is by definition a part of the area in which most professionals and other knowledge workers are operating. Fields of action with low uncertainty, or where the knowledge required to evaluate problems and solutions is easily accessible, do not provide the space necessary for the development of socially recognized expertise (Beckman 1989). This means that the results of work are frequently very difficult to evaluate, at least for those outside the sphere of experts concerned: 'In many cases, the quality of what is delivered can only be assessed by other professionals within the same area of expertise, which is precisely the reason why society accepts professional associations taking charge of peer reviews, licensing, and sanctioning of inappropriate behaviour' (Løwendahl 1997: 36).

In practice such quality evaluations seldom take place. Often, perhaps, the client has an opinion about whether a problem has been solved or not, but even if he or she is happy with the outcome, it is not certain that a group of experts evaluating the job would agree with him or her upon its quality, or that there would be consensus within the expert group. The quality assurance of professional associations is frequently uncertain, and the judgement of other experts on what has been delivered in terms of professional service may vary.

Bédard and Chi (1993) cite reviews of work in auditing which compare the decisions of expert and novice auditors. They indicate no relationship between expertise and consensus in high-risk and less standard situations, and the experts' level of agreement was lower than that of novices. This does not mean that experience and knowledge do not matter. They also cite several studies showing that experts may exercise superior judgement, and in one study the correct solution to a problem was observed more by experienced auditors than less senior. Experience and knowledge often do not, however, necessarily reduce differences in terms of assessment of complex problems.

In much auditing work, as in many other cases of knowledge-intensive work, the criteria for how to evaluate the work done are unreliable or absent entirely. Mozier (1992), for example, remarks that 'judging the quality of an audit is an extremely problematic exercise' and says that consumers of the audit service 'have only a very limited insight into the quality of work undertaken by an audit firm' (p. 2). Also referring to accounting firms, two other researchers claim that 'There is a high premium on idiosyncratic knowledge of the client, great difficulty in monitoring performance and developing clear performance contracts' (Fichman and Levinthal 1991). Within advertising work representatives of clients and the advertising agency very often have different evaluations of a particular proposal for an advertisement (Alvesson and Köping 1993). The work results of computer consultants are often the object of uncertainty, and 'agreement on problem definitions and solutions requires active communication and negotiation' (Deetz 1998: 156). A study of the construction of the Channel Tunnel found that the perceived role and significance of engineering consultants diverged heavily between the consultants themselves and the permanent staff (Henriksson 1999).

While the consultants 'frequently put across the notion of being the committed rescuers who salvaged the project from complete failure', many of the people they said they were helping frequently accused them of 'having done more harm than good'. One person said that 'You can't expect them to do nothing, and what they do is they end up redesigning the project. Everybody was vying for position, everybody was justifying their fee . . . The added value was nil many times' (p. 146).

We can hardly evaluate who is 'right', but the impression is that it is very difficult, based on the stated judgements of a number of actors involved, to evaluate the impact and contributions of the engineering consultants in the case (Henriksson 1999). The impression, once again, is that complexities and uncertainties make it very difficult to arrive at a shared evaluation of the results of the efforts of the people involved, typically perceived as highly knowledge-intensive. A study of a management consultancy project to change the administrative system of a client similarly led to highly diverse assessments of the outcome and the consultants' competence and contributions. While the consultancy and client project managers saw the project as mainly successful and thought that the consultants had done a good job, although not as much was implemented as had been intended, other people involved expressed a more negative verdict. Another consultant and, in particular, two other managers from the client company thought that the project was rather problematic in vital respects. The two managers were critical of the performance of the consultants (Alvesson and Sveningsson 2003). Similar tendencies to diverse opinions are well known by people familiar with the review process in social science. An article I submitted a few years ago led to the contradictory verdicts of 'brilliant' and 'quite simply, incompetent' by two presumably qualified members of the research community. Of course, this is exceptional but variation in assessment is fairly common.

Some knowledge-intensive service firms standardize their products and, for example, in the field of management consultancy it is increasingly common for firms to develop methodologies for systematic work (Werr *et al.* 1997). However, the idiosyncrasies of clients and the considerable amount of interaction between consultants and their clients in the production process add to task uncertainty and to the difficulties of evaluating the quality of results and the performance of the knowledge-intensive company.

Because of the difficulties of evaluating the performances of many knowledge-intensive forms of work and the close interaction between consultant and client, market control can often be relatively ineffective. 'Because of the esoteric body of knowledge, as well as the intrinsic opacity of agent behaviour and indeterminacy of outcome, however, analogous market control mechanisms are either ineffective or not at all present in the principal–professional context' (Sharma 1997: 780). This implies that the marketing mechanism is not necessarily very effective in screening out actors with bad performances and assuring the long-term survival only of those who are helpful to clients.

In product development work the situation is somewhat different. Here the end results are less ambiguous in the sense that different evaluators may agree more on the qualities of physical products. Drugs, aeroplanes, and mobile phones can be tested in terms of performance. Frequently, however, a large part of the work processes and their partial outcomes are not easy to assess. In the pharmaceutical industry it may take ten years or more before the success of a particular product is clear, and even then it may be as much an outcome of successful marketing as of intrinsic product qualities contingent upon R&D work. Before the market finally gives its verdict, there are many instances where assessment of the work and results must be made, and here ambiguity is often salient. That careful tests and, perhaps finally, the market may provide more or less strong indications of the quality of a particular product does not rule out the possibility that ambiguity will characterize many R&D processes and different points in the decision-making process.

In general, however, the ambiguity of work results may have the strongest explanatory power for service work within the 'softer' areas. Frequently, the idea that 'knowledge solves problems' in a straightforward and self-evident way appears oversimplistic, even rather naive, as the work results are often almost impossible to evaluate for the non-expert and even difficult for the expert. How can anyone tell whether a headhunting firm has found and recruited the best possible candidate or not for a certain position? Or if an audit is of high quality? Or whether a proposal by a strategic management consultant is optimal or even helpful? Of course, sometimes it may be obvious whether something works or not (e.g. after the intervention of a plumber), but in the context in which the concept of knowledge-intensiveness is used the issues are normally not that simple. Here we are dealing mainly with complex and intangible phenomena. Even if something seems to work after the intervention of a consultancy organization, it might have worked even better, the improvements might have lasted longer, or the cost of the intervention might have been much lower if another organization had carried out the task.

Summary

In this chapter I have questioned some dominant ideas according to which knowledge brings clarity to fuzziness and is a problem-solving capacity that creates positive outcomes. Instead I have emphasized ambiguity as inherently related to complex issues in which the perceived need for 'knowledge' is significant. I have argued that some of the distinctiveness of KIFs lies in the complexities and ambiguities characterizing their claimed core product or service offer (knowledge), what they are doing (working with 'knowledge' compared to behaving in ways that are loosely connected to this quality), and the results of their work. Knowledge-intensive organizations are thus 'ambiguity-intensive', i.e. 'clarity' and 'order' are not the best words to use in providing accounts of the work and contribution of knowledge-intensive organizations and workers. Saying this, however, is not contradictory to acknowledging that ambiguity exists in all organizational life, which is clearly the case (Feldman and March 1981; Jackall 1988; Martin and Meyerson 1988). I am definitively not saying that knowledge-intensive organizations have a monopoly on this label; this category is neither unitary nor unique. Service work is often said to be characterized by its intangible nature (Grönroos 1984; Normann 1983). This is debatable in many cases (the material component of restaurants, transport, etc. is considerable), but in knowledge-intensive work where the significance of easily inspected tangible elements is highly limited, the ambiguity becomes salient. Even in product-focused companies R&D processes include much ambiguity and considerable uncertainty regarding what is good and promising and what are the mechanisms behind positive outcomes. Focusing on ambiguity may be particularly fruitful in the study of knowledge-intensive organizations.

Emphasizing ambiguity as a general feature not only of knowledge but also of contemporary societies and organizations in general gives a different understanding of why experts go beyond simple acceptance that sophisticated knowledge brings about good results. One may engage experts because there are institutionalized norms saying that one should do so (see Meyer and Rowan 1977). Experts provide legitimization. In the context of uncertainty, the appointment of consultants may also make it easier to avoid responsibility when it comes to 'blame-time'. As Jackall (1988) points out, managers want to avoid making (difficult) decisions and are inclined to involve many people in them in order to distribute the blame if the decisions appear misguided in retrospect.

There are thus good reasons to explore dimensions other than those commonly associated with KIFs, emphasizing ambiguity and various responses to it. It is simplistic and misleading to assume that KIFs are based on reliable knowledge and esoteric expertise (symbolic analytical skills, embrained knowledge) that solve problems and produce valuable results. Incorporating ambiguity as a key dimension challenges and reframes conventional understanding of the nature and management of knowledge-intensive organizations.

Chapter 4   Image and Rhetoric

THE expectation that objective reality speaks for itself may make sense in situations that are very simple and clear. In contemporary business and working life these circumstances seldom are. In knowledge-intensive contexts, in particular in service work, managers and workers must devote attention, energy, and skills to dealing with how to present their knowledge, work, and organization and produce positive expectations and assessments of themselves and their work results. This is very much a matter of the management of expectations. Themes like image, rhetoric, and symbolism become significant. The idea that 'corporate brands' can increase the company's visibility, recognition, and reputation in ways not fully appreciated by product-brand thinking has become increasingly popular (Hatch and Schultz 2003). I am not convinced that the terms 'corporate brand' and 'branding' differ very much from 'corporate image' and 'image management', and will favour the latter pair of terms.

Of course, knowledge-intensive firms (KIFs) are not the only institutions in which people have good motives for carefully considering image (corporate brand) and rhetoric. As Cheney and Christensen (2001) note, there is a general 'growing problem of *being heard* in a communication environment saturated with corporate messages' (pp. 232–3). However, the invisible nature of knowledge and the uncertainties around decisions to hire a KIF for a particular service or to purchase their products, combined with ongoing uncertainties around the work and the outcomes of it, make image issues significant in this kind of business.

This chapter starts by discussing the meaning of image in a working life and organizational context and the image-sensitivity of KIFs. An exploration of some basic versions of image management is then followed by a section emphasizing the role of, and some major themes in, KIF rhetoric.

The Concept of Image

The concept of image is tricky to define and use. It is sometimes used to refer to somebody's inner picture of a particular object, and at other times it refers to the communicated attributes of an object. In the former sense, an image is primarily created by an agent for his or her own sake. Image can then be defined as 'the subjective record of sense-experience (which) is not a direct copy of actual experience, but has been "projected", in the process of copying, into a new dimension, the more or less stable form we call a picture' (Langer 1957: 144). In the second sense, the image bears the imprints of a *sender* trying to project a certain impression to an audience. It can, of course, be argued that the image exists some-where 'in between' the communicator and the audience. An image is then a result of projection from two directions. Especially con-cerning corporations, products, brands, etc., the images of interest from top management's point of view are emerging in the presence of particular efforts to produce an impression. As Bernstein (1984) puts it, image 'means a fabrication of public impression created to appeal to the audience rather than to reproduce reality' (p. 13). An image is then at least partially a creation with the aim of producing a certain believable impression. It must not be perceived as untrue, and the manufacturers must avoid producing images that might too easily be proven false. Boorstin (1961) stresses that 'An image is ambiguous. It floats somewhere between the imagination and the senses, between expectations and reality' (p. 19).

I use the concept of image to refer to something affected by the intentions of particular actors (e.g. a company), for whom the image is singled out as a particular concept and target for instru-mental action. The image is not a tightly integrated part of a referent, but is loosely coupled to it. This view is in harmony with that of most authors concerned with corporate images (e.g. Bernstein 1984). Image, in this sense, plays an increasing role in organizations and economic life, primarily in the way that cus-tomers and other external actors view an organization, but also for the impressions and sentiments held by employees. This is espe-cially the case for large and complex organizations with little transparency and where the individual employee typically has a limited overview of the broader patterns. Personal experience and direct observation are not sufficient to form beliefs about the entire company and its characteristics. Individuals then become likely to take seriously the systematic representations of the work organization mediated by the management, which has access to resources of centralized communication (Alvesson 1990).

Image-Sensitivity

The ambiguity of knowledge and the work of KIFs means that 'knowledge', 'expertise', and 'solving problems' to a large degree become matters of beliefs, impressions, and negotiations of meaning. Institutionalized assumptions, expectations, recognitions, reputation, images, etc. matter strongly for how the products of knowledge-intensive organizations and workers are perceived. Reputation is the most important factor behind the choice of consultants (Clark 1995) and has a strong impact on corporate results (Greenwood *et al.* 2003). Reputation is based on first-hand and mediated (third-party) sources. We have here one of the most significant and interesting aspects of knowledge-intensive organizations, in particular in the service sector, one that makes them worthy of study as a particular category. It is extremely important for those claiming to be knowledge-intensive to nurture an image of being so. The image—as a specific target for management action—becomes crucial in the absence of the existence of tangible qualities available for inspection.

Organizations that are heavily dependent on the relevant sector's view of them—abstracted from specific assessments of particular actions, services, and products—can be referred to as image-sensitive. In such organizations there is typically a heightened awareness of, and managerial focus on, the organizational image (corporate brand). Companies and other organizations may be more or less image-sensitive. That large PSFs may be highly sensitive to image is illustrated by the collapse of the accounting firm Arthur Andersen after the Enron affair in 2002. The mass media broadly exposed the firm's failure to conduct a satisfactory audit and perhaps even their attempts to camouflage illegal acts within the client company. This exposure had drastic worldwide consequences.

Image becomes vital as a substitute for the absence of reliable indicators of the skills and knowledge of the personnel. In a sense it compensates for the difficulties in finding out what knowledge workers actually do and for evaluating their results (Alvesson 1990). In situations of high market uncertainty—it is difficult to assess what one is getting for the money spent—it is likely that an actor will choose an exchange partner based on social status (Podolny 1993). It is especially important in the management of expectations and as a surrogate for more reliable indicators on what a firm can offer. Greenwood and Empson (2003) point out three business advantages following from a good reputation:

- The demand for a firm's services and products increases, which means that it can charge more.
- The marketing costs are reduced: clients are more inclined to respond positively to marketing initiatives and they may actively seek the assistance of the prestigious firm.
- Reputation may also bring about competitive barriers, in that clients will only consider and select from a limited set of firms with a good reputation.

A good reputation also means that it is possible to attract and recruit better employees or do so for less costs: people may want to work for a high-status company as it may boost their self-esteem or may be thought to increase their value on the labour market at a later stage in their career.

Image can be managed on different levels: professional–industrial, corporate, and individual. Image may be targeted in specific policies, acts, and arrangements, in visible symbols for public consumption, but also in everyday behaviour within the organization and in interaction with others. Thus image is not just of importance for marketing but also during and after production. Clients' estimation of the quality of service may be affected by the image of the company whose performance is being evaluated. If the corporate image indicates that a good performance may be anticipated, one is probably more inclined to perceive an ambiguous outcome positively; on the other hand, the gap between high expectations and an outcome that is perceived as not so good may lead a more strongly negative assessment than in cases where the image was less positive in the first instance. So strong deviations from a good reputation may be extra costly for companies not able to deliver.

Image Management

Image management takes place at different levels, from efforts to manage the reputation of an entire industry or occupation to individuals trying to nurture a particular view of themselves. The efforts of an occupation or an industry to establish itself as a profession or to get acceptance for claims to being like a profession can be seen as image management at the macro level. In this book my interest is mainly in the corporate, work group, and individual levels.

Macro-Level Image Management

The general scepticism about many knowledge-intensive occupations is an important aspect of the background to the interest in image issues in many organizations and associations. Important issues are directed towards the fact that many services are seen as very expensive and as not always delivering substantial results. These image problems make firms in management consulting, law, accounting, and advertising very aware of the significance of reputation. They also encourage people to try to counter negative reputations and nurture an image of being solid and reliable. Professional associations and links with universities represent professional–industrial strategies to deal with this problem. By emphasizing intimate connections with institutional structures such as specific educational and research institutions, licensing arrangements, disciplinary procedures, etc., trust and legitimization are created. One can argue that the project of professionalization is mainly about creating a positive image, of people belonging to a particular occupation, that they are bearers of specific knowledge and moral commitments, carefully checked and guaranteed by the bodies of the profession, authorized by the state.

Organizational-Level Image Management

At the *organizational* level different acts and arrangements of management are intended to affect the organization's image. Of course, everything a company does—and much that goes on beyond its control—affects its image. Of interest here is mainly what it is explicitly aimed at image management. Most activities are not exclusively about influencing the external world's impressions of the company—what is intentional image management and what is not may be hard to tell. Certain parts of management are, however, of interest to address under the label of image management. These arrangements, acts, and use of language are not, however, exclusive properties of management. All employees, to various degrees, 'do' image management—sometimes in line with top management's intentions, sometimes not—in their interactions with various audiences, ranging from customers to neighbours: 'The whole organization from top to bottom and across functional units is involved in realizing the corporate brand, along with the audiences the brand is meant to attract and engage' (Hatch and Schultz 2003: 1045).

This dispersed participation in the carrying out of image management is more pronounced in service work than in manufacturing and especially salient in professional or knowledge-intensive service work. The image produced is very much an effect of how employees appear, act, and talk in highly visible settings (e.g. public appearances and internal formal meetings involving people that do not interact on a daily basis) as well as everyday situations.

This does not mean that certain centralized decisions and policies are not significant. Top managers and specialized units, such as marketing and public relations, deal with the mass media and produce promotional material and activities—from advertisements to sponsorships. Top managers also play a major role in strategic decision-making, even though strategies are far less commander-directed in many PSFs and other KIFs (as will be explored in Chapter 6). Strategies may be image-focused or at least carry strong implications for corporate image.

Some *strategic* decisions may be strongly motivated by image considerations. Being big and well known may indicate success and reliability. Size and fame are therefore extremely important for many KIFs—and here we perhaps have a major, although certainly not the only, explanation behind all the mergers and acquisitions in accounting, management consultancy, and other PSFs.

Some mergers, acquisitions, and reorganizations appear to be motivated by a desire to present a favourable impression before introduction on the stock market. Interviews with managers in IT companies indicate that a major purpose of mergers and acquisitions is to increase the company's stock value.

Question: Are there a lot of things like that in this business, doing stuff in order to look good on the stock market?

Yeah, I think so. It's, you can see it in the companies that are introduced as Internet companies now. Take Intercom Co., which was introduced now, it's an incredibly good job, starting up a company with that volume with profitability and all, but it's not very much bloody Internet if you ask me. It's the six last months of marketing before the introduction on the stock market that has given the company its Internet image. It can be 20–30 per cent. They have got 100 people, it's just providing manpower. Sometimes you hear the analysts muttering about this, indicating that you can question it. Anyway, they came in and they were listed to double the value.

The scale of the business is of great importance in this kind of context:

But the IT companies, especially the ones that want to be introduced on the stock market, it is volume you know. What kind of volume or quality of the volume, it's just covering up and rolling in.

In Sweden a firm with a few hundred employees seems to have a clear advantage since its size facilitates synergies, it makes the company well known on parts of the Swedish market, and, not least, it enables the company to staff big projects without any problems. However, it is uncertain whether there are any significant economies of scale in increasing the business to more than about a few hundred consultants. A very successful elite US law firm took the strategy not to employ more than about a hundred people, which makes possible its high quality and reputation (Starbuck 1993). There are problems associated with large size that are fairly distinctive of KIFs, particularly PSFs. Greenwood *et al.* (2003) argue that the increasing complexity that normally follows from increasing size means that formal control to some extent replaces participation in decision-making, reducing autonomy and the motivational benefits of partnership. Lowendahl (cited in Greenwood *et al.* 2003) talks about 'substantial diseconomies of scale in professional service firms'.

One manager stressed that 'we didn't get any better after merging with Ditto company, and neither did we when we were fighting with Infogood later on'. Another manager argued that economies of scale are quite insignificant in the IT business, once a certain volume has been reached:

I don't think there are any major economies of scale. We have bigger volume. It might be possible to get rid of some administration, but on the whole it's very little. Perhaps it's possible to do that anyway, trimming down the administration. I think CCC did that in 1993 when business was bad; they were doing a lot of rationalizations in the administration then. In practice, it doesn't make any difference if we were 1100 or 2000, what matters is the ability to take, or not take, get or not get big contracts, big customers, at least you'll get that with that volume.

This can partly be connected to the importance of image. Lacking clear criteria for measuring quality, volume is perceived as a kind of quality indicator. As size sometimes can be pumped up it is, however, questionable whether size says anything about quality. But marketing is strongly facilitated if the firm is large and its name well known. Large size and being well known also facilitate recruitment and may assist employees in their identity work (a theme addressed in Chapter 9).

Decisions to get certain clients in PSFs that are well known and prestigious may also be motivated by image reasons. Clients are appreciated not only for the money and the learning following from specific assignments, but also for the fame and glamour they may contribute to organizations they associate with. They are valuable resources in marketing.

A Case Illustration

Image management at the meso level may take many forms and may be focused on corporate artefacts (material objects expressing cultural meaning), specific actions, social practices, and rhetoric. The case of a computer consultancy company, CCC, is informative (Alvesson 1995). The company wanted to portray itself as a progressive, non-hierarchical, people company, informal, flexible, and creative, with good communication and relationships with its clients' managers and personnel.

In terms of artefacts, CCC loaded the corporate building and its interiors with as much image-communicating corporate symbolism as possible, from clouds painted on the floors and the avoidance of straight corridors to locating top management close to the reception: this was supposed to express values appealing to the 'whole' person and to promote an image of creativity, informality, and anti-hierarchy.

The business concept of the company seemed to fulfil internal and external functions intended to shape how various audiences were to view the company. It was defined as combining strategic and IT knowledge in order to improve the business of clients. It attracted attention and was frequently pushed by the managers. Some of my interviewees considered that the official business concept accurately described reality rather well and that CCC's successes were largely a result of close adherence to the concept. Here are some typical responses:

Linking the development of a new system to the customer's business concept and area of operations is our basic philosophy.

I don't believe we are any better [than other companies] from a purely technical point of view. We are better at some things. And that is precisely the fundamental business concept: management and computer development. But we are no better at computer development, perhaps worse in some cases. But on the management side—our way of handling customers—that's where we are better.

Our target group is corporate managements, not data processing departments.

The business concept here signals the organizational identity (Albert and Whetten 1985), and is seen as expressing what is understood to be the essential characteristics and distinctiveness of the company. But other interviewees give a different picture of the company. A consultant who had worked for CCC almost since the start said:

We are supposed to be computer consultants, combined with management consulting, and this has been part of our business concept for several years. But Christer, Hasse, and John [i.e. CCC's founders] represented the management side. They didn't recruit people at a lower level with that orientation; they wanted computer consultants—programmers and systems analysts.

In an interview with a former manager of the company conducted ten years after my initial study and after his departure from the company, the former manager claimed that

What we live by in the consultancy business, really, is resources and volume. It isn't the brilliant analysts in the front line that we live by, but it is the bulk, the middle field. Systems administrators and programmers, that's what we lived by then. We were covering up and pretending that we were working in a project at CCC, but we seldom really had to take any major risks in the project. It was running billing [ongoing debiting], it was just a way of covering volume consulting. But that's not the way they worked in our England subsidiary. They believed in it, 'here comes the new view of management and IT', and we were talking about it in Sweden, but we didn't do it much, but they believed blindly in it, and it went to hell too [laughter]. It is volume that it's all about! It's bulk!

The manager said that

it was a cleverly dreamt and cleverly nurtured myth, I am claiming a bit maliciously. But I do think this is true. And I would not say that it was wrong, because the myth worked during the entire '80s. That is not a black mark against us. If the consultants thought that we were good at combining management and IT—fine. Then they were happy about it, worked in their projects, and earned money through programming, because that was what it was really about.

This illustrates that image management is at least sometimes far from just presenting a fair or even slightly 'improved' picture of a company. It is perhaps often better seen as a combination of a wish to present a positive and appealing picture, ambitions, and a more or less realistic idea of where one is going. But is it perhaps also an outcome of management's desire to deceive the customers and/or the personnel?

Image Management as Intentional Deception?

Whether managers frequently simply try to deceive various groups by means of misleading communications of their company is hard to say. Such practices may be dangerous and harmful, and most people are probably not that cynical, although a society characterized by intensive marketing of brands and images may fuel just that attitude (Boorstin 1961; Jackall 1988). Issues around image frequently stand ambiguously to what actually goes on in a company. The borders between reality and ambition, realism and wishful thinking, being honest and wanting to inspire, fact and fiction, are often hard to draw. Typically, managers try to represent their companies in as bright colours as possible, perhaps sometimes thinking or hoping that 'visionary' statements one day may come true. But as the case illustrates, managers may well communicate fabricated versions of what the company stands for and aspires to be that have very little connection with what they actually think the company does.

Hatch and Schultz (2003) warn against allowing discrepancies between how various audiences perceive an organization. They see it as vital to link closely strategic vision—the central idea of top managers about what the company will achieve in the future—with organizational culture—the values, beliefs, and meanings of the employees—and corporate images held by various stakeholders. They argue that alignment between perceived corporate image and organizational culture magnifies awareness about the nature of the corporation and what it stands for. A gap between a focus projected by image management and organizational culture as manifested in everyday meanings and actions may create problems—confusion, cynicism, distrust—both internally and externally. In particular, in knowledge-intensive service work, where there is a strong interface between knowledge workers and the client, any deep discrepancy between the image systematically communicated by management and what is expressed by the workers may kick back and undermine efforts to create a positive image. Undermining trust may be harmful. On the other hand, the high level of ambiguity creates considerable space for the development of different pictures, which are not necessarily compared or checked. The quotations above signal how management can successfully manipulate the beliefs of subordinates and, possibly, clients.

Micro-Level Image Management

The significance of image also affects the disciplining of the workforce at the *micro* level, e.g. the everyday behaviour of individuals. It is here that the actual beliefs and meanings of employees, more or less affected by normative control, are expressed. Some of what is expressed is influenced by an ambition to shape perceptions of what can be expected from the company and its employees. In a study of one of the (then) big six accounting firms, Covaleski *et al.* (1998) found that the appearance of being 'professional' was highly significant for the career prospects of accountants. One person, identified by his superiors as a 'revenue stream', reported that his success was closely associated with imitating the behaviour of his mentor and his mentor's mentor, both of whom were partners. There was a strong focus on physical appearance in order to give a strong impression of being tightly disciplined and accountant-like. Virtues such as being clean, proper, impersonal, objective, conventional, disciplined, predictable, and reliable are, presumably, communicated. One interviewee mentioned a reprimand from a superior for cutting his lawn in his free time without a shirt, which was seen as improper. Another had a feedback session that focused less on his work behaviour than on the fact that his superiors had observed that his tie stuck out a bit under the collar, and that this was not 'professional appearance'. (For similar documentation, see Grey 1994, 1998.) A study of Swedish advertising workers indicated much effort in projecting the right appearance, with fashion-conscious, casual but elegant clothes, frequent changes of dress, etc. (Alvesson and Köping 1993).

Highly visible meetings with people in senior positions making vital decisions while being remote from projects and lacking intimate knowledge of them are also significant in terms of image production. Powerpoint presentations seem to be a key event for image management in consultancy firms' encounters with clients. A young management consultant I interviewed remarked, with a deep sigh, that he felt as though he had spent half his work life preparing and delivering Powerpoint presentations. In these, a highly structured, rational version of what is supposed to be accomplished is presented, persuasively gaining acceptance for a proposal. A study of the preparations for a meeting with a potential client in an advertising agency revealed the most detailed preparations and worries, including the hair-length of one of the key people from the agency, the composition and colour of the fruit on the table, and two spelling errors on the overhead (Alvesson and Köping 1993).

Of course, careful and extensive presentations aimed at providing a credible and impressive image of what is to be done and what has been done may not always work as intended, and may even backfire. One manager in a company commented upon a project with a large consulting firm:

when I try to inform them about things I try to put it as tangibly as possible, and find the core issues. And then G and G Consulting tries to present enormous amounts of information. It's like heaps of pictures, lots of information. It's hard to actually analyse what is being said. They're professionals when it comes to making Powerpoint presentations—no one can object to that. I'd say that they have probably presented more overhead transparencies in order to push our system aside than the total amount of our systems documentation.... they have produced enormous amounts of paper.

I don't know what we paid them last year, but it's this many pictures and very few deliveries.

In science-based work such as pharmaceutical R&D, importance attaches to having a doctorate and being active in scientific communities by writing articles in scientific journals and attending conferences. The doctorate can be seen as a reflection of competence, but participation in the rituals of the scientific community is not solely motivated by product development and commercial reasons. Industrial scientists feel that in order to get full credentials and have full access to scientific networks and informal information, the image of being a 'complete' scientist is called for.

Of course, knowledge workers do not have a monopoly on jobs in which image management is important. People in many service sectors also need to act as representatives and present a good face, although this is often more episodic, brief, and may concern issues of appearance more than impressions of intellectual ability or knowledge (Thompson *et al.* 2001). Knowledge workers, in this respect, are more similar to managers, in particular perhaps those wishing to impress their superiors. Arguably, using opportunities to present and nurture a particular image is vital here.

Rhetoric-Intensity: The Claims to Knowledge

In view of the notoriously ambiguous character of (a significant part of) knowledge-intensive work and organizations, the demands of the agents involved in terms of providing convincing accounts for what they do become central. Rhetorical skills and rhetorical acts become highly significant for the constitution of the company, its workers, activities, and its external relations. It is central for regulating impressions and images, although the latter is also very much a matter of using material symbols and producing image-enhancing acts and establishing relationships that symbolize corporate success.

Comparatively 'non-ambiguous' organizations (involved in clear-cut products and a great deal of operations and many employees' work content), such as fast food and railway companies and nail manufacturers, and occupations, such as typists or machine operators, can be managed without very developed rhetorical skills. This is not to say that ambiguity is absent or that persuasive talk is not needed in these organizations, only that this talk is less salient and that material aspects of work often limit the scope and need for rhetorical skills. Of course, service work often includes much verbal interaction, but the tasks do not normally call for or even allow mastery of more elaborated language codes. For example, the rhetoric involved in typical utterances by air stewardesses—'good morning', 'what would you like to drink?', 'coffee or tea, sir?', and 'goodbye'—is not salient. But organizations and jobs that score highly on ambiguity—such as the ones we are addressing here—cannot be managed without this rhetoric. 'In the face of competing knowledge bases consultants have to appear authoritative by convincing prospective clients that their expertise is worth buying in. They must persuade clients of their definition of the situation and persuade them to collaborate on the basis of this analysis' (Clark 1995: 91–2).

A management consultancy firm is thus quite different from a bus company in its 'rhetoric-intensiveness'. The latter is hardly in the business of rhetoric. The former, together with most knowledge-intensive organizations (including universities), is. One could say that they are 'knowledge-claims-intensive'. This does not, of course, imply that these organizations are *only* in this business. Clearly, much more is needed in order to succeed than possession of rhetorical skills.

There are good reasons to resist a clear-cut objectivist or realist dualism between, on the one hand, rhetoric, ideology, symbols, and other 'non-real' elements and, on the other, the real, the true, substance and other 'non-invented' stuff. However, a strong rhetorical, relativist, symbolist, postmodernist, or subjectivist thesis, in which all distinctions between reality and appearance are viewed as fictions, is also unsatisfying. I am certainly not denying that we can sometimes sort out the real from the fabricated. Most interesting research questions for social science, however, do not fit easily into such a pattern of thinking. We seldom have an interest in questioning obvious issues (although occasionally things may be less obvious than they appear). The constructed-ness of reality and the reality of construction, the realness of symbols and the symbolic character of reality, should be borne in mind (Peters and Rothenbuhler 1989)—especially, perhaps, when the knowledge-intensive is studied.

Rhetoric, then, is not external to the core of knowledge-inten-siveness, but is its core. Rhetoric does not simply mean persua-sive talk in some kind of opposition to 'reality' or 'truth', but refers to elements of arguing and persuasion that may, or may not, be backed by 'facts'. Seldom can these be separated from a rhetoric aiming to convince sceptics that a particular claim simply is based on, or reports, 'facts'. Even scientific reports are rhet-orical products (Calás and Smircich 1988; Watson 1995). This book is certainly not just presenting logical arguments and data but expresses efforts to persuade the reader through a variety of moves and tricks. When referring to other studies they are either—typically—invoked in a way that simply supports my point, or they are referred to in order to show weaknesses and problems in positions less clever than my own. This is unavoid-able. The unavoidability of rhetoric in many areas of human life does not mean that everything is rhetoric or that this term is equally relevant and carries interpretative power in all corporate and work contexts. An aspect that differentiates many KIFs, especially in the service sectors, from other kinds of company is the *degree* of elaboration of the language code through which one describes oneself or one's organization, or regulates client-orientations.

In many KIFs talk and conversation are a crucial part of the work day (Deetz 1990). Complex problems and difficulties in making assessments call for negotiations of meanings around problem definition, work processes, and evaluations of progress and solutions. Certain types of management consultant are also very much in the business of working with vocabularies and developing or encouraging specific sets of meanings. This kind of consultant can metaphorically be described as a broker of meaning. Here the profession is viewed as speciali-zing in the production and delivery of linguistic artefacts

(Czarniawska-Joerges 1988, 1990[1]). The consultant is a travelling broker 'who sells tools for producing meaning, and therefore the control, which is needed for collective action' (1990: 142). Unlike the esoteric expert type of consultant, working more like a doctor or engineer, who claims that labels in improvement activities must be authoritatively attributed by the consultant, the broker wants to engage the locals in labelling work and meaning production. Apart from the shared use of a vocabulary clarifying what exists and what calls for improvement, much energy in the consultancy process is spent creating metaphors indicating new ways of understanding issues and thus some energy and enthusiasm. Consultants here work as teachers, as sparring partners, they are 'idea-makers' or, when the creativity of the locals is unleashed, 'idea-cultivators' (1990: 142). The rhetorical part of work is significant here: the metaphors used and cooperatively produced must be persuasive, even seductive.

A Dutch study observes that clients as well as consultants are eager to connect and disconnect themselves respectively from fashionable and non-fashionable labels. The knowledge that consultants sell must appear to potential clients to be up to date. 'Through the close contacts with potential and present clients, consultants are quick to pick up signals about their customers' preferences, which leads consultants to adopt or shed labels' (Benders and van Keen 2001: 46).

This use or disuse of labels may have little or nothing to do with the actual work of the consultancies. Of course, this 'substance' certainly matters. But without being labelled in the correct way, it is difficult to get paid for doing it. The study also underscores the significance of framing competence and work through effective rhetoric, but also the temporal nature of the rhetorical effectiveness of a particular vocabulary.

In technically oriented KIFs, such as in computer consultancy work, communication and interaction are significant for the successful discharge of projects—which, according to my interviewees, fail more often on non-technical than technical grounds, e.g. through confusion and misunderstanding in the project, from

[1] Czarniawska-Joerges uses the term 'merchant'. For my purpose I feel that the term 'broker' works better.

unclear or changing demands from clients, and from users not accepting solutions.

Often, however, the need for persuasive talk is strongest in those situations in which people try to gain acceptance for claims for something abstract and important. Sometimes professionals try to distance themselves from the more practical and technical issues and associate themselves with 'strategic' themes. A study of marketing departments in UK companies offers a nice illustration. The people in the marketing departments had problems in establishing themselves as a key group for corporate success worthy of putting their imprints on the company's strategic orientation. Tensions around marketers' efforts to establish their breadwinning credentials are partly a matter of difficulties in 'convincing the doubters that marketing is based not on superficial slickness but on entrepreneurial substance and that in difficult times it is marketers who deliver the goods' (Chalmers 2001: 66).

The marketing people in a computer systems company tried to distance themselves from promotional activities and move the terminology away from marketing language. They talked about 'business teams' as synonymous with sales teams and substituted 'business manager' for marketing manager. The head of the unit, formally known as the marketing planning manager, proposed the term 'business management' as appropriate for their work by referring to their responsibility for safeguarding the 'integrity of the business' and for the non-promotional aspects of marketing, including management of gross margins and profit, and 'ownership' of commercial relations with suppliers and business monitoring activities. The company had a strong culture of accountants, technicians, and salesmen, but 'not any real culture of managing a business' (p. 72) and this niche was for the marketing unit to occupy, people in this function hoped. The senior marketing people tried to divide the marketing department into two sections, one involving promotional and more routine tasks, serving sales, delegated to junior employees, and a more active, entrepreneurial role, managing the business part, which they themselves should occupy. This division had strong gendered undertones, where being a marketer in the first version connoted a less valued masculine status. The business manager's marketing version was one of an active, entrepreneurial and masculine, 'breadwinning' role, characterized by initiative and leadership. This image was clear in the accounts of sales people, represented as impulsive, in love with being flattered, and not necessarily rational or profit-oriented in their work. This image contrasted with the image of the business (or marketing) manager as rational, cool, and able to master his passions. Chalmers did not study in detail how this rhetoric was actively used in relations with other groups within the company—of which top management, of course, was the most important audience—but the use of this rhetoric as part of the building-up of a shared aspired identity, and mobilization to talk and act within the group of marketers, is in itself of importance. As Broms and Gahmberg (1983) point out, auto-communication is an important part of organizational life. The sender is also the recipient of the message.

There are different kinds of discursive resources—words, scripts—that are employed in KIFs and (other) more or less professional settings in order to produce convincing accounts for why clients should pay very high fees for something they can't assess particularly carefully in advance. Parts of these revolve around knowledge; others go outside or beyond a knowledge discourse and refer to more 'subjective' traits and orientations, such as creativity, social skills, ability to manage process, or intuition. A closer look is called for.

Rhetoric of Knowledge

Discourses on professions and other knowledge-intensive workers and organizations are characterized by their persuasive powers. The literature on management consultancy as written by practitioners of the trade often presents a rather idealistic picture, portraying the consultant as a highly competent and rational professional with integrity and self-control, possessing unquestionable expertise suitable for solving different kinds of management problem in practice. This representation is also expressed in statements such as 'the nature of the work, which is the application of knowledge learned through extensive training and experience to a series of incrementally different but complex situations, is unique' (Howard 1991). Such a positive, rational view also comes through in the claim that 'the quality of what is delivered can only be assessed by other professionals within the same area of expertise, which is precisely the reason society accepts professional associations taking charge of peer reviews, licensing, and sanctioning of inappropriate behaviour' (Løwendahl 1997: 36). In the *Danish Encyclopedia* it is said that 'the professional consultancy function is characterized by objectivity and integrity in relationship to customer and client' (cited in Poulfeldt 1999). Implicitly, it is claimed that people in a consultancy role score much higher in terms of cognitive rationality and moral virtue than other mortals. These expressions can to some extent be understood in terms of rhetoric and as an expression of the self-promotion of professionals and managers of professional organizations, accepted and reproduced broadly in society and also by many researchers. (For a counter-view, in which the formal status of a profession is viewed as an outcome of power and politics rather than superior expertise, see Collins 1990.)

In some knowledge-intensive fields scoring high on a scale of official professionalism (state authorization, ethical committees, etc.), practitioners can draw upon institutions which take care of much of the persuasive work. Close connections to universities, scientific institutions, and recognized professional associations carry in themselves much of the persuasion needed and indicate that the 'profession' has something fine to offer for which clients should subordinate themselves and pay a lot of money.

An implication of this is that the focus changes from an emphasis on formal knowledge to persuasive strategies that can be used to convince all concerned of one's expertise and superior rationality, which are to the benefit of one's clients. It is rarely a matter of plainly demonstrating one's knowledge in a simple and clear-cut way. Knowledge or core competence is still vital, but this becomes rather a matter of knowledge for the sake of being socially recognized as an expert, i.e. knowledge about how to act in an 'expert-like' way. The persuasive or rhetorical element is vital. Being perceived as an expert is more crucial than being one; indeed, 'being' an expert is, in terms of social relevance and success under market conditions, an outcome of social validation. Of course in order to act credibly as an expert often calls for considerable experience, skills, and self-confidence. Rhetoric presupposes knowledge.

Formal (theoretical) knowledge has considerable prestige and symbolic value in Western society, indeed in the entire world, and firms and professionals use this terminology for identity as well as image-enhancing purposes.

Other Kinds of Rhetoric: Unique Selves and High Morality

Not all the persuasive strategies and tactics of KIFs emphasize knowledge. Sometimes this particular quality is to some extent downplayed while virtues such as creativity or process skills are emphasized, and these are closely related to more personal, subjective qualities. These are not just then seen as idiosyncratic characteristics of specific individuals, but may also be presented as abilities produced or reinforced by specific professions and organizations. My two case studies of a computer consultancy firm and an advertising agency indicated the significance of discourses stressing personal, subjective orientations facilitating social interaction and creativity.

In the computer consultancy case, managers and consultants did not stress knowledge—in terms of technical skills or education-based knowledge—as very central. The shared orientations of the personnel were emphasized. At a meeting for new employees one manager said that, among his consultancy staff, there were people with all kinds of background from nuclear physics to hairdressing. He thus communicated that formal knowledge was not that crucial. Of course, people had some higher formal education and practical experience in computer work, and about two-thirds of all employees had a university degree. This was published in, for example, annual reports. Still, the internal managerial philosophy rather strongly emphasized social orientations, communication abilities, and flexibility as characterizing the company (Alvesson 1995). The personalities and orientations of employees were claimed to be central, and these qualities were viewed as outcomes of a highly selective recruitment policy and the philosophy, corporate culture, and general emphasis on an ability to handle social relations in computer consultancy work at a corporate level. Whether people in the companies actually 'had' or were guided by the espoused cultural orientations is hard to say, and is of less interest for my point here, but they were salient in their accounts of themselves and their work, and they presumably often made an impression on clients and others, which contributed towards convincing them of the unique competence of the company and its people.

This company thus put strong emphasis on a rhetorical strategy in which its ability to master social relations and interactions associated with projects and client–consultant relations was made credible through organizational talk (and action) that stressed the organization's special features. Its ability to 'manage projects' was underscored by rhetoric emphasizing the company's refined ways of dealing with the difficult social and communicative side of computer consultancy work. When describing the highly diversified set of tasks, the broadness of the skills involved, and the rather messy situation that characterize projects, this rhetorical strategy highlights not technical expertise or knowledge but the 'people' side of projects. Ambiguous work can be described in many ways. The version that the work involves only moderately complicated programming tasks and the management of highly complicated social and organizational situations that call for some computer knowledge and rather more social and project management skills is certainly not the only one available, and many other companies use other forms of rhetoric.

In the advertising case, some people complained about lack of knowledge, ignorance, etc. within the occupation despite the fact that, within the agency we studied, about a third of all employees had a university degree (typically in business administration). At the same time one interviewee, the founder of the agency we studied, emphasized that knowledge is very important in work, while 'without knowledge one is just but a freely floating artist' (Alvesson and Köping 1993). On the whole, however, advertising people did not emphasize knowledge as what they contributed to the firm. The impression was that they could function with relatively modest 'knowledge'. Instead, a somewhat 'non-rational' understanding was expressed. Typical discourses stressed the subjective orientations of the workers and the particular working climate of their organizations. In terms of talk and appearance (e.g. attire) advertising people indicate that they are aesthetic, sensitive, emotional, and individualistic. These personality traits and subjective orientations are put forward as signs of their fine-tuned intuition of what appeals to consumers and their creative ability to communicate to them in ways beyond the capacity of the client organizations (who occasionally expressed the opinion that they could have produced the advertisements equally well). According to their self-representations, advertising workers are special and different from employees in bureaucracies. This belief is important in forming the identities of advertising people and the rationale for clients paying for their services (Alvesson 1994). In a study of marketers—the purchasers of the work of advertising people—one person saw jargon as a key resource that people outside the advertizing field lacked:

We deal with people who are professional marketers in the creative agencies that we use, and by and large the qualities they bring to bear in things do not appear to be extraordinarily better than the people that we have working... Almost the best bit about it would be that we would know the jargon (chuckling), and if we could have the hands up on the jargon, I'm sure it would do the trick. (Chalmers 2001: 143)

In other jobs, such as psychotherapy, social work, and some organizational consultancy, people refer to their personal qualities as a key feature of work (Beckman 1989). The individual—rather than abstract knowledge and intellectual skills—is sometimes represented as a tool, although cultivated in professional training. More broadly, it is sometimes stated that professionals in general are special, while such 'work and organization either attract or develop unique individuals' (Howard 1991). Such discourses about the self may be seen as part of the self-understanding and identity work within a profession, but also as a way of promoting one's own labour power in the absence of more tangible signs of reliable knowledge or results.

In R & D based KIFs, where the centrality of a physical product may offer more instances for saying yes or no to various claims of what is good and what works, the need for persuasive talk is sometimes less salient than in service work, where clients must be worked on and with. But even in some R & D settings there is downplaying of the knowledge background of people and an idealization of having the 'right' orientation in work. As an interviewee in a large high tech company, named Tech, expressed it: 'A lot of people we hire into this company, at least the ones that stick around, have basically the same mindset. Someone who is innovative, enthusiastic, willing to work hard, who isn't hung up on structure, and who has absolutely no concern with educational background' (Kunda 1992: 73).

In this company technical expertise certainly is significant, but it does not tell the entire story of what makes the company succeed, and this shared talk on the nature of Tech people really has persuasive and productive effects, shaping people's orientations. I will address this further in Chapter 9, on identity.

A different type of rhetoric refers to the cultural values of the profession and/or the firm. Here it is not so much unique individuals and forms of subjectivity that make people capable of accomplishing certain things, but the shared orientations associated with the collective (profession or firm). The definition of consultants found in some encyclopedias and books on the trade that stress objectivity and integrity can exemplify this. A further example of this kind of rhetoric and how it is used in a particular context is provided by Greenwood *et al.* (2002) in a study of the transformation of the accounting profession in Canada from being a single profession to a multi-disciplinary profession. This change involved the redefinition of chartered accountants from being not merely accountants to becoming 'business advisers' instead. As such chartered accountants are to draw upon a broad set of diverse skills and services to offer to their clients and employers.

This involved a redefinition of the profession and efforts to make the members of the occupation as well as their clients, employers, and other groups accept this change. It was here emphasized that chartered accountants had the necessary expertise and the right value set for the change, including objectivity, integrity, and service: 'Instead of defining itself in terms of a substantive core of abstract knowledge, the profession became defined by its values of objectivity, service and expertise. By implication, the jurisdictional domain to which these values could be applied became fluid and open to reinterpretation. Hence professional integrity would be sustained despite expansion of the profession's boundary' (Greenwood *et al.* 2002: 72).

A key element here is thus the claim that chartered accountants can be trusted even when expanding their range of activity because of their high ethical standards.

The three discourses—around knowledge, subjectivity, and ethics—are normally combined in KIF and professional rhetoric. Sometimes it is possible to see extreme knowledge-focusing, rationalistic or knowledge-downplaying, subjectivity- and intuition-celebrating discourses at work in the corporate and self-representations of people in PSFs and other KIFs. I think it is less common to find a high ethical level discourse dominating—clients want more than just talk about moral trustworthiness, although it was salient in some of the argumentation of the Canadian chartered accountants. Firms and workers draw upon two or all three discourses, to different degrees and in different situations. The need to explain what one is capable of doing in a way invoking trust calls for a repertoire of discourses, functioning as resources for persuasive talk. Knowledge is often crucial, but firms often think they need to distance themselves from a strict knowledge-focusing discourse indicating that they may offer something more than just the application of university-based, formal knowledge and the fairly standard knowledge of the certified professions. Pure rationality is often not sufficient. Talk about more individualized or organizationally idiosyncratic orientations such as creativity, intuition, and social skills adds to the persuasive powers. Since there is sometimes suspicion of KIFs, partly associated with the problems of assessing their contributions, convincing people of their moral credibility using rhetoric emphasizing a strong work ethic around service-mindedness and integrity becomes important. The popularity of the slogan 'client orientation' can be understood in this light. It says little about knowledge and competence, but indicates a form of subjectivity as well as a moral orientation that is geared to making the client less anxious about the good intentions of the service provider.

Rhetoric and Management Control: Consultants Doing 'Integrated Services'

Let us move on from rather general comments and illustrate how seemingly neutral and rational ways of representing what an organization is doing can be seen as rhetoric effectively shaping expectations and even exercising powerful management control.

Deetz (1997) has provided an in-depth analysis of the ways in which an IT service group within a large company changes its form and defines its business concept (mission statement) in a different way. The service group AIMS, comprising about ninety people, defined itself as achieving 'integrated business solutions performed through a consultancy arrangement', the latter element involving a partial redefinition to the employer. Deetz interprets the role of the conceptions of 'consultancy' and 'integrated solutions' in terms of their persuasive powers and effects on personnel, ruling out alternative ideas on how to define their position and task. The idea of doing 'consultancy'—rather than an alternative position of being internal consultants or a support group, at least partly internally funded—was seen as prestigious and appealing. It was understood as breaking down a bureaucracy of fully funded service units, to improve employee motivation and general effectiveness. It also meant having to do much internal marketing, being subordinated to the price mechanism and an increased dependence on clients—aspects less ideologically and practically positive for the unit, but these alternative meanings were marginalized and never aired as a consequence of the ideological power of the idea of being 'consultants'. A similar effect characterized the contrast to 'integrated services' involving larger projects, namely 'smokestack' services, and the carrying out of smaller tasks, such as customer-requested applications requiring a specific skill. The terms 'consultancy' and 'integrated' were thus seen as signalling something good, and exercised strong rhetorical influence. Deetz points out that both terms seem concrete, and yet contain enough ambiguity to cover many different things:

The terms written together make a good start to any document that denotes a unit that is different, coherent, cutting edge, and knows what it is about. The terms' power resides in their apparent normalization and articulation with dominant themes in business. (p. 196)

At the same time, the terms reveal very little. 'Integrated' seems to say something clearer and more distinct than services, but actually does not:

To say 'services' invites the question of what services, to say 'integrated services' already implies an answer of all services, thus seeming to make the follow-up question unnecessary. 'Integrated' adds little specification to 'services', telling how they are offered but not what they are. The analytic power of the adjective is to divert attention from what is unclear, the services themselves. The term 'integrated' thus distinguishes in the sense of adding value rather than adding clarity to the difference. It more stops the discussion with its implied value and clarity than adds to it. (p. 196)

This kind of vocabulary has a marketing value as it creates a misleading clarity and persuasive effect in a situation where it is difficult to define what one can actually do. It also has an internal control effect as it allows 'the dominant coalition to control interpretive processes and to enhance their power at the same time' (p. 197). In the company the emphasis on consultancy encouraged employees to become 'client-oriented', and to subordinate themselves to the clients' demands. The emphasis on 'integrated services' meant that those mainly doing 'smokestack' work—mostly female employees—were marginalized. Compared to the more protected and autonomy-guaranteeing partly funded organizational situation, managerial power was also reinforced by the new definitions of the organizational situation and what is most valuable. Through being 'consultants' people became more accountable to their managers. Through viewing 'integrated services' as the ideal, the autonomous work project declined in status, and managers as coordinators and integrators became more central.

This example illustrates the significance of persuasive conceptions and talk in this kind of business, where representations of what is actually done are open projects and the possibilities are many. Rhetorically effective statements about the business counteract experiences of ambiguity and openness, in relationship to external audiences as well as within the organization.

Summary

Knowledge seldom speaks for itself. KIFs, in particular in the service sector, are highly sensitive to image. Image management—carried out by top management but also by all employees on an everyday basis—is very important. So is corporate rhetoric. The nature of the work calls for persuasive strategies to account for what they can do, and what they actually do and have accomplished. Claims of managers and workers in KIFs about themselves, their capacity, work, organizations, and results need rhetorical support. Knowledge workers are language workers.

A division of labour, in which PR departments and top management act as rhetors while the rest of the organization keeps quiet
and does mainly productive work with physical outcomes (type
letters, boil potatoes, drive trucks), does not fit most KIFs. An
important aspect here is that communication about the firm and
what it stands for cannot just be communicated externally but
must also work internally. Frequently messages go both ways; for
example, communication seemingly directed at external audiences functions also as a message to people within the organization, mobilizing them as communicators for the organization
(Cheney and Christensen 2001).

A strict separation between having knowledge and marketing
it—between a core competence and a separate task of persuading
various audiences about knowledge-intensive organizations
having it—is misleading. Knowledge does not exist in a vacuum,
as something fixed and packaged, ready to be sold and distributed, even though many authors on knowledge and knowledge-
intensive organizations prefer such a reified view. Knowledge resides in persuasively expressed models.

I have pointed to three discourses—around knowledge, subjectivity, and ethics—that are normally combined in KIF and
professional rhetoric. Knowledge rhetoric often dominates, in
particular in R&D KIFs. In this sense KIFs can be described as
knowledge-claim-intensive, i.e. rhetoric focuses on claims to
being highly knowledgeable. Sometimes elements that go beyond
or are on the margin of knowledge are emphasized, such as
creativity, flexibility, and process skills. As a consequence of high
market uncertainty and fear of opportunism on the part of KIFs,
in particular in the service sector, moral rhetoric is often used. The
key term 'client orientation' can be seen as a signal expressing
the moral virtues of professions and PSFs. As Greenwood and
Empson (2003) note, it is possible that professional partnership
firms—exclusively dominated by people within the profession—
enjoy certain market advantages as clients may perceive them as
free from separate owner interest and that the dominance of
professional values may make them more reliable than companies subordinated to capitalist interests.

It is worth noting that knowledge is not always brought forward as salient in the image management practices and rhetorics
used by firms in describing their work and themselves. Other

aspects are also, and occasionally even more, significant in KIF persuasive strategies and tactics. Therefore, seeing KIFs in terms of 'agents of knowledge' may be not so much misleading as an overly rational and partly reductionistic view. In many cases person-bound, subjective qualities and moral virtues are presented as equally or even more significant than 'knowledge'.

Chapter 5 Socio-politics of Knowledge Work: Social Connections and Interactions

As a socially constructed phenomenon knowledge does not exist on its own, but is dependent on social recognition. Without being perceived and recognized by others knowledge does not, for all practical purposes, appear as such, at least not in market and organizational contexts. A company that claims to be in the knowledge business—being able to offer services or products with a sophisticated knowledge content—calls for the specific or institutionalized confirmation and support of significant others. Parallel and partly overlapping work with image management and corporate and professional rhetoric call for the establishment, maintenance, and development of favourable social relationships.

On the ideal market it is only the product or service—and its quality and price—that matters: who is selling and delivering it is irrelevant. Of course, such an asocial orientation is an ideal type, appearing only among actors with full information about what is exchanged. When the quality or value of a commodity is difficult to assess, the perception of who is offering it becomes important. In conditions of high market uncertainty in which actors exchanging with KIFs typically operate, in particular in the service sector, perceptions of partners and the nature of the social relationships involved become crucial. Podolny (1993) shows, in a study of investment banking, that the greater the market uncertainty, the more likely organizations are to engage in transactions with those of similar status.

Many researchers emphasize that knowledge development is dependent on social interaction and on broad areas of contact with knowledgeable others. A favourite theme for authors writing about functionalist knowledge and organization is that social networks and interaction between people and institutions that are 'objectively' experts or knowledge-intensive lead to more knowledge and innovation (e.g. Newell *et al*. 2002; Nonaka 1994; Wikström *et al*. 1993). I agree that this is often the case, but the main point I am making here is very different and revolves around the image aspects of visible networks and connections. I am emphasizing the symbolic aspect of interactions and relationships, which is significant especially for service providers.

The rather heterogeneous aspect of the dependence on significant others for validation—the relational character of knowledge-intensiveness—involves (*a*) (being perceived as) having links with bodies that confirm one's knowledge-intensiveness, (*b*) forming and maintaining specific ties with specific clients and customers, and (*c*) orchestrating the interactions involved in carrying out work in socially and politically fine-tuned ways.

Social Links with Others Known for Knowledge-Intensiveness

Relational–interactional issues are relevant on different levels. Professionals receive considerable recognition and authorization from professional bodies. As a layman, one 'knows' that a person is knowledgeable because other knowledgeable people have declared that person to be so. An expert belongs to a community of experts, and authorization and membership of associations are often the criteria for expertise. For members of the recognized professions this is, of course, necessary, and certification is formally regulated. In a corporate context this is far from sufficient: no company would be satisfied with using just any certified accountant or lawyer for an important task. For most clients of the occupations and firms that are broadly defined as professional without being officially recognized and certified—e.g. engineering, management, and IT consultancies—it hardly matters whether they belong to an association or whether the people have a standard route to their positions as qualified 'professionals'. Since these formal issues and the connections that precede and legitimize them are less crucial, for most KIFs relationships and indications of inclusion other than formal membership in or authorization by professional associations become more vital. For firms claiming to be knowledge-intensive it is very important to have (or be broadly perceived as having) the right—advanced and demanding—

clients, joint partners, and other organizations in the network. This is sometimes seen as important because it facilitates the development of new or better knowledge (Wikström *et al.* 1993). In some industries, such as biotechnology, close collaboration and informal contacts outside the formal organizations are crucial (Kreiner and Schultz 1993). My main point in this chapter is that connections are important because they can be used to support the focal company's credentials and claim to knowledge-intensiveness. Of course, it is vital to acknowledge and consider that 'A firm's portfolio of collaborations is both a resource and a signal to markets, as well as to other potential partners, of the quality of the firm's activities and products' (Powell 1998: 231).

My emphasis here is on the second, signalling effect of network. As Håkansson and Snehota (1989) suggest, the invisible assets of firms 'consisting largely of knowledge and abilities, fame and reputation, are mainly created in external relationships. Furthermore they cannot be separated from these relationships' (p. 193).

Knowledge as a social construction is maintained, developed, and communicated through such interactions, and the best way of indicating that a knowledge-intensive company deserves this label is to point to prestigious customers or partners well known for *their* knowledge. A consultancy firm refers to having the 'right' client and the client refers to the use of the 'right' consultants. Different organizations 'prove' that they have advanced knowledge by linking up with the correct organizations. Different organizations 'prove' that they have advanced knowledge by referring to the organizations they are collaborating with. An example of this is when senior people from large consultancy firms write pop-management books with academics, thereby showing their collaboration with and solid anchoring in academia and research (Suddaby and Greenwood 2001). Through such mutual confirmation internal and external audiences 'know' that advanced knowledge is there.

A Swedish public organization in the industrial policy field suffering from legitimacy problems tried to improve its position by presenting itself as in the field of knowledge integration, invoking the names of universities, bank managers, and auditors who had taken part in courses the organization had arranged for entrepreneurs. The courses could have been run without the involvement of these other organizations. By trying to locate itself at the centre of such a network, the organization made an effort to improve its status and profile (Ramfelt 1993). The success of this enterprise was doubtful, and many of the institutions involved seemed more interested in the funding provided by the public organization than in being perceived as engaged in a tight network with it. The image of the focal organization didn't seem to improve. However, that organization's intention is well in line with the significance of belonging to the right club as an indicator of one's worth.

As mentioned above, by definition only insiders can evaluate who is very knowledgeable in a way that is broadly credible. Within the professions the criteria and rules for evaluation are determined by the professionals themselves (Jamous and Peloille 1970). Even though other knowledge-intensive occupations that are less professionalized have developed less of an aura of mystique and are more vulnerable to the evaluation and opinion of outsiders, they are still strongly dependent on the recognition of other insiders. Outsiders rely on those insiders to determine what is rational and valuable. The play within a relatively restricted field then becomes important. The assessments of the market are partly viewed as inside-based, to the extent that the clients are seen as knowledge-able and are assumed to choose and continue to use the better product or service. But frequently the client may not have a deep knowledge of the subject, and considerations and circumstances other than knowledge-ability—e.g. reputation, internal politics, ambiguities, and coincidences—may account for the choice of partner and the forming of links and networks. So 'insiders'—organizations collaborating, for example, by using PSFs—may not necessarily be well informed and 'rational' but may be read as such.

The overall symbolic function of networks is thus significant in contexts weak on visible signs of 'substance'. By being perceived as having close ties with others perceived as being knowledge-intensive, one's own status is confirmed. Sometimes joint ventures are partly motivated by the value of being able to show that one has a close partnership with another technologically advanced actor. This can be seen as a strategic–symbolic issue.

Developing and Maintaining Social Relationships

Partly for this reason, but also of course in order to get and keep customers generally, managing social relationships is important. So it is especially crucial for knowledge-intensive service firms. Organizations in exchange relationships develop structural as well as individual attachments. Structural attachments are procedural (rules to manage the relationship), economic, and technical arrangements that make the exchange relationship possible in the first place and thereafter make it run efficiently. Individual attachments relate to personal skills, knowledge, and interpersonal relationships developed by specific individuals who are central to the collaboration, typically doing boundary spanning work (Broshak 2001). While structural attachments are normally not very dependent on specific individuals, interpersonal attachments are an outcome of key individuals interacting and forming bonds. Professional service personnel invest in learning how to meet the idiosyncratic needs and requirements of clients (Sharma 1997). Fichman and Levinthal (1991) found, for example, that auditing firms typically make investments in relationships with clients and make efforts to generate social attachment. The significance of individual attachments means that when certain key individuals leave, the organizational relationship will dissolve. In professional service contexts this means that when the key contact person of the client organizations leaves or is promoted, the interorganizational relationship is jeopardized. The departure of a key contact person within the service firm may have the same effect. This can be explained through the loss of the binding powers of interpersonal attachment and bonding as well as the investments of time and energy to make the collaboration work. These investments have no value outside the specific interpersonal relationship, and with its termination the client will have less reason to maintain the relationship with the service provider (Broshak 2001).

In the absence of something very specific to offer or tangible results that can be inspected in professional service work, how the social process works comes to represent how the work is done. Talk about and other representations of the (ambiguous) 'core' work process become central. 'A key objective for consultants is to manage and manipulate the interaction process in such a way that they convince clients of their value' (Clark 1995: 53).

Relationship-specific knowledge is embodied in organizational procedures and routines or in individuals. In the absence of the availability of competition parameters such as price (which tends to be less significant for knowledge-intensive business) and quality (which is, as I have said, hard to evaluate) personal relationships and ambiguity reduction through personal contact become particularly significant.

For knowledge-intensive organizations, especially in the service sector, relations and 'relations knowledge' are important. Covaleski *et al.* (1998) refer to one employee in an accounting firm who observed that his 'emerging identity of being "chargeable" was less associated with possessing expertise and wielding knowledge than with managing business relations with clients' (p. 317). In another study of a Big Six accounting firm Grey (1994) reports pressure for those aspiring to be partners to exploit their private life in order to develop and maintain business contacts. In a computer consultancy company, CCC, the slogan of treating everybody as a friend was part of management rhetoric. Many social activities of a climate-shaping character were institutionalized. In some of these clients were invited to participate. Others were primarily used for internal purposes but with the idea that the social skills developed could be used in interaction with clients (Alvesson 1995).

Familiarity and personal knowledge do not guarantee the capacity to evaluate clearly the competence and contributions of a knowledge-intensive company, but knowing the company and its personnel is one way of reducing the uncertainty experienced by the client. Clients of knowledge-intensive service firms are often inclined to remain with those they have experience of, as unknown firms would only exacerbate the felt uncertainty and anxiety. Consequently, investment in and maintenance of an established relationship become crucial.

This is in practice not easy to accomplish, even where people put in great effort, including exploiting their private lives. Relationships between PSFs or KIFs and their clients are not always harmonious. There is frequently mutual scepticism between them. Pressure from the client to cut costs and minimize the use of their own qualified personnel in joint activities, and demands from top management of the consultancy company for high margins in the project, are sources of tension in consultancy work. Deetz (1997) reports of a case of an IT unit where a significant degree of 'emotional labour'—working through, controlling, and exhibiting the 'correct' feelings—in client relationships was called for. Many clients were almost abusive and placed higher demands on the consultants than on their own employees. Paying high fees made them feel entitled to demand effort and sacrifice that they would not ask of their own personnel.

Marketing

The significance of maintaining good business relationships brings us to the marketing and selling of knowledge-intensive or professional service work, a complex area that calls for the use of considerable resources, including, in many businesses, the most senior people. Sales are frequently the most significant work area for senior people in PSFs and the criteria for promotion to partner and, within this group, pay and prestige. As observed by Robertson and Swan (1998), 'those consultants who are best able to market their skills and expertise both internally and externally are much in demand' (p. 557). In some PSFs meeting sales quotas is the variable that management pays most attention to (Empson 1998).

This emphasis on marketing reflects how difficult it is to market professional services. It is partly about the uncertainty of what is being offered, and partly about the ambiguity of the needs of the clients and the potential for PSFs in certain fields to find a very large number of areas of improvement. Often it is far from clear to what extent there is a problem to be solved or suboptimal performance to be improved through the enrolment of expertise. The challenge for PSFs is sometimes to convince clients both that they are underperforming in certain respects and that the PSF concerned can help them with the problem.

Since PSFs—and R & D based KIFs to be contracted for large development jobs—cannot simply exhibit their product for inspection and testing, they must sell promises. How do they get their clients or customers?

If they have a sufficiently good reputation, or a strong corporate brand, then clients themselves sometimes approach the supplier with a problem. Previous experience with a particular consultancy often also increases the likelihood that the client will take the initiative. In most cases PSFs must do a great deal of active marketing with clients in order to sell.

This is always easier when clients and service providers have an established relationship, which reduces the uncertainty. In the absence of such previous contact and perhaps even more so if the PSF does not have a strong brand name, sometimes radical measures are taken. PSFs may offer not to be paid for the time spent, or to be paid only a moderate amount, but to share the profits of a particular assignment; for example, to receive half of the higher revenue or the cost savings that will be produced. This, of course, calls for very precisely defined assignments and measurable outputs, and does not appear to be very common, although some consultancy firms say that they are moving in this direction. An interesting approach to marketing was taken by a firm that lacked the network and was a relative newcomer in a highly competitive segment of the consultancy market. The firm, Land, developed a sales process called the 'pilot project' process.

Sales leads were generated by business development officers who established initial contact with potential clients. The objective was to persuade clients to allow Land consultants to spend a few weeks based at their companies conducting pilot projects, for substantially discounted fees. During this period, the consultants identified the most important issues to be addressed, developed a potential project plan, and quantified the potential financial benefits that would accrue if the client employed Land consultants to carry out the project. The primary objective for the manager of the pilot project was to encourage staff at all levels of the client organization to accept that their firm had an acute problem and that they needed to employ Land to help them to solve it. (Empson 1998: 124)

The interviews indicated the manipulative elements in this sales work. One said that 'the pilot project was about 10% content and 90% emotion' and another that it was all about 'how to move a £200 000 sale to a £2 million sale' (p. 124).

A large part of all marketing of PSFs is conducted when carrying out a current assignment, i.e. finding new assignments with an already existing client. Compared to Land's approach, this can be referred to as 'hidden marketing'. Consultants keep their eyes open for new possibilities and try to convince their clients of further needs for their services. As one manager of an IT consultancy firm I interviewed expressed it, 'we get paid while we do our marketing work'.

But sometimes the hidden marketing is not well disguised and clients may be irritated by efforts of consultants to seek further business opportunities while carrying out a project. One manager in a client company observed that the consultants spent time outside the project they were hired for:

> They then start to work outside the FIS-systems, approach other people in the organization . . . in order to sort of market themselves over there, because they realize that here is more money to make than here . . . I felt like a sheepdog. G and G Consulting people were the sheep, I had to go out and catch them . . . Their task is not to go out and find new possibilities here but their task is to do what the contract is saying . . . you will do this.

Another manager in the same company remarked that 'consultants are like rabbits, if you don't have the situation under control they'll reproduce uncontrollably, it's in their interest to make as much money as possible' (from Alvesson and Sveningsson 2003).

The use of a variety of contacts and indirect relations is generally very important for PSFs in order to find more assignments. A senior consultant in a large management consultancy talks about ways of getting new work in a large company, Great Insurances (GI):

> We have entered the organization through a certain channel and we have started to work there, but we simultaneously try to attack other parts within Great Insurances, and to further develop our engagement at GI, actually in other business units, in staff functions and things like that. In parallel with this project, which we run and deliver and try to enhance in line with the general rules of the art, we try to find new possibilities there too.

> Q: How do you work in order to find the possibilities?

> We try to make them easily accessible by learning about them, reading annual reports, talking to people. It is always easier when you have an ongoing project because you have a quite different stock of information. But we're trying to be proactive, thinking one step ahead and trying to

think of what we would have done if we were in GI's executives' place and what we think they ought to do. And then we try to sell it to them.

It's about having those contacts with people, on different levels in the company. That's where you get the most information and therefore it's difficult when you don't have an ongoing project. So to a certain extent there are more cold calls when you phone them and want to present the company or present something that we have done in a similar company somewhere in Europe or the US or wherever it might be. And you try to start off by building this network, a network of contacts in the company, in order to be able to produce something good, something that both they and we believe that they need.

Some PSFs use a 'promiscuous' strategy of seeking new and changing partners as this provides learning opportunities that broaden experience and knowledge that can be exploited in efficiently run projects with new clients (Jones *et al.* 1998). Most firms want more clients, but often they have good reason to pay specific attention to existing ones. Existing clients are the most important and profitable source of work for a variety of reasons. They typically mean lower marketing costs, as established contacts and knowledge of the client are crucial in order to get more work. Good access to information sources in the client company is important. During ongoing projects consultant firms have the opportunity to learn about potential additional work and can then sell while being paid by the client. Project work may also be carried out more effectively and thus more profitably owing to earlier learning and mutual adjustments that make work run smoother and with greater trust (Clark 1995: 77; Maister 1993). Relationship marketing is therefore very important: time and energy are typically put into the maintenance and development of relationships with existing clients.

Frequently the formation of business relationships follows a social rather than a rational logic, or perhaps rather a fusion of social and rational elements. People who leave consultancy firms sometimes use them as clients, at least when the process of departure has not been a negative one (as may be the case when somebody leaves after having been denied promotion to partner). It is often important for KIFs to manage the departure process in a way that adds to the building of positive networks. Active freelance assistance of people who are encouraged to or want to leave is thus often a source of future business as the former staff may be more inclined to recommend their old company, which they know and understand. It is not unlikely that this will facilitate cooperation between client and consultant. Compared to companies that rely less on personal contacts, management of departure may be a significant area for KIFs (Alvesson 2000*a*). An interesting example of how client relationships can be established is that of a management consultancy company that created a steady supply of assignments through sponsoring and leading a network of consultants and plenty of activities, from courses to workshops. Most of these were internal consultants, and as they knew and had benefited from the seemingly altruistic consultancy company running the network, they were strongly inclined to bring it in when they perceived the need for help.

The complexities, difficulties, and great significance of selling in many professional service areas mean not only that enormous efforts and key competence are invested in sales activities, but that a great deal of irritation and suspicion is created. Consultancy firms are often perceived as strongly oriented towards selling, consistently looking for sales opportunities. They are believed to find 'needs' of clients that correspond to their speciality. Wallander, a former CEO of one of Sweden's largest banks, writes that 'organizational consultants seem often to perceive the very reorganization as a strengthening sauna experience' and adds: 'they have it all wrong' (2002: 36), arguing that it takes a very long time to build up a functioning network of working relationships in an organization and that the eagerness of consultants to restructure may, if accepted by top management, seriously destroy this.

Orchestrating the Interaction Process

Another cornerstone of carrying out knowledge-intensive work is the management of interaction processes. This is most significant, of course, in service work. Here it is normally a matter of a close cooperation between the service supplier and the client. They typically work together in problem definition and the choice of solution, and often also in the implementation of it and the redefinition of problems and changes in solutions that take place over time. 'With intangible deliverables and unclear client demands, the quality of the client's expectations, partly steered by the PSF during the project, becomes absolutely crucial to the perceived quality of the final output' (Løwendahl 1997: 33–4). The strong component of face-to-face interaction with the client is a core aspect of professional service work (Maister 1993). Success in orchestrating interaction processes is of course connected to the forming and reproduction of the social bonds central in networks.

Similar to the position advocated in this book, Clark (1995) argues that 'the distinguishing quality of the consultant–client relationship lies less in the currently available metaphors for professional/institutionalised assistance, counselling or exchange, and more in the interaction between these two parties' (p. 94).

According to Poulfeldt (1999) the clients of management consultants emphasize six elements as central to successful work: adaptation to the situation, the significance of the process, personal fit, active involvement (from the client), professional competence, and consultancy competence. It is worth noting that many of these elements concern social interaction.

Not all PSFs emphasize social relations and social skills as key aspects of their work. One partner in a large auditing firm, Sun, said that 'People come to us if they want a hard-nosed bastard to help them out. They don't want a trusted business advisor or a friend. A Sun client will say, "Don't ask me about my golf handicap, just fix my problem" ' (cited in Empson 2003: 10).

This position, emphasizing an instrumental, rather masculine position, is probably a minority one. Most organizations in the field seem to emphasize social skills. In a computer consultancy company it was generally believed that the technical aspects were less crucial for the success of projects than the social ones: getting along, clarifying expectations, negotiating shared understandings during work, and getting acceptance for solutions were critical (Alvesson 1995). In an advertising company relationships with clients were also seen as very important to address, but much more difficult to handle. To develop a good proposal was sometimes easier than getting the client to accept it, the advertising people complained (Alvesson and Köping 1993). Clients were portrayed as cautious, lacking stamina, and sometimes irrational; for example, rejecting a proposal because the wife did not like it.

One management consultant argues that to appreciate and be close to the client's situation becomes more and more central the more senior one becomes. A well-developed *fingerspitzgefühl* (sensitivity to context) is vital in order to get an agenda through in the absence of direct power:

You learn how to establish...Some interview you might not do in order to collect facts but in order to establish something. It might be necessary to talk to everybody in all business areas in order to make them feel involved. [It's important] that you have a good relation with somebody at the customer company who can point out who's got influence and who's not. Sometimes it turns out that you develop a very good relationship to a person who has this network at the company where all decisions are made at the tennis court or in the sauna. So the only way for me to put my ideas through is to tell him what to bring up at the next round of tennis. (senior consultant)

One consultant emphasizes that it is of utmost importance that one works very closely with the client's personnel, and that substantial resources in the form of time and people are also invested by the client company:

That they, from top management level, are sanctioning and sponsoring the project, so there's a will among the customers involved to actually participate in the project, so that we're not just some kind of resource there, but working together with them instead. It sounds like a cliché but there's a difference between sitting there as a resource doing the job and working together with people from the customer. Either there is good support from top management and then you have some people who work full-time in the project, or you don't have good support from top management and then you sit there as a resource, just being a pain in the ass. So that is probably the most important thing. The expectation I have is that the customer feels that this is very important and sets aside resources to work with this and that it is prioritized from a high level in the organization. That is probably the most important thing, actually. (consultant)

In many projects there are differences with the client company over the extent to which the PSF is seen as a positive resource and what the consultants are expected to do. Frequently consultants feel that the client's personnel are sceptical about their presence:

In a small project there might be two or three people involved, and you might do an investigation of some kind. A pre-study is common, then, in those situations. It is common for top management to sanction the project but they haven't had time to establish it yet, and then you enter as an alien in the company, so it's a very tough job, incredibly tough, because then you need to tell people all the time why you're there, so it's very tough to get going and work in a good way then, so that's tricky. You have to explain all the time why you're here, and then you are confronted with scepticism. I don't know if it's any different if you're from a Swedish consultancy or from an American one. Sometimes people are sceptical to Big Consultancy, Big Consultants and things like that, and it is very hard to deal with that attitude and you often encounter it in small projects. In large projects the project is known for some reason, there are always people from the customer side who's participating, and then the project is established in a whole different way, and then you don't need to argue about why you should help me, but it comes more naturally. (consultant)

In knowledge-intensive service firms maintaining a good relationship with the person who is responsible and purchasing the service involves much more than doing a good job in some technical sense. Often there is a political game going on and the service provider is expected to be prepared to provide political support, including letting the client take the credit for any perceived good result and accept that the blame is ascribed to the service provider (Fincham 1999; Jackall 1988: 141). The client here is not the entire company that is hiring the PSF, but the particular individual who is making the key decisions around the choice of the PSF. The interests of this individual and the client company as a whole may diverge considerably, but from the point of view of the PSF it is the key individual that one benefits most from satisfying.

Of course, managing the client relationship is to some extent a part of a professional-functional concept of knowledge. Problem-solving involves not just the application of technical knowledge on a given problem, but the development of a shared understanding of what the problem is. Gaining acceptance for the proposed solution and working with implementation issues also call for social interaction and the use of social skills. Dealing with resistance to change, conflicts, and organizational politics call for process skills. In some cases, such as management process and organizational development consultancy, interaction 'knowledge' *is* professional-functional knowledge in itself: the very topic of the assignment is to influence people in terms of thinking, values, and orientations. The interaction aspects pointed at here, however, go beyond this kind of professional-functional knowledge and are often not primarily about solving an 'objective' problem or accomplishing results that increase the profits of the client company. The construction of the work and interaction cannot be boiled down to such simple and straightforward matters as an 'objective' problem and a solution. Non-functional elements include keeping the client on the hook, keeping him or her happy (more than serving the client organization as a whole), acting in a politically sensitive way for one's own benefits, preserving the image of knowledge-intensive work being carried out, and using all kinds of means of securing a personal relationship. All these elements appear particularly in the many cases where it is not possible to demonstrate superior capacity.

Consequently, the management and manipulation of social relations and belonging to the right association or informal network of knowledge-intensive players are vital elements in demonstrating one's capacity in the absence of clear-cut and solid proof. The orchestration of social processes in an image-conscious and politically sensitive way is important to compensate for the intangible, ambiguous character of the service being offered. Social relations and personal knowledge sometimes dominate market transactions and matter more than quality- or price-based competition.

The Politics of Management Consultancy Projects

Politics is a crucial part of business and organizational life. Political issues and conflicts are frequently elevated in situations that are outside established relationships. Many consultancy projects address fairly technical issues that are not necessarily emotive issues, although the relationship between the workforce and its managers, on the one hand, and the consultants, on the other, may be characterized by suspicion, and tension around problems of responsibility and the attribution of praise or blame. Managers of departments may prefer resources to be allocated to them rather than spent on expensive consultants.

Additional political problems enter the picture when management consultants are used as troubleshooters. This is not rare: consultants are often used when a senior executive spots suboptimal performance. At minimum some blaming, loss of prestige, and weakening of position are at stake when issues around unsatisfactory performance are put on the agenda and become the target of highly visible intervention. More often, highly substantive issues also become involved: promotion, demotion, career options, loss of resources or jobs, the overall direction of the organizational unit concerned, perhaps of the entire company, and so on. Jackall (1988) reflects on general tendencies among management consultants:

The further the consultant moves away from strictly technical issues— that is from being an expert in the ideal sense, a virtuoso of some institutionalized and valued skill—the more anomalous his status becomes. He becomes an expert who trades in others' troubles. In managerial hierarchies, of course, troubles, like everything else, are socially defined. Consultants have to depend on some authority's definition of what is troublesome in an organization and, in most cases, have to work on the problem as defined. As it happens, it is extremely rare that an executive declares himself or his own circle to be the problem; rather, other groups in the corporation are targeted to be 'worked on'. (p. 140)

We are dealing with a strong client here, one who rules and directs the consultant, the latter being correspondingly weak, sometimes viewed as a 'whore in stripes', according to some of the managers interviewed by Jackall.[1]

The plurality of interests in organizations makes it difficult simply to aim at client orientation. For consultants a long-term relationship with a limited number of clients is very important. Typically clients use people they have experience of and whom they trust. Trust here is tightly connected with the demonstrated ability of a consultant to act in a way that supports the interest of

[1] O'Shea and Madigan (1998) provide narratives supporting this kind of client–consultant relationship.

the person paying for the service. When it is blame-time or praise-time, consultants may often be wise to accept blame for what has gone wrong and give considerable credit to their client. Consult-ants frequently complain that they are used as scapegoats, but recognize that they are also paid for this. For consultants acting as traders in trouble to be successful it seems plausible that they should be context-sensitive and skilled in problem-solving of a special kind. The centrality of political awareness and subordin-ation to power structures runs directly against most claims of professionalism building on objectivity, neutrality, and auton-omy. The term 'client orientation' thus often glosses over rather complex situations and may hide a variety of different, possibly conflictual orientations in relationship to the plurality of interests and views in the client company.

In order to understand power and politics, it is important to note the significance of the consultant's dependence on and sub-ordination to the senior executive paying for the consultant, who is typically working on other people. Normally the consultant is guided by the client in defining the problem and task ahead and in how to go forward and get more information and solve the problem as perceived—or at least presented—by the client. A particular politics of professionalism is involved here, since professionalism gives the process some legitimacy, and self-identification as a professional prevents the consultant from becoming too involved in the political issues. However, this notion of professionalism becomes relatively superficial in the present context as heavy dependence on the client and the client's definition of what should be done in politically heated situations is at odds with how professionalism is normally defined in society.

Typically, to manage in a limited time and in what may be a highly political environment, consultants may be forced to rely on corporate formulas combined with skilful gathering, collation and feeding back of knowledge and ideas generated by the organization itself. This may be further constrained by the need in effect to act as justifiers of policies already preferred by the senior client executive, paying the piper and expecting to call the tune. In this guise, a plausible reinforcement by a prestigious adviser, charging enough to be listened to, is a catalyst for change, which cannot be propelled with sufficient force by the champion from within. (Ramsay 1996: 165)

It should perhaps be pointed out here that politics is very much part of normal organizational life and consultants do not necessarily differ from managerial and other groups in firms. Internal actors are also mobilized as resources and participants in political struggles. We should be careful not to exaggerate the differences between consultants (and other PSF externals) and client personnel. However, the former often enter in situations where politics is amplified and may therefore frequently operate in politically contested situations, and may be wise to work in politically conscious ways. As they are easy to get rid of, they are more vulnerable and sensitive to holders of top positions, unless they have a strong market position or high integrity, in which case they may emphasize their independence and take the risk of losing the client. Against the notion of the professional as typically an independent, neutral subject with a high degree of integrity, the politics of consultancy work and the strong mechanisms leading to compliance, sometimes concealed behind the label 'client orientation', are also important to underscore.

Power Dynamics in Client–Consultant Relations

Jackall (1988) writes that the management consultancy industry 'fuels executive anxiety with a never-ending barrage of newly packaged schemes, all highly rational, most amelioristic' (p. 141). Other authors also take this aspect seriously, particularly in relationship to perceptions of fundamental changes, turbulence, and a repeated and strident bombardment of calls for radical change in managerial values and skills (Clark and Salaman 1996; Sturdy 1997). With every new management fashion, existing managerial competence and practice is viewed as obsolete and great efforts to close the gap between current abilities and a more optimal, up-to-date orientation, e.g. being 'entrepreneurial', are encouraged. Management fashions, as promoted and exploited by consultants, then trigger and reinforce the anxiety that creates receptivity towards the employment of consultancy services then supposed to remove the anxiety. 'Consultancy is fuelled by their provision of a sense of reassurance to management and at the same time reinforcing or creating insecurities' (Sturdy 1997: 397).

The metaphor of consultants as agents of anxiety and suppliers of security can be used to illuminate this understanding of management consultancy (Alvesson and Johansson 2001). This metaphor portrays the consultant as strong and the client as uncertain and experiencing a gap between needed, up-to-date skills and actual knowledge. But a crucial force behind this is powerful managerial discourses—e.g. on business process re-engineering, quality, or the new economy—that are capable of shaking up the client. The consultant can then draw upon and reinforce this anxiety and exploit it.

Sometimes the power asymmetry in relation to the client is assumed to favour the consultant or consultancy firm owing to her or its knowledge or status in a specific area (Løwendahl 1997; Sharma 1997). In such cases it is thus substantive knowledge—or at least beliefs about it—rather than knowledge how to inject anxiety that matters. Løwendahl (1997) argues that the very rationale of PSFs is that they 'create value through processes that require them to know more than their clients, either in terms of expertise or experience in similar problem-solving situations' (p. 32). This seems reasonable, but sometimes PSFs are used as additional rather than superior labour, e.g. to increase manpower temporarily in managerial or IT work owing to extra workload. And even if the PSF has (or is believed to have) a specific form of expertise or experience, it does not necessarily mean that the relationship with the client as a whole is asymmetrical in favour of the former. Sometimes the client may be in a more powerful position and simply tell the professional what to do (Fincham 1999), showing little respect for the superior expertise of the professional but having specific ideas about what the professional should do. Often consultants need objectives, guidelines, and active support from the client, including the allocation of sufficient time, interest, and resources from client management and personnel in order to carry out the task effectively. Also, when the expert is perceived as possessing superior technical expertise, his or her task may be predefined fairly strictly by the client and exercise autonomy and influence only within a highly constrained area. In advertising, for example, it is not uncommon for clients to reject the proposals of an advertising agency and show little respect for the agency's judgement and proposals (Alvesson 1994). Sometimes the client and the consultant may be in a symmetrical relationship: the client being receptive to suggestions, without being confused or uncritical, and the consultant offering either expertise or input to a dialogue. This situation is frequently said by consultants to be the normal one, but it may overemphasize harmony and symmetry and is probably only sometimes a valid description.

Of course, the client is typically in a much stronger financial situation with the knowledge-intensive service company very eager to satisfy him or her. Sometimes PSF workers are very compliant.

Sometimes it's a matter of having some courage. To place demands on the client and say that there is a too heavy focus on delivery. To be able to say: 'No, we're not going to do this. It will be no good.' On that point we have to get better, we must dare to say that 'this won't be good. We will deliver this date, but the solution is not good.' We must dare to say it ... I think there's a need for some courage among those who sit with the clients, to be able to say, 'No, we're stopping this project' from our side. (management consultant)

The general, idealistic notion of the professional taking an independent position as an adviser acting with the client's interest as the guideline does not necessarily say much about the majority of the relationships between clients and consultants (or other experts). Consultants are often inclined to accept the demands of the client: financial dependency outstrips any (perceived) knowledge asymmetry that would make the client inclined to bow to the authority of the consultant.

We can conclude that the power relationship is a complicated matter in this type of work. The knowledge worker may attain expert status and place the client in the position of a layman, but the client may also be central and turn the consultant into hired labour very willing to do what the client proposes. The clients of, for example, consultancy firms, advertising and market companies research, and architects are frequently highly professional themselves. Business services are thus different from the professional services to laymen of, for example, physicians, dentists, and psychotherapists, where the client is typically in a weaker position than and strongly dependent on the professional. The large number of clients means that professionals are typically not financially dependent on single clients. In PSFs the degree of financial dependence on each of what are often a limited number of significant clients can be high. Even a large PSF may get a large part of its business from a single client, which makes the former vulnerable and compliant. We must be careful not to exaggerate the status and power of 'experts', which may well be used to support managerial labour in a subordinate capacity as much as adding something qualitatively superior.

Summary

In many KIFs organizational image and rhetoric are significant areas of managerial work and important elements of corporate success. Image and rhetoric provide guidance and resources for how social relations and interactions are handled. At the same time the creation and maintenance of networks with prestigious institutions, social relations, and everyday behaviour are vital to the realized corporate image and for credible rhetoric. In KIFs, in particular in the service sector, three kinds of social relations thus call for careful management.

1. Becoming part of and remaining in the right kind of network. Networks and associations are in this context not only of interest in relation to 'substantive' issues, e.g. knowledge creation and business opportunities, but also for symbolic and marketing reasons. Being associated with other institutional actors—having prestigious firms or universities as clients, suppliers, or partners—offers strong support for credibility and self-esteem. Networks and contacts can be mobilized in image management and corporate rhetoric. At the same time effective image management and rhetoric facilitate inclusion and continued membership in these networks. Similarity of status seems to be an important mechanism behind the search for partners in at least professional service work (Podolny 1993).

2. Careful handling of social relations in specific work contexts. To develop and maintain social relationships with specific key personnel among clients becomes very important in PSFs, where neither price nor quality are crucial variables—

simply because price is not of primary concern in very many KIF contexts and quality is very difficult to assess. The market does not offer sufficiently clear information about various service providers and their expected contributions. Since quality and competitiveness do not matter very much in decisions about who to hire, image and personal connections take the upper hand. These provide a sense of security and indicate some form of reliability. Keeping the client's key people happy becomes central. Also within project-based organizations, as most KIFs are, personal networks and support are important as assignments vary and it is essential to find the right people to work with. In a large management consultancy company surviving was seen as a matter of 'teaming upwards' with a successful senior person so that the likelihood of being asked to work on interesting and career-enhancing jobs increased. Kunda (1992) also reports, in a study of a large high tech company, the significance of having a variety of good relationships for getting new assignments after finishing a project, in particular if it was seen as unsuccessful and discontinued. The ad hoc nature of work means that connections matter strongly compared to more 'rational' and predictable selection and manning principles associated with human resource management systems and bureaucracy.

3. The careful orchestration of political and social processes in complex projects. Here issues of social adaptedness and political *fingerspitzgefühl* (sensitivity to context) are central. Ad hoc settings characterized by varied social configurations where actors are sometimes dealing with unknown or ill-defined problems in collaboration with new people—from the client or one's own company—call for social and political skills. In many PSFs ongoing projects offer the best position for further sales of service. But too strong a sales interest can easily backfire as the client's personnel may react negatively.

It is important to emphasize that image and rhetoric do not relate only to overall social and institutional connections, superficial campaigns, arrangements, and advertisements, but can also to a great degree be seen as ongoing outcomes of the behaviour and talk of managers and other employees of a company in various everyday encounters. Image management is thus very much a matter of getting employees to act and interact in line with the impression that corporate management wishes to make. A key element here is to talk persuasively in specific ways. This calls for management to influence the organizational culture and identity of personnel, a theme that will be developed later (primarily in Chapters 7 and 9).

Chapter 6   Management and Organizational Control

WHAT is the role and significance of management in KIFs? One could argue that the conventional functions of management (planning, coordination, and control) and the general characteristics of managerial work are also relevant to understanding KIFs. KIFs are far from homogeneous in terms of management and organization; nevertheless, it is typically believed that management issues are different in most KIFs from those of many other firms. I reviewed some of the distinctive features of KIFs in Chapter 2. It can be added here that managers of PSFs interviewed by Løwendahl (1997) claimed that models for the management of manufacturing companies are of limited, if any, relevance. The basic idea of management, as conventionally understood, that of a separation between the planning and execution of a task, is hardly at all a key feature of KIFs. KIFs in this sense by definition are non-managerial: the more it makes sense to talk about knowledge-intensive activity, the less it becomes relevant to employ a (conventional) management model of thinking. Still, there are activities and functions that the concept of management productively illuminates. Since the degree of knowledge-intensity is not always extremely high in many KIFs, there is sometimes space for top management to put its imprint on the organization.

In this chapter I shall go more deeply into some areas of management and work organization where the characteristics of KIFs are distinctive. The chapter starts with a more general discussion of the often limited role of management in terms of strategy, and then points to other areas that are important for management in KIFs. Image management and efforts to develop and strengthen certain ideas of organizational identity are addressed, as are issues of organizational control. Here the interplay between management and client control is emphasized in the case of PSFs.

Human resource management (HRM) will be treated in the next chapter while knowledge management will be addressed in Chapter 8 and some ideas on personal identity and how managers try to regulate the identities of organizational members will be further treated in Chapter 9. The present chapter then addresses some more general aspects around the management of KIFs, while the following three chapters dig more deeply into three areas that are arguably of special significance in this highly people- and sometimes knowledge-intensive field of work and organizations.

General Management and Strategic Decision-Making

Management in most KIFs is strongly affected by the nature of the tasks and qualifications of the employees, both tending to weaken the significance and positional power of top management. In PSFs, based on partnerships, there are frequently tensions between collegial decision-making exercised by the partner peer group, and positional power exercised by managing partners (Greenwood *et al.* 1990; Hinings *et al.* 1991). In the professional partnership 'strategic direction is weak, and the strategic process is one of negotiation, consensus building, and iteration. Implementing a strategic decision depends on widespread acceptance and professional conviction rather than on corporate manipulation of resources, rewards, and sanctions' (Greenwood *et al.* 1990: 750).

Leadership in the context of strategic and other broad organizational issues is frequently not salient in KIFs. Owing to the complexity of work, senior managers frequently do not understand what actually goes on and cannot rely on simple indirect, quantified performance indicators to manage the process. To be innovative, the whole organization must balance the tension between determination and emergence. Large, complex organizations tend to give priority to the former:

To control the wide variety of activities under them, managers rely on abstracted and generalized criteria, but these obliterate the unique aspects of an innovation. Because senior managers are detached from the situated specifics of work, they may force a uniform development time on all innovations regardless of differences, intervene in day-to-day problem solving even though they are not familar with the issues and impose rigid controls when delays crop up. (Dougherty 1996: 429)

Often the majority of employees are capable of acting autonomously, and single individuals can sometimes take initiatives that affect the direction of the entire company—as when a PSF employee gets a large contract with a new client which is then followed up by similar assignments. This means that the space for key figures at the top is often limited. A managing partner in a large management consultancy company that we studied refers to his co-partners as his 'bosses'. Frequently the managing partner in a partnership-based company has limited influence. There has been a change within professional service firms in the direction of greater managerialism, e.g. departing from pure models of partnerships towards strengthening management and strategy and creating a more integrated firm (Greenwood *et al.* 1990; Morris and Malhotra 2002). But sometimes this is difficult. Even a law firm developing strategic plans and management systems and trying to concentrate power in the hands of a managing partner was still seen by people in the company as similar to a fashionable store: 'a flash brand on the outside with a lot of franchises on the inside' (Morris and Malhotra 2002: 16). Løwendahl (1997) refers to managers viewing the management of PSFs as like 'herding wild cats' and 'making ten or twenty racing horses pull a cart together' (p. 63). This calls for talent in negotiation and persuasion, but as most KIFs are capable of tolerating a fair degree of diversity, not all the horses have to pull the same cart or exactly in the same direction. There is, however, as will be explored below, the matter of counteracting too much diversity.

In some cases, however, there are one or two central actors, often the founders of the firm, that have a guru status and these people may have considerable influence in KIFs and PSFs (see e.g. Alvesson 1995; Empson 1998; Kunda 1992; Robertson 1999). Leadership may also be significant under those conditions where a major change is called for (Boxall and Steeneveld 1999). Great persistence and persuasive powers may be needed, and as people in the organization are used to acting and thinking comparatively independently, the opportunities for exercising formal authority and imposing sanctions are limited. This means that

some kind of consensus—or at least the support of a large majority—about the change must be accomplished.

The need for strategies and regulating constraints for employees are weaker in PSFs than in many other organizations. As
Løwendahl (1997) writes, PSFs 'evolve through processes in
which the flexibility of adding new clients, services and competent professionals is absolutely crucial' (p. 63). Strategies are
typically less deliberate—less planned and centrally controlled,
with decisions followed by implementation as distinctive steps—
and more emergent—more spontaneous and an outcome of the
actions of various actors acting and deciding almost simultaneously (Alvesson 1995; Mintzberg and McHugh 1985; and
Mintzberg and Waters 1985). However, some direction is needed
where critical issues are concerned, such as recruitment of new
professionals and the portfolio of projects and clients served. To
utilize, build upon, and expand competence is vital, and it is risky
if this is totally ad hoc and opportunity-driven. Strategic management here becomes more an umbrella setting than a command-
like structure (Mintzberg and Waters 1985) and involves the
development and communication of a consensus-based vision,
broad objectives, and a set of priorities (Løwendahl 1997). Miles *et
al.* (1997) argue that in the 'cellular organization' the entrepreneurial, self-organizing, and ownership elements of work must
be supported by a bold managerial vision and by a philosophy
that emphasizes investment in human resources.

Although many management issues about making strategic
decisions, exercising detailed control over subordinates, and
making a large bureaucratic machinery work are less important
for top managers in KIFs than in many other organizations, there
are some management tasks that become even more significant in
KIFs than in other organizations. These may include:

1. creating social integration within the company by managing
   boundaries and creating the feeling of a common purpose
   and community around an organization's identity;
2. working with an indirect form of control, i.e. normative control, by reinforcing common beliefs and values, e.g. trying to
   influence, maintain, and develop organizational culture;
3. working with client orientation among employees and the
   satisfaction of important clients. This includes nurturing

relationships, and managing the expectations and perceived quality of important clients. This is most critical in PSFs and in some product-focused KIFs ordering tailor-made systems and products;

4. working with the development and reproduction of a corporate image and a shared feeling of organizational identity, and providing support for ongoing image management by all employees;

5. recruitment, motivation, retention, and mobilization of employees, and long-term competence development—creating and developing knowledge and also the motivational base of the organization;

6. improving the use of knowledge by building upon existing knowledge and stimulating innovativeness through the combination of various competences (knowledge management).

The last two themes are addressed mainly in Chapters 7 and 8. The fourth theme, image and identity, surfaced in Chapter 4, and identity will be addressed further in Chapter 9 so here I shall only touch upon them briefly. I shall concentrate on the first three topics in this chapter.

Image and Identity

Many KIFs put emphasis on their distinctiveness and originality. In Chapter 4 I addressed the issue that the services and results that the client pays for at least in PSFs do not speak for themselves and cannot be inspected before purchase—and product-creating KIFs that produce something unique to a specific customer (e.g. a prototype) are sometimes in a similar situation. In this context image (corporate brand) is important to nurture.

The product will be judged in part by who offers it—not just who the vendor corporation is but also who the corporation's representative is. The vendor and the vendor's representative are both inextricably and inevitably part of the 'product' that prospects must judge before they buy. The less tangible the generic product, the more powerfully and persistently the judgment about it gets shaped by the packaging—how it's presented, who presents it, and what's implied by metaphor, simile, symbol, and other surrogates for reality. (Levitt 1981: 97)

Some image management can be centralized and carried out through specific policies and initiatives, e.g. by establishing collaboration and communication with certain partners and clients, developing formal structures that look good from the outside, using material symbols such as corporate building and dress code, advertising, etc. These are tasks for top management, PR, and marketing departments. But image management also calls for the support and active input of employees. This is the case particularly in service work, where employees represent the primary interface with clients and other collaborators. If the everyday behaviour of employees and what they communicate in various situations is not commensurate with the image top management is trying to create and maintain, the latter will be undermined (Hatch and Schultz 2003).

Organizational identity roughly in line with image is thus important in order to make image management possible through the mobilization of internal resources that communicate the right message (or at least do not communicate anything that undermines the desired image). As image is (as addressed in Chapter 4) about a fairly superficial impression and is influenced by instrumental acts designed to create a certain impression, there is no necessary one-to-one relationship between the external and internal communication about the nature of the organization. Questions of identity such as 'Who are we? and 'What is distinctive about us? are related to but not exactly the same as questions of image such as 'How do we want others to see us?' and 'How should others perceive our distinctiveness?' But if the disparity is too wide, the image aspired to cannot credibly be sold to the environment, at least not those parts of the environment that one is closely interacting with. Image management in after-sales situations and for the successful mastery of ambiguities during work, and intimate interactions with clients and partners, call for in-depth image management, and this is related to how employees construct their organization and themselves as members of the organization.

In addition to being important to the creation of image, issues of organizational identity are also, of course, of significance in shaping the self-understanding and mindset of the workforce in more internal work contexts. Identity here relates closely to organizational culture (Alvesson 2002*a*). Material that moulds organizational culture—stories, rituals, corporate artefacts, myths, jargon, etc.—is used in internal and to some extent external communication, building and maintaining more or less distinct, more or less broadly shared sets of meanings and symbolism. Many KIFs have clear, sometimes spectacular, cultural manifestations of this kind, strongly emphasizing their distinctiveness and gathering people around a common identity (Alvesson 1995; Grugulis *et al.* 2000; Kunda 1992; etc.). Of course, most cultural meanings do not concern the identity issues of 'Who are we? and 'What is distinctive about us?',[1] but in relationship to image management, organizational identity can be seen as an important corresponding internal set of issues fuelling—and sometimes undermining—managerial efforts to sell a particular organizational image. Frequently identity talk involves messages and beliefs about the elite character of the firm, in terms either of claims to employ the 'best people' or of claims to have organizational conditions that facilitate high-quality work (Alvesson *et al.* 2001). Boosting ideas about superiority in certain areas in external as well as internal communication leads, when credible, externally to expectations of high-quality work and internally to high self-confidence, which facilitates convincing behaviour and rhetoric.

Although organizational identity and culture overlap, some firms have no distinct corporate culture (Starbuck 1992, 1993). This does not prevent them from having a distinctive organizational identity associated with an aura of prestige and quality. Some senior partners in a law firm studied by Winroth (1999) tried to push for a firm-specific way of doing things, but what this was supposed to indicate remained vague. Nevertheless, the firms had a fairly distinctive sense of organizational identity, associated with corporate history and a reputation for quality. Ideas about distinctiveness and key characteristics thus follow not from unique values and meanings associated with organizational culture, but from being superior, having the 'very best' clients, etc.

---

[1] Cultural meanings may concern all aspects of organizational life, including technical and administrative systems, and gender and ethnicity issues— themes that may not be invoked in definitions of identity or seen as distinctive of the organization, and thus only loosely connected to organizational identity.

Organizational Control

Some researchers, referring to notions such as common industrial recipes or tendencies to isomorphism, claim that organizations within the same industry tend to adopt similar solutions and to become more or less homogeneous (e.g. Boxall and Steeneveld 1999; Maister 1993). It is often believed that 'knowledge work is best conducted in "organic" and informal settings, with egalitarian cultures and where horizontal, as opposed to vertical, communication dominates' (Newell *et al.* 2002: 98). Although I agree that knowledge work often thrives best in such contexts, I also think that there are strong empirical indications on knowledge work carried out under very different conditions.

Management may involve a multitude of different forms of control. Varying modes are used, ranging from hierarchical and bureaucratic modes of control, such as monitoring behaviour, to pecuniary rewards, such as pay and promotion, and non-pecuniary rewards, such as confirmation, status, and assignment to appealing tasks. Most organizations use the entire spectrum, but in very different ways. Some KIFs have relatively strong hierarchical and bureaucratic features (Akehurst 1994; Covaleski *et al.* 1998; Kärreman and Alvesson forthcoming); others, probably most, exhibit the opposite qualities (Alvesson 1995; Kunda 1992; Morris and Empson 1998; Starbuck 1992). The former tendency is partly related to size. Moreover, firms working a great deal with the reuse and implementation of known solutions and not doing much innovative work can sometimes deviate substantially from the organic organizational form (see Mintzberg 1983 on the concept of professional bureaucracy). A partnership system, at least where the ratio of partners to non-partners is high, also seems to fuel a hierarchical structure by making the step between partners and others significant (Maister 1993). There are considerable differences between KIFs in terms of hierarchy and leverage, particularly in large organizations involved in large projects structured and supported by methodologies and procedures, where junior people under supervision may carry out a large proportion of the work.[2] In certain professions, including

---

[2] Leverage refers to the hierarchical competence structure of work done by a combination of senior and junior professionals. In project teams firms try to integrate the skills of senior people with the efforts of junior people. Using the

law and accountancy, the hierarchy is typically weaker, and frequently the ratio of partners to non-partners is lower, although there is variation within those professions (Greenwood *et al.* 1990). However, within the fairly large partner group a collegial orientation is more prevalent than in companies where the chief executive and the board of directors are clearly above the rest.

The long-term prospects of promotion and wealth associated with becoming a partner do seem to make junior professionals more inclined to accept subordination at the same time as collegial control among partners flattens the top of the hierarchy. In some service firms chargeability is a significant measure (Covaleski *et al.* 1998). Here quantifiable performance measures are central and are backed up by incentives in the form of monetary rewards but also by loss of status, humiliation, and guilt resulting from failure to reach objectives. These and the degree of achievement are sometimes made public within organizations. Frequently the effects of power are far-reaching and the people subjected to control feel under great pressure to deliver. In most R&D companies short-term sales and other quantifiable targets are typically not available or not very useful, at least in the most knowledge-intensive parts of the organization. Efforts to structure development processes in periods and to establish templates for how long a specific task should take are used, but often not with any great precision owing to the uncertainties involved.

Despite the variation, control targeted at the values, ideas, beliefs, emotions, and self-image of people characterizes much management in KIFs. Some of this control may be similar across firms, as part of a broader industrial–professional culture, so it does not necessarily imply the existence of a unique organizational culture. Similar ambitions to manage or engineer culture can characterize the management in many firms. Industrial and occupational cultures and recipes may influence how managers try to shape the values and ideas of subordinates at the organizational level. A considerable amount of self-organization on the

supervision and support of the senior person, the juniors can contribute above their competence level. Since the firm charges rather highly for the service of the junior professionals compared to their pay, this surplus, in combination with the often large number of juniors compared to seniors, means that juniors are quite profitable. Therefore, firms often try to use work models and relationships where as many junior professionals as possible work together with one or a few seniors and perhaps a couple of 'medium-experienced' professionals (Maister 1993).

part of employees is necessary, which calls for some degree of influence on cultural orientation and identity in order to make people inclined to do the right thing voluntarily, and in the absence of monitoring.

While in much professional service work socialization and a common framework and set of values based on the profession or organization takes care of a large part of the control in some firms, the situation for R&D work in large organizations is more complex and calls for a wider set of balancing between different objectives and work principles.

Dougherty (1996) lists four sets of activities central to the innovation process:

1. Conceptualizing the product to integrate market needs and technological potential. The ability to manage this linkage and its inherent tension between inside and outside must permeate the entire organization, since resources from various functions are involved. A variety of resources must accommodate multiple sets of market–technology linkages.

2. Organizing the process to accommodate creative problem-solving. This means that, in order to coordinate highly interdependent activities, 'innovators must understand the constraints in other functions, anticipate others' needs, and use dense, two-way communication to process fragmentary information' (p. 427).

3. Monitoring the process. 'Despite the fanciful sense of unfettered freedom for innovation sometimes found in the organization literature, evaluation is necessary for innovation, since random "variation" will not produce comprehensive design or thorough problem-solving' (p. 428).

4. Developing commitment to the effort. This is about mastering the tension between freedom and responsibility, calling for key people who are committed to innovation and professional enough to see it through. But as these people are involved in other activities and groups, and work with people with a 'normal' orientation to the project, it is important that the organization as a whole is characterized by supportive orientations and is capable of embodying the tension between freedom and responsibility (p. 425).

Dougherty (1996) emphasizes the role of a shared system of beliefs leading to a code of conduct that gives a foundation for and facilitates the more specific guidelines and orientations that are used to control the process. Central here is an organizational identity 'that combines internal and external issues' (p. 432). Communication based on consultation (not command) is also important, and its content consists of information and advice (not instructions and decisions) and a view of the organization as process, enabling people to shift their boundaries over time. Dougherty also stresses that collective accountability needs to permeate the organization as a whole. This can be accomplished by training people to take broader roles and by encouraging lower-level employees to participate in framing rules for decisions.

In order to facilitate communication of the 'right' corporate image, identities, and cultural beliefs and meanings, managerial thought and actions well in tune with occupational culture are necessary. All this goes beyond what traditional management of a bureaucracy and simple output control can accomplish. Even in those firms trying to standardize their products, 'client involvement adds to task uncertainty, requiring professionals to create their roles to some extent in the course of a client assignment' (Morris and Empson 1998: 619). Bureaucracy does the trick to a lesser degree than in many other work organizations; it is, of course, relevant and has a strong presence in many KIFs, but it sometimes has a 'softer' impact since people have to adapt to circumstances and become used to exercising judgement and feeling confident about bending rules when appropriate (Kärreman and Alvesson 2004).

Clan Control

Management control in this kind of company is a complex affair. The difficulties of employing rules and using performance measures and the need for a more flexible approach lead many authors to emphasize cultural–ideological or 'clan' control rather than bureaucratic or market-like (output) forms of internal control (Alvesson 1995; Hedberg 1990; Kanter 1983; Kunda 1992; Wilkins and Ouchi 1983), although, of course, not without contradictions and tensions.

Ouchi (Ouchi 1979, 1980; Wilkins and Ouchi 1983) talks about a clan when using the term 'culture' to refer to the properties of a unique organization. Ouchi has in mind not just any kind of culture, but a functional, organization-specific one similar to what many others refer to as 'corporate culture'. It involves a deep level of common agreement on objectives and a high level of commitment. It may also lead to the regulation of complex exchange relations between employee and employer. In situations where performances are not easily identified or rewarded in a short time-span, e.g. in much R&D work, it is important to have a corporate memory and a shared framework in order to understand people's efforts and contributions. The clan contributes to this, according to Ouchi. It accommodates great complexity and ambiguity, allowing for diversity of behaviour or style, and avoiding the dysfunctions of forms of control that reward a narrow range of behaviour or measurable results.

Apart from achieving control in situations where other forms of control really do not work, the clan has advantages in the form of intrinsic motivation (low monitoring costs), high commitment, and flexibility. While market-like forms of control mean that people focus on what they are rewarded for—and do not do much beyond what is measured and rewarded—and bureaucracy leads to compliance and a tendency to do only what is prescribed, the clan tends to encourage a wider engagement and a more positive spirit. This more positive orientation outclasses the narrowness and instrumentality of market and bureaucratic forms of control.

However, the clan form of organization has significant costs and is in most cases very difficult to create. Clan information systems cannot cope with heterogeneity or employee turnover. The clan also calls for a homogeneous and stable workforce; otherwise the cultivation of a shared framework, which is at the core of the clan, will not be possible, at least not to any degree. While contemporary working life fairly often exhibits much heterogeneity and turnover in the workforce, clans are not at all common.

How are clans produced? Ouchi, like other authors addressing the management of organizational cultures, mentions the use of rituals and ceremonies as well as selective recruitment, socialization, and training. How meetings are structured and filled with content, how stories are told, also matter. A problem with clans is that they are most needed in complex, turbulent situations where it is frequently most difficult for management to exercise the degree of normative control needed to produce them (Alvesson and Lindkvist 1993). Clans call for stability and low mobility. On the other hand, the domination of a single profession or occupational group makes it easier to develop similar, organization-specific values and orientations in KIFs than in most more heterogeneous organizations.

'Outsourcing Management': Client Control

In KIFs and PSFs working directly for a client, client control is a significant part of the overall control structure. More generally, customers are increasingly used as a source of control in business (du Gay and Salaman 1992). Management brings forward the client as an evaluator of performance and the employee is encouraged to satisfy the customer rather than the supervisor, risking sanctions if there are indications that this has not been accomplished.

Client control can be exercised in three ways. The most obvious one is when the client makes explicit demands, referring to a contract or demands not formally regulated. The client then acts like a manager, supervising the service or product supplier. The second is when the PSF internally emphasizes client orientation, and views making the client happy as a major objective. The client is not directly exercising control, but the explicit focus on satisfying the client becomes a major element of control. Sometimes this is accomplished through the use of client satisfaction examinations: the client is interviewed by senior people from the PSF and the (dis)satisfaction noted is reported back to the project manager or stored in the corporate memory and plays a role in wage-setting and promotion decisions. A third version of client control concerns more abstract constructions of the client and how employee attention and motivation is mobilized by being presented with an image of the client. Here it is the general notion of client orientation, and beliefs about what that would mean, rather than specific input or the reactions of specific clients, that matter. Client orientation, then, is part of the organizational culture and as such guides people without necessarily including much of a reality-check in the form of the open-minded testing of the client. It is the idea or even fantasy about the client that

exercises governance. Assumptions and anticipations are important here.

The three forms of client control, of course, frequently intersect,
but they may carry varying significance and if one is important,
then the others may be less salient. If there is, for example, a
strong degree of client orientation within a company (in the
third and perhaps second of the three versions)—if people have
common ideas about what this means and attach great value to
it—then the client may not need to make explicit demands and
there is less need to control people through formal client assessments, as they are already very eager to please the client. (Control
is then needed not to steer effort, but only to check work quality.)
Client orientation takes precedence over active mobilization of
the client as an explicit source of control, though the latter may
occasionally be invoked in order to support the former, e.g. by
fuelling organizational cultures through moral stories about poor
behaviour upsetting clients.

Management is active in three different ways in relationship to
the three forms of client control. In the case of direct client control
there is negotiation and agreement between client and management of the PSF (or other KIF) on how the project should be run.
Although workers in PSFs often say that they want to be in charge
of a project, they need instructions and support from the client.
The more the client takes the lead, the less s/he can blame the PSF
for a disappointing result. In the case of client satisfaction control,
management signals that this will be carried out and the client is
mobilized as a judge of the work. Interviews or questionnaires are
used, and the feedback is passed on to those involved; the client's
verdict may also be registered and may follow these people
throughout their careers within the organization. In the case of a
more general emphasis on client orientation as a key value, there is
management of meaning around this: managers produce slogans,
tell stories, and engage in constant reminders to the people doing
work for clients. The three ways of accomplishing client control—
within the overall frame of the contract—then take place, respectively, during a project (client supervision), after a project (client
satisfaction control), and prior to a project (socialization). These
are the three classic ways of accomplishing organizational control
(Perrow 1979). What is of interest here is that the client is mobilized in these respects, although in the third case it is managerial

representations of the client that are active and it is thus still a fairly classical form of organizational control.

Fulfilling contract requirements and/or making the client happy are objectives that often discipline consultancy personnel even more than in traditional hierarchical situations where a manager stands more clearly and directly in control. Sometimes these are harsh. Deetz (1997) reports a case study of an IT group (AIMS, also referred to in Chapter 4) in which the personnel subordinated themselves to very demanding clients: 'In this surrogate management situation, not only did AIMS employees lack normal worker rights since they complied voluntary to meet the client's needs, but they were also expected to placate clients and maintain friendly, supportive relations' (pp. 198–9).

The management of AIMS deplored difficult clients and offered support to the personnel. Nonetheless, 'The command to please the client as a part of the consultancy "self-employment" and a reward system supporting the command enhanced consent to management control that was accomplished through clients rather than directly through AIMS managers. The customer relation thus controlled more powerfully than management could have' (p. 199).

Deetz draws attention not only to how the client is very active and demanding in setting objectives, monitoring progress and placing high demands on consultants, but also on how people in the PSF construct the notion of the client as something that one has to comply with. The client is not simply assessed realistically based on experience, and expectations of the wishes and demands of the client occasionally checked, challenged, and negotiated. The consultancy–client construct in this case makes the consultant very compliant.

Anderson-Gough *et al.* (2000) add to Deetz's study by showing how trainees in a large accountancy firm not only respond to specific clients or base their judgement on empirical tests—real-life encounters—but invent ideas of the client which then become true, at least in terms of control effects. Apart from the client having a concrete expression in the shape of people and premises visited in work assignments, this notion also had 'an abstract and symbolic significance when invoked to justify general requirements of behaviour' (p. 1171). There was a great deal of discussion and references to prototypical clients, implying how to behave and on what to focus attention. The client discourse was thus used as a control device, and not only from the top down, implicated 'in a wide array of power-effects, especially those relating to time-keeping, appearance and conduct' (p. 1171).

Here we find, as an example of the third version of client control, a general and abstracted client orientation that goes well beyond 'real' clients. As this abstract client is assumed to expect a certain behaviour, dress, and vocabulary, one does not deviate from the assumed correct way of appearing and performing, to test what the client really wants or is willing to accept.

Summary

In this chapter I have addressed some vital aspects of management in KIFs and organizational control. Previous chapters have also addressed management issues, e.g. the systematic attention of managers and other senior actors to image and to the development and anchoring of a specific rhetoric and mastery of organizational symbolism to be played out internally as well as in relations with clients. In the next two chapters knowledge management and the management of (efforts to regulate) identity will be addressed, although in these two chapters, as in the previous ones, more than just management aspects will be addressed.

Management in KIFs is, of course, very much a matter of the management of people and culture. Strategic issues cannot easily be dealt with in the same way as machine bureaucracies, where centralized decisions carried out by autocratic management at least sometimes may be carried out irrespective of a high degree of support from broader groups of people. Most KIFs are much more pluralistic, and many people can choose to deviate from the route proposed by top management. Sometimes there are departures from stated firm objectives and strategies, and organizational fragmentation resulting less from conscious choices about autonomy and more from people drifting in different directions owing to the relative ineffectiveness of formal and hierarchical forms of control. Generally, a high level of participation, the active support of large groups of people, plus considerable tolerance for variation characterize most KIFs, in particular PSFs. Accountancy firms are sometimes described as 'an archipelago of islands' and their management as 'an exercise in molecular management' (Greenwood *et al.* 1990: 733). Generally, professional partnerships are characterized by their emphasis on collegiality, autonomy, and widely distributed authority. Some firms, however, such as Big Consulting (addressed in the next chapter), do differ from many other partnerships through their far-reaching hierarchical structure and the dominance of a relatively small group of partners.

Apart from at certain stages such as the foundation and early expansion of a firm and during crises calling for conflict-ridden changes, leadership is probably a less important aspect of KIFs than of many other organizations. However, in organizations in which one or two strong individuals are simultaneously founder, owner, and chief executive, those people may have a strong grip over the firm.

KIFs tend to be characterized by stronger inputs of normative control than is common in most other organizations. Some KIFs do rely heavily on technocratic forms of control—soft rules and procedures as well as measurement by performance indicators—but these are included in, and fuel, normative control by operating in a non-mechanical way, influencing the ideas, expectations, and subjectivities of people (Alvesson and Kärreman, forthcoming). In PSFs and some other KIFs working for a special client in a business-to-business situation around a particular product, client control is an important part of the steering situation. The client may act as a directing force (foreman), as an evaluator of results, and/ or as an abstract, imaginary source of a particular orientation (client-centredness).

Chapter 7

Human Resource Management and Personnel Concepts

PERHAPS more than anything else, KIFs stand out from most other organizations because of the extreme significance they place on the quality and motivation of their personnel. Some KIFs in the R&D sector are relatively capital-intensive, and many PSFs are heavily dependent on their image (corporate brand) or the network relationships they have developed, in particular around the client portfolio. This does not prevent personnel issues from being the most significant factor. Consequently, personnel issues call for careful attention. I have touched upon this theme in several chapters, but now is the time to focus on it more systematically. In this chapter I try to look somewhat deeper than usual and draw attention to what are referred to as the personnel concepts of organizations. This provides the starting point for human resource management (HRM) strategies, and is based on a more or less organization-specific understanding of the prototypical organizational member that one aspires to recruit, retain, and motivate.

The chapter starts by pointing to two principal ways in which 'human resources' make a crucial difference: the human capital advantage versus human process advantage. I then address the significance of competence and of key personnel. Subsequently, the idea of personnel concepts is introduced and explained. This idea then serves as an integrative framework for HRM policies and practices in organizations that are ambitious in their methods of dealing with personnel. I then relate this to and discuss the need to achieve a relatively high degree of loyalty to the organization among personnel since the absence of such loyalty can be very costly to the employer. One element here is the possibility of the profession as an alternative source of identification and loyalty, perhaps weakening the ties of professionals to the organization or in other ways creating problems for the latter. The chapter then discusses the use of more specific combinations of rewards and motives that organizations may work with in relationship to employees as part of a distinct, more or less integrated way of achieving retention, motivation, and development.

I shall also go into depth in addressing two firms I have studied, and illustrate some of the themes addressed in this chapter, in particular the personnel concept, but also some of the management and organizational themes that were treated in the previous chapter.

Human Capital Advantage Versus Human Process Advantage

As repeatedly emphasized, that personnel and their motivation and competence are developed and utilized is crucial for KIFs. In terms of the employees and their effectiveness, it is possible to distinguish between human capital advantage and human process advantage. The former refers to the employment of talent, the latter to 'difficult-to-imitate, highly evolved processes within a firm, such as cross-departmental co-operation and executive development' (Boxall and Steeneveld 1999: 445). In terms of human capital, the crucial issue is to recruit and retain personnel with the best qualifications possible, given the nature of existing and potential tasks. The best company is the one able to employ the best workers. This means that a lot of resources go into recruiting, selecting, and rewarding—with wages, interesting tasks, and career prospects. The human process advantage is more about creating preconditions for synergy effects. Designing work organization and supporting methodologies, working with social relationships, team-building and composition, a supporting organizational culture, and a strong sense of organizational identification may be central ingredients in such work, creating an effective human process. Here the organization and what it does with people in the form of governing their thinking and behaviour, and the resources it provides, is vital. Their performance is viewed more as an organizational outcome than as the result of input in terms of the knowledge, experience, brains, and drive that individuals bring to work in the form of capacities.

Of course, all organizations need both human capital and human process in order to work. But as resources are not endless

and one can't have everything, the two elements may be prioritized differently. At one extreme is the effort to go exclusively for
the best and the brightest; another is to be satisfied with those
sufficiently good—as good as possible, given the budget for
wages—and also adaptable and cooperative and put a lot of
resources into optimal systems and procedures. This, of course,
overlaps pricing strategy. The employment of the best people is
often easier in upmarket kinds of consultancy work and in certain
advanced R&D projects. In firms characterized by less unique
and more routine work, in which earlier solutions can be drawn
upon, it makes more sense to focus on improving and controlling
human processes. Most firms by definition have limited resources
for recruiting and retaining (what are perceived as) very good
people and lack the reputation or type of work needed to be seen
as a really attractive employer.

One version of maximizing human process advantage could be
not to focus on systems and procedures, but to develop a corporate culture or clan, facilitating cooperative work and a smoothly
functioning organization. A clan can, in principle, coexist with
well-developed systems and structures and even the recruitment
of the best and the brightest. And as shared a cultural orientation
is partly, or even mainly, a consequence of organic developments
and elements beyond management control, it is not a zero-sum
game. Systems and procedures can also be a source of common
meanings and, through these artefacts and the development of
meanings around them, be a part of corporate culture. Different
forms of control can intersect (Kärreman and Alvesson
2004). Nevertheless, management time and skills as well as available resources frequently mean that some trade-offs between the
three strategies—best people, strong systems, and supportive
cultures—are called for. The best-people approach calls for extensive recruitment, selection, and retention activity and very high
individual rewards. The systems and procedures approach calls
for fairly adaptive people and large resources put into technocratic work. The clan or corporate culture approach calls for
selective screening and hiring of people—where values and personality matter almost as much as technical competence—and
a lot of managerial skills and energy as well as resources
put into collective activities, with the management of meaning
and rewards encouraging the 'right' orientation. While the

emphasis may differ widely—see the two cases presented below—there is always some balancing between elements: getting the best people possible (within constraints, such as financial resources and the budget for wages), as well as having systems and procedures in place and creating a shared orientation in the organization, are on the agenda in almost any KIF. No company can neglect either human capital or human resources advantages, but they can vary their priorities, often based on a mixture of strategic choices and constraints on what they can do.

Competence and Key Personnel

Even though process-facilitating arrangements sometimes play a big role, the people dimension is generally the most important in KIFs. These human resources—people—contribute much more than their labour. The significance of their networks and relationships is often great: 'The professionals bring to the firm their expertise, their experience, their skills in relationship building and maintenance, their professional reputation, their network of professional peer contacts, and their established relationship with past, present and potential clients' (Løwendahl 1997: 41).

While client contacts are of significance in the professional service industry, networks with peers and other institutions are equally if not more important in science-based industries such as biotechnology and pharmaceutical companies.

A particular problem for many KIFs, especially in the service industries, is to retain their key personnel, therefore, making commitment and loyalty significant (Alvesson 1995; Davenport and Prusak 1998; Deetz 1998; Løwendahl 1997). While it is a standard problem for all firms to attract, retain, and develop competent personnel, this issue is amplified in many KIFs. This is a result of two circumstances:

- Personnel are by far the company's most significant—sometimes only significant—resource. Capital and equipment are normally not of great importance in PSFs, although the need for capital is increasing somewhat as mergers and acquisitions and internationalization become more common. Capital plays a greater role in R&D companies. Still, one may

    say that highly qualified personnel are of greater signifi-
cance in KIFs than in most other companies.

- In many cases an established company might risk entire
  groups leaving their employment and forming a new company, taking old clients with them and emptying the former
  company not only of important personnel but also of clients.
  This risk is, of course, most salient for consultancy firms and
  other PSFs. It is less of an issue in KIFs that rely on capital
  (equipment) and that claim a monopoly on knowledge products through property rights. But here also the defection of a
  key group of engineers or scientists may have devastating
  effects.

As Maister (1982) writes, PSFs compete in two markets simultaneously: the 'output' market for its services and the 'input' market
for attracting and keeping the professional workforce. These
markets are closely related: loss in one may affect the other. For
many high tech and science-based knowledge firms there is no
direct link between the departure of key personnel and that of
clients, but here too the inflow and retention of qualified personnel is crucial. For this reason many such firms are located in areas
close to large universities, which facilitates the recruitment of
good engineers and scientists.

Drucker emphasizes the dependence of organizations on personnel, and the strong bargaining position of large groups of
knowledge workers: 'In knowledge work, the means of production is now owned by the knowledge worker. They are mobile
and can work anywhere. They keep their résumés in their bottom
drawer. Consequently, they must be managed as volunteers,
not as employees. Only the unskilled need the employer more
than the employer needs them' (cited in Kreiner and Mouritsen
2003: 233).

The significance of retention issues is illustrated by a quotation
from an executive who says that 'Many people say all our resources go down the lift in the evening after a day of work, and
that the firm is then empty. That is why I see it as my primary
concern to make sure that they want to come back tomorrow'
(Løwendahl 1997: 24).

For many KIFs it is important to secure people's satisfaction
with and loyalty to the company. In some PSFs, based on the

up-or-out principle, too great a commitment to the organization may, however, be problematic for the employer as people may be less inclined to read signals and accept that their careers would benefit from leaving the organization. But in these firms a certain degree of loyalty and commitment is also important to secure, for most personnel and for most of the time.

The personnel concept then provides the starting point for how (some) KIFs—and other organizations—eager to succeed on the 'input' market identify, target, and work with the appropriate segment of the labour market. The personnel concept—if well thought through and followed up by carefully designed and applied work principles—is one key element behind the likelihood that resources will come back the next working day. Of course, they do so because of specific, more or less tangible reasons: high pay, a good work atmosphere, identification with the organization, career prospects. If these specific factors are anchored in an integrated line of thinking and practices, including communicating what the organization is offering and why this is especially valuable, there is a greater likelihood that the specific rewards and advantages will be perceived more clearly and positively, while what may be perceived as not such positive workplace features will be focused on less, and the links to the organization will be strengthened.

The Relationship between the Profession and the Organization: Tension or Harmony?

There have been discussions around the possible tension between professionals and their employing organizations (Bacharach *et al.* 1989). Professionals have been assumed to be caught in a potentially contradictory position between bureaucratic (organizational) and professional objectives and values. This has sometimes been believed to limit loyalty to the employer. Gouldner (1957), for example, distinguished between locals (oriented towards the organization) and cosmopolitans (oriented towards the broader values and ideals of the professional community), and saw these as quite diverse and, to some extent, competitive orientations. The ethics and occupational culture of the profession have been thought to interfere with organizational loyalty and with relations between management and professionals. Many of the stated characteristics of the 'true' professions would point in such a direction: autonomy, client orientation, strong collegial cohesion, and a particular ethical code. This would presumably then call for conscious and systematic efforts among managers to reduce identification with and loyalty to the profession as a source of reduced commitment to the employing organization.

It appears doubtful, however, whether the conflict between profession and organization is particularly salient in most contemporary organizational settings. The available literature on professionals as well as on KIFs does not indicate any serious contradictions in this respect (Alvesson 1995; Deetz 1995; Grey 1998; Kunda 1992; Wallace 1995). Earlier views on the matter were probably partly a reflection of a great bulk of professional work being carried out by autonomous, self-employed professionals, which created a particular non-bureaucratic ethos, while most professionals nowadays work in medium-sized and large bureaucracies of which some are (labelled) professional and some are not. These professionals probably typically develop fewer traditional orientations. In addition, the great proportion of the population receiving higher education and the increase in the number of people who could be categorized as professionals in one sense or another reduce the space for this group to be perceived as very special or to expect treatment radically different from other employees. If people belong to a small, exclusive group of people who outclass the large majority in terms of education and status, they may develop a sense of self that makes them difficult to govern and the environment may feel that they are superior and deserve extra respect. However, having a university degree and a professional job is today for most people not extraordinary. Higher education has expanded dramatically and is highly inflated. There is some, albeit inconsistent, evidence of tendencies towards a deprofessionalization and proletarianization of many professions (Burris 1993, ch. 5). Fores et al. (1991) point out that professionals may fit nicely into bureaucracies in terms of common ideas about rationality and order. They argue against the idea that professionals have strong cosmopolitan orientations that lead to conflicts with administrators, quoting a study of hospitals by Green, who found that conflicts within the medical profession were more salient than conflict across the doctor–administrator divide. Studies of lawyers (Wallace 1995) employed in bureaucracies showed no conflict between professional and organizational commitment. Other studies indicate a high degree of compliance with the company and little independence in relationship to clients. Anderson-Gough *et al.* (2000) found, in a study of trainee auditors, that the discourse of client service 'has little to connect with issues of independence, public service or, for that matter, ethical standards' (p. 1169).

There may be conflicts between professional (ideological) and bureaucratic *modes* of control, but this does not mean that there are any strong conflicts between the commitments to the two institutions of professions and firms. If the employing organization meets professional expectations and goals, commitment to the former will follow (Lachman and Aranya 1986; Wallace 1995). As Herriot and Pemberton (1995: 46) write, 'professionals don't lack organizational commitment. They are as loyal as the next person, provided that the organization honour their side of the bargain they have struck with them.' One could add here that even though there are no necessary conflicts between professional and organizational commitments, there may be differences within the overall category of knowledge workers. Many knowledge workers do not belong to the traditional professions, which may reduce any possible inclination to conflict associated with a strong commitment to the profession. In *some* cases the orientations of the profession may make people less inclined to follow organizational arrangements and more inclined to put some premium on autonomy or a follow route that is not necessarily commercially optimal. A study of a medium-sized Swedish law firm showed considerable difficulties in making the lawyers take seriously the idea of operating as a joint, integrated firm (Winroth 1999). Although this reflects their view on what is most interesting and important in their (individual) work more than (dis)loyalty to the company, it also illustrates that certain organizationally important issues become marginalized as a consequence of professionals following their interests. These priorities are partly a consequence of professional identities that are antithetical to taking management and organization seriously. In some R&D organizations there is a tension between what management believes to be commercially most important and the inclination of scientists to give some priority to what they find most interesting from a scientific point of view (Alvesson and Sveningsson 2002). This seems not primarily to be a matter of conflict between profession and organization so much as that no professions emphasize non-commercial goals for scientists in industry. It rather reflects how socialization within the scientific community makes people find some aspects more interesting than others, and to some extent downplays commercial concerns and matters of application.

The ambition to integrate the 'souls' of employees into the more commercial and administrative sides of work—something knowledge workers may find less interesting—calls for influencing their identities and trying to link them with the organization as a whole. The socialization and long-term inclusion of people then call for consideration of their background and efforts to develop HRM and cultural forms of control that can stimulate some 'de-purification' of professional orientations. This is relevant, at least for those organizations that are ambitious and systematic in their way of dealing with the problem of knowledge workers being too 'knowledge-focused', giving priority to interesting professional work sometimes at the expense of organizational interests. Marketing talk and customer-oriented forms of control are, of course, relevant here, but can be more or less integrated with HRM and identity-focused forms of cultural control.

To conclude, then, without denying the possibilities of professional–bureaucracy conflicts there appears to be no reason to see the most typical characteristics of professionals in organizations in terms of tensions between loyalty to the profession and to the bureaucracy. In many firms commercial ideals are dominant and there is a synthesis between conventional corporate management and a professional model of partnership (Greenwood *et al.* 1990; Morris and Malhotra 2002). It is, however, quite common for knowledge workers, including those who score high on conventional criteria for being professionals, to find some work associated with their key identities more interesting than what is seen by top management as commercially and organizationally optimal. In most cases the professionals would probably agree upon the importance of commercial goals and making the organization effective, but may not let this fully influence their personal priorities.

Personnel Concepts

The ways firms operate in terms of trying to develop and utilize particular human capital and human process advantages are grounded in more or less careful thinking about how to attract, retain, develop, shape, and motivate personnel. There is variation between companies in their recruitment strategies, how they combine rewards and other satisfying elements in the work contract, as well as strategies for training, development, and promotion—and sometimes the termination of employment. As will be showed below, there is also considerable variation between how KIFs allocate resources to and work with HRM issues. Firms may invest more or less money, and more or less managerial attention and time, in different types of rewards, other motivating elements, and in building and utilizing workforce competence. Firms also vary in how they communicate—externally to potential job candidates but also internally to the workforce—their version of what they offer and draw attention to their respective strengths.

This can be described in terms of specific HRM arrangements and one can compare firms issue for issue: from the desired profile of new recruits to career structures and to what senior managers do—or do not do—in terms of devoting time and energy to shape a positive workplace climate. But one can go further than that and look at the HRM ideas and strategies *behind* the specific arrangements. This can be described in terms of HRM strategies, portfolios, or archetypes. But it is also possible to go one step further, behind the strategies and specific resource allocations and the HRM packages that the employees encounter. I propose the term *personnel concept* to refer to a company's basic ideas about the starting and anchoring point for HRM (Alvesson 2002*b*). This notion goes beyond the HRM area as conventionally defined. My idea is that variation in personnel concepts simultaneously reflect, are part of, and reinforce particular logics and organizational configurations with regard to personnel issues. The personnel concept refers to an idea or conception of employees in relation to the organization and the effort to define the motivational and developmental basis for the employee–employer relationship, which an organization develops and uses as a starting point for and key theme in personnel–HRM strategies. The idea of personnel concept overlaps with terms such as 'psychological contract', but goes beyond this. The personnel concept incorporates

- an idea of the company's basic conceptualization of the kind of employees it wants to attract;
- what it offers (mix of rewards and other benefits) to the employees, and how these are being stimulated and developed in terms of competence; as well as
- an active shaping of the motivational–identity orientations of employees through HRM and other organizational structural arrangements and the communication of cultural beliefs and meanings.

It thus involves a model of the (ideal) employee and a more or less integrated system of ideas and practices for recruiting, motivating, retaining, producing, and exploiting him or her. Such a model may revolve around satisfying and developing work tasks as the core driving force for people and lead to certain priorities and a certain willingness to turn down tasks in order to attract, retain, and make employees feel committed to the company. Or it may be based on the idea that material rewards and incentives are crucial for the people that a company wants to hire and so that the company might pay high wages and allocate less managerial time and financial resources to other benefits associated with the work situation. It may be based on the assumption that development and learning are mainly accomplished on the job, through carefully chosen assignments and the composition of work groups, or that formal, planned training and education are a key element, or that knowledge-sharing and supportive organizational cultures are the major vehicle behind personal development and increased competence.

The personnel concept may influence not only HRM systems and specific personnel issues but also the work organization and work structure, the company's operations, and the kind of competence and results it aspires to.

It is open for discussion whether all or most organizations have a distinct personnel concept. Many organizations follow established conventions and templates for HRM. In those cases where an organization is just following institutionalized structures and lines of thinking, the personnel concept does not add much to our understanding. Here we may speak of a weak or even absent personnel concept. KIFs have strong reasons to think through how they conceptualize their employees and how HRM strategies and tactics should look. A number of firms seem to be fairly ambitious and reasonably original about this theme and can thus be said to have developed and be working within a more than 'minimalistic' personnel concept. A 'real' personnel concept then presupposes (*a*) some degree of independence and original-ity in thinking about personnel, (*b*) some possibility of profiling the motivational–identity basis of the employee and organization, and (*c*) a certain degree of coherence between HRM issues, the employees' orientations towards work and organization, and the organization's structure, culture, and ways of working.

My purpose here is not to examine the broader relevance of the idea of the personnel concept for organizations and working life in general, but to use this idea to illuminate some basic HRM themes in KIFs, in particular those that are distinctive in what they offer and communicate in relationship to how employees are recruited, retained or dismissed, shaped, and motivated.

Modes of Managing Loyalty

The significance of the personnel concept can be seen in relation-ship to the importance of managing loyalty for KIFs. Even though firms do not often need to fight a battle with professions for the souls of the employees in KIFs, they often—as explained above—have other good reasons for tying personnel—in particular the most qualified and most promising people—to the firm. Lack of loyalty may not lead just to loss of personnel or people being opportunistic at work, but may also mean that they defect to competitors or start a business of their own, taking clients with them or in other ways risking losses to the former employer on the output market. It is perhaps the risk of this simultaneous dual loss—on input and output markets—that makes loyalty among large sections of employees of KIFs so significant and contributes to the relevance of the personnel concept.

Within the general category of loyalty, it is possible to distin-guish between *instrumental loyalty* and *identification-based loyalty* (Alvesson 2000*a*). The two concepts have similarities with Etzioni's notions of utilitarian and normative compliance (Etzioni 1964).

Instrumental loyalty corresponds to what Habermas (1984) refers to as the system, which operates in a formal, depersonalized manner, and its principal media, money and formal power. Calculation is here the dominant logic. Identification-based loyalty relates to the life-world, e.g. the level of the experience of social reality, in which personal and shared meanings are central. Key features include meaningfulness and involvement.

Typical means of reassuring instrumental loyalty are legal agreements and money, as well as other compensations. Present and future (anticipated, promised) benefits lead to loyalty. Legislation as well as specific contracts may reduce the opportunities for employees in PSFs to leave a company, taking the company's clients with them. Deferred compensation plans may also be used to manage the middle-level 'external value' problem in some PSFs (Maister 1982). The partner system used in many industries and organizations, such as law and accounting firms, ties senior people together through detailed legal and economic arrangements partly contingent upon shared interests. The system often seems to achieve a tight discipline, in particular in large firms (Covaleski *et al.* 1998; Grey 1994).

The partnership system probably often includes elements of identification-based loyalty as it builds upon as well as creates a long-term relationship. Being a partner implies a certain social identity that not only reflects but also tends to increase cohesiveness.[1] In some firms, particularly large ones, there is strong pressure to perform and optimize financial results from the large body of partners whose individual income is dependent on the performance of others. In other firms, particularly small and middle-sized ones, people can use their position as partner to give more priority to non-financial qualities, such as interesting work tasks. Løwendahl (1997) refers to engineering firms, where maximization of profit and income is *not* the key issue in the same way as stimulating and developing work tasks.

Purer forms of identification-based loyalty do not primarily involve the means of money and contracts, but are a matter of perceived similarities, shared positive emotions, and social

---

[1] Social identity refers to the definition of oneself through the use of a social category that one identifies with, e.g. the firm, the profession, or another, perhaps more informal, group. More about this in Ch. 9.

bonds. They may also function on a more cognitive level: self-definition is then defined in social terms as part of how one conceives oneself rather than as affiliation with and attraction towards a certain group of people (Turner 1984). Emotions are, however, sometimes significant in the normative control of KIFs. There are feelings of belonging to a community of people whose shared social identity follows from their being employed by a particular company. Feelings of community may revolve around a positive corporate identity—if people are proud of the company and what it stands for—or around social cohesion among the people in it. Quite often normative control and corporate cultures involve a combination of these two elements (see Alvesson 1995; Kunda 1992). These two means of managing loyalty—a positive corporate identity and close social relations among people in the company—may also operate independently. Some firms may be in a position to make a strong case for being seen as unique, excellent, progressive, or just distinctive in an interesting way, and may thus facilitate identification with the company without doing much of a purely social or collective character. A successful US law firm described by Starbuck (1993) seems to illustrate this case, as does the management consultancy firm Big, addressed later in this chapter.

In order to create the perception of a distinctive corporate identity a company may emphasize its history and current practices or vision and direct attention to a (better) corporate future. In any case, organizational symbolism—stories, myths, vocabulary, symbolic management, corporate image, etc.—is vital. Other firms, perhaps in particular smaller ones, may have difficulty in successfully developing a rhetoric about their distinctiveness or excellence, but may instead develop a strong rhetoric about interpersonal bonds associated with being part of a company representing a socially cohesive community (Alvesson and Köping 1993). The first version may be said to represent an *institution-based* road to identification-based loyalty through relying on the institutionalized nature of the organization (Selznick 1957). An institution is characterized by being infused with value, so that it is seen as representing more than just its instrumental value. An organization that is institutionalized is viewed by its defenders as standing for something special that is important to nurture. The second version marks a *communitarian-based* way to loyalty between members of the organization and thus indirectly to the employer. While the second relies heavily on interpersonal relations and affective bonds, the first means that identification with a group can arise quite separately from interpersonal interaction and social cohesion (Ashforth and Mael 1989). The combination of these means of control—managing the rhetoric of the distinctiveness and greatness of the company and managing the collective of employees as a community—may be referred to as *social-integrative management* (Alvesson 1995). This involves connecting the community with the company or, alternatively, coupling the company (as an abstraction) to specific social situations and group relations. It may take the form of efforts to engineer broadly shared ideas about an extra-ordinary corporate culture including strong cohesion and close social relations, which is seen as progressive and unique for the company concerned. Emotions as an object of control are significant here (Van Maanen and Kunda 1989).

The means of achieving instrumental loyalty do not directly address identity. This kind of loyalty may be seen as a way of reducing uncertainty around the issue of identity in the corporate context. Management does not compete with other sources of identification on the identity arena, but relies on more impersonal means of securing compliance. Of course, the person who is driven by money and career prospects may develop an identity around these issues (a person may define herself as a vice-president earning $150,000) but the problem of competition between different kinds of social sources of identification is reduced when management succeeds in achieving compliance through the use of utilitarian means. Identity is then indirectly affected, but is not the object of management control, at least not intentionally. The personnel concept may summarize how managements of organizations address loyalty issues: Should priority be placed upon instrumental rewards or identification-based routes to loyalty? Should management try to align the two or emphasize one route? In order to create identification, when this is a conscious objective, are success and status symbols used or should a strong feeling of community be targeted? How does one handle possible contradictions?

Reward systems and motivations

The specific rewards and other attractive features associated with employment and perceived good performance are, of course, highly significant for the employees' responses and their bonds to the organization. There is considerable disagreement between researchers regarding the role of instrumental motives, probably reflecting researchers' assumptions (and their own values) as well as empirical variation. Many authors emphasize promotion to partnership as a major motivator. In some KIFs ownership has replaced partnership as a crucial issue and may change the choice from one of promoting people to partner, to a matter of the size of ownership. While partners are typically outnumbered by non-partners, most or even all employees can own shares in the company even though one or a limited number of senior people may own the majority of shares. According to some researchers, drawing upon studies of engineering consultants, 'employee ownership is enormously significant' (Boxall and Steeneveld 1999: 457). Apart from the financial and influence dimension of ownership, it also contains a strong symbolic element: being an owner is a source of feelings of inclusion, trust, and identification with the company. One can imagine that partnership means a merging of the individual and the firm in some cases, when the partner identifies very strongly with the firm.

One assumption behind emphasizing the powers of organizations to shape people's motives, identities, and perceptions of what is valuable at work is that there are not just universal or individual drivers behind motivations and priorities but also a strong cultural influence. Part of this influence is organizational. The personnel concept points at how values and motives are constructed at the workplace level and that HRM practices not only respond to or trigger needs, wants, and motivators, but also contribute to their creation. This is a way of understanding the variation around what people emphasize as important in work for satisfaction and commitment.

In many KIFs the financial side of employment is downplayed, while the intrinsic aspect of work is emphasized. Kunda (1992), in his study of a large US high tech company, concluded that instrumental motives were not very significant: 'the importance of economic rewards is underplayed, even frowned upon' (p. 90).

Løwendahl (1997) also reports that many professionals (including co-owners and managers) emphasized that their priorities were to help clients and have fun rather than to make profit and maximize their incomes.

The significance of interesting and stimulating work tasks, of learning and development and a positive professional work environment, must be mentioned. The extent to which a company offers appealing work tasks and development possibilities, or rather, facilitates meaning construction processes that lead to positive evaluations of the work and prospects for learning in comparison to other options, is often crucial to the ways in which choices around exit and loyalty emerge. One company working with R&D consultancy projects gave a great deal of leeway to people to pursue their own interests and to control their own work time, which made it a very attractive employer for many people (Robertson 1999). Often, interesting work means that the instrumental aspects, including the significance of pay and other rewards, are downplayed (Alvesson and Lindkvist 1993). The significant rewards for project managers may not be higher wages so much as a chance to participate in what they see as very good projects (Kanter 1983).

In many cases this vital part of the experience of work is difficult for management to control, as market demands and competition in most industries do not offer a surplus of dream projects. In the case of the R&D consultancy firm that I just referred to, the space for people to do creative projects with somewhat uncertain commercial bases had its costs. Although a large proportion of the job tasks of KIFs is relatively qualified work there are sometimes assignments that people have limited enthusiasm for. There is, for example, a tension between doing something novel and challenging, or reusing earlier solutions and doing similar kind of projects to those one has done previously. The strongest satisfaction often comes from work involving a lot of knowledge exploration, while the market frequently favours more efficient work based on knowledge exploitation. Clients are seldom prepared to pay for the service providers' self-fulfilment. As Fosstenløkken *et al.* (2003) write, 'when competition is tough, margins are squeezed, and PSFs seek to reuse and modularize knowledge as well as solutions, internal competition for the best arenas for knowledge devolopment may also become extremely tough'

(p. 875). In science-based companies there is a similar issue, mentioned above, as the scientists sometimes want to do work that pushes knowledge forward—rather than do what is viewed as commercially more important. The conflict between very interesting work and commercial constraints is often pronounced, and if the work tasks are viewed as far from optimal, the employees' loyalty to the firm may be undermined.

As Pfeffer (1981) points out, it is primarily the symbolic sphere of corporate life that management may control, at least if one accepts market constraints and is not prepared to sacrifice revenue for the benefit of more satisfying work. Of course, under favourable market conditions firms sometimes turn down tasks seen by personnel as boring or stressful, but this is a far cry from regularly choosing only those tasks that the personnel find clearly interesting. Even though the job content is crucial, for how people react to the instrumental as well as institutional and communitarian aspects of the total employment situation, management may often direct their efforts to issues of motivation that are easier for them to control, e.g. reward systems and career decisions.

Companies can attract and retain qualified personnel through a mixture of means, e.g. wages, other financial benefits, and career prospects, giving them the most satisfying work tasks, possibilities for learning and development and, frequently overlapping, a positive organizational climate and good social relations. Financial arrangements such as partnership or shareholding in order to tie in key or even major groups of employees to the organization are not uncommon in KIFs, especially professional organizations such as law and accountancy firms. Pay scales and other reward systems that are regarded as fair in the long term may be another method of securing long-term exchange relations. In complex work settings such as KIFs, this may call for the existence of collective, fine-tuned frameworks for how to evaluate performance and a corporate memory that makes it possible to keep track of people's contributions over time. This is the benefit of clans within the context of exchanges and transaction costs (Wilkins and Ouchi 1983).

In many KIFs there are ambitious attempts to create environments and attitudes that result in the development of socio-emotional ties among employees with each other and towards the company (Alvesson 1995; Grugulis *et al*., 2000; Kunda 1992; Van Maanen and Kunda 1989). Such workplace environments and ties counteract an interest in narrower instrumental rewards such as salaries and, to some extent, promotion (Alvesson and Lindkvist 1993).

Two Illustrations

I shall illustrate most of the aspects of management addressed in this and the previous chapter with two cases from the professional service sector. I shall, to some extent, emphasize the idea of personnel concepts and indicate how it may illuminate two typical ways of structuring the employer–employee situation and also affect wider organizational priorities and patterns (following Alvesson 2002*b*).

Let me first say a few words about the two firms Big and CCC. There are many common features between the two, at least if one looks at the Scandinavian branch of Big, a large multinational company. Both have about 500 employees and were founded ten years before the time of the respective study (Alvesson 1995; Alvestson and Kärreman, forthcoming). Both are consulting firms combining management and IT (although Big's assignments include more management and strategy, and CCC is mainly involved in IT). Both employ mainly younger people, with an average age of about 30 (CCC) or slightly below (Big). More than 80 per cent of the personnel are knowledge workers or professionals, working as consultants or in other qualified capacities, e.g. with knowledge management. Often projects are carried out at clients' workplaces, meaning that the employees of the consultancy firm have more contact with the client's personnel than with those in the 'home' firm (outside the project concerned), although Big's employees seem to be more distant from their clients' personnel.

Big Consulting

Big Consulting is an international IT and management consultancy company with more than 20,000 employees. The company relies heavily on technical expertise spanning the IT and management fields. It offers a broad supply of services from strategic advice to assistance with implementation of strategies and organizational changes.

The company is broadly viewed as efficient and reliable, working instrumentally, and focused. It draws upon a wide range of experience and resources internationally. Big Consulting's strongest competitive advantage lies in its capacity to deliver the solution on time (a rare phenomenon, particularly among IT consultancy firms) and their particular work procedures. A wealth of systems and procedures produce substantial standardization in methodology, and also in talk and appearance. There is also homogeneity in recruitment: new recruits typically come directly from business and engineering schools. All this contributes to a distinctive organizational identity, and the corporate image is well in line with this. Its employees also are fairly well trained in communicating the corporate brand in everyday interactions. The large size of the firm means that it is fairly well known, and this contributes to making its brand strong.

The firm often delivers at a fixed price, meaning that there is a strong focus on cost-effective work, limited scope for flexibility, and a strong imperative to deliver with as little use of resources as possible.

Big has highly qualified personnel, according to themselves, and this is broadly confirmed by clients, competitors, and the informed public. They are less important as unique, irreplaceable individuals as most work is carried out in groups. The team is the key organizational unit. Every project and customer contact is organized around a particular team. Thus, management control revolves generally around team management. As a consequence, the individual is typically rather insignificant, at least as an organizational resource. On one level the individual is highly visible within the organization: it is the individual who is carefully evaluated, rewarded, and punished (by deferred pay rises or promotion). But on another level the individual is hardly visible at all and appears as a team member.

We have been extremely delivery- and process-oriented in our way of working: putting the team together and getting competence on different levels straight than looking at that person who has just come off a similar project and now wants to develop. We try to improve but still it is like that: oh, now that person is free and we have an empty hole there.

The firm gives priority to the development and utilization of human process advantage through a technocratic system producing synergy effects and individuals developing values and orientations in tune with this system. These well-elaborated systems are partly made possible through the size of the company, meaning that it can afford the investment and exploit the results broadly.

The organizational hierarchy is strongly pronounced formally, with several career steps and associated titles (from analyst and consultant to manager, senior manager, and then partner). There is high leverage in the firm, i.e. comparatively few senior, highly qualified people in relationship to junior consultants. This is made possible by the high degree of standardization of work tasks and availability of systems and procedures for carrying out work. People at least at junior level experience the hierarchy as strong and say in interview that they have little contact with partners, feel small compared to them, and do not know what they are doing. People refer frequently to the titles of other people, see these as reliable indicators of competence, and seem to have great respect for and compliance with formal hierarchy.

At Big Consulting employees are expected to work their career. Big is also at pains to develop and sustain an elitist image. They claim that they recruit the 'best people', and that they are an 'up-or-out' company. Employees typically respond by viewing Big as a vehicle for their personal career. The relationship between the company and employees seems to be somewhat calculated and instrumental. Some people join the firm because it is considered to be an advantage to have worked there for a few years. The mainly instrumental loyalty of those staying and working up through the hierarchy is, however, not entirely one-dimensional as people also identify with the firm and there is a sense of international belonging involving a certain degree of community.

In Big the highly structured approach to HRM and organizational structures can be seen as promoting a technocratic orientation in projects. A particular identity and mentality is produced in recruitment and evaluations: clear criteria, homogeneous rules and standards, predictable outcomes. Arrangements and acts aim at the minimization of uncertainty, surprises, and deviations from rules and norms. People are fairly homogeneous and with very few exceptions have the same educational background.

Perhaps the most vital criteria are results from technical universities and business schools and a full acceptance of the prevailing conditions of work and career (Bergström 1998). Big employees sometimes complain that they are perceived as lacking in imagination and not very good in establishing close relations with clients.

The personnel concept of Big is based on an idea of an individual strongly interested in performing, eager to be assessed and to improve, make a career, and earn a high and increasing income. The company offers its employees a great deal of training and development options and a clear career ladder, with fairly frequent promotions based on performance and maturity assessments. Wages are emphasized and are seen as based on careful assessments. Titles are viewed as important, as is status based upon position in the formal and carefully regulated hierarchy.

The company's emphasis on rationality and procedures, a strong focus on measurements, reliable delivery, and hierarchies harmonizes closely with the personnel concept and the HRM arrangements contingent on it. We can say that these produce a form of subjectivity well in line with the technocratic structure guiding work: instrumental, calculating, performance-oriented, and efficient (Alvesson and Kärreman, forthcoming).

CCC

CCC works with various IT consultancy projects. Projects of various sizes exist, employing from one person for a short time, to a dozen people for over a year. CCC is placed more in a middle-level market and is not as expensive as Big. Most projects are charged by man-hour, so that the imperative is to work as many hours as possible rather than, as in Big, to minimize the number of people and clock-hours spent on an assignment. CCC has tried to expand internationally, but with limited success, so that it is mainly working in the domestic market, with subsidiaries in a few neighbouring countries.

One advantage of CCC is the excellent network of founders of the company and the establishment of close links with some well-known client companies. In CCC there is a strong emphasis on good social relations and communication as key ingredients both in internal relations and in client relations, on all levels. Technical issues are downplayed somewhat. It is not here that claims are made about the company's strength.

The company tries to convey an image of being original, informal, creative, good in establishing contacts and creating positive work relationships, and good in communicating. CCC has a distinctive profile among its clients and within the industry. Efforts to sustain the image of linking IT questions with strategic issues have been moderately successful (see Chapter 4). Internally, considerable efforts have been made to create and sustain a corporate culture that supports these claims. These have been fairly successful in affecting employees' perceptions of what is distinctive about the company and the meaning of being an employee here. The interest in human resource issues and corporate culture is very strong in the firm, defining itself as a people company. The founders spent much time thinking through what is important for people to function well at work, and were systematic, ambitious, and skilled in carrying through the results of this understanding.

As part of a people-oriented management style, hierarchy is downplayed in many respects, including minimization of visible status symbols. Senior people behave rather informally and try to reduce social distance across levels. As one interviewee expressed it, even junior consultants expect to have a beer with the chief executive. The employees have a strong influence on hiring decisions. They are also consulted in the selection of managers and can, in principle, veto candidates, although this can in practice be difficult. Top management's influence is to a great extent carried out through cultural control, although as always a wider spectrum of means are sometimes used. The company tends, however, to be quite informal and not to rely heavily on formal control mechanisms.

The company does not allocate many resources to competence development or seem to view technical competence as very important. Some of the rhetoric even says that IT consultancy seldom fails because of technical issues: what is decisive is how social relations are handled. People are recruited because of personality and attitude as much as excellent IT competence.

In order to attract and retain people and to produce positive work relationships within the company and with clients, it is important that the employees feel satisfied and that the managers are well informed about their work and life situation, CCC's top management argues. The structural arrangement of the company, with subsidiaries employing a maximum of fifty people each, is partly based on the idea that the manager of every subsidiary should know every employee, and that people should develop a group feeling associated with the subsidiary.

In CCC there is an assumption that the well-being of employees directly influences the quality of their work. One of the strongest aspects of the company is its ability to make employees feel satisfied. The chief executive even said that 'if there is anything that we are good at it is this, we are damned good at this'. An element in this is to make the employees see the company as a 'family'. This can be illustrated by the allocation of space in the corporate building. The consultants, i.e. the third of all who are not located at the clients' workplaces, have only limited individual office space at their disposal. People sit tightly together. The social areas in CCC's building are, however, large and appealing. CCC has a high profile in social activities in which people in the company invest much energy and emotions, e.g. corporate celebrations. The company's tenth anniversary gathered together all employees over three days on an island in the Mediterranean.

Loyalty is achieved by encouraging strong identification with what is represented as a progressive, unique, and successful company. A distinct corporate culture—a rich fabric of values, beliefs, and ideas expressed through slogans, symbolic managerial behaviour (such as informal interaction and disclosing information about sensitive issues), and material artefacts (such as the building)—is important here. This means that the competitive advantage of the competence of CCC lies very much in culture-driven human processes, while it is weaker in human capital (as the aggregation of skilful people) as well as in human process advantages following from technostructural arrangements (as in Big).

What keeps CCC together and expresses its distinctiveness and forms the bonding between individuals and organization through a managerially led community is even more strongly expressed in client relations. HRM and client management, i.e. the management of the consultant–client, interface rather than intersect. In CCC the approach to personnel is seen as directly reproduced in the relationship to the market and in project work. As

expressed by one of the senior consultants, 'The company suc-
ceeds in making people feel happy with the company and then
they also feel better in the work they are doing and the job also is
performed a bit better, and then our customers are also happy.'

By encouraging a non-hierarchical relationship and demystify-
ing senior managers internally, CCC also hopes to encourage
consultants to establish relationships with and to take the initiative in relationship to senior people in client organizations. The
engineering of cultural ideals internally then forms the basis for
the engineering of client relations.

CCC's personnel concept, and the rewards and management of
motives that follow from it, focuses very strongly on the social
individual as part of a distinct corporate culture. The company
tries to recruit people who are willing to give more to the workplace than just labour power. Work should involve close social
relations and a lot of fun. The workplace climate is crucial, and it
is important that people are happy at work. People—at least those
people that fit into CCC—want to be part of a community. Ex-
pressiveness and emotions are vital. The whole person should be
included. Hierarchies and other distance-creating structures
should be minimized. Wages and titles are not major sources of
satisfaction in the company. Managerial time and resources are to
a much higher degree invested in social events and community-
building activities than used to pay people above average.

The entire company is to a high degree built up around this
view of human beings. The organizational structure is designed
to facilitate community relations and specific competence is also
based on social and communicative skills rather than technical
ones and instrumental rationality.

Market and Community Models for Employer–Employee Links

Legge (1999) discusses images of employees in the corporate
world and social science, based on marketplace and community
conceptualizations. The values associated with the former are
individualism, free choice, and economic rationality, while com-
munitarianism has its background in collectivism, social consensus, and social rationality (including social bonds and loyalties).
Legge argues that there are five major images of employees: as
customers, resources, and commodities (market-based), and team

and family (community-based). The three market-related images are present in both firms—labour is sold to clients, making the commodity metaphor relevant—but are more salient in Big, while the family metaphor is more strongly imprinted on CCC. In Big experiences of community are perhaps better indicated by the term 'club' (used by interviewees in this company). The team metaphor has a similar relevance in both firms. One could say that Big offers personnel a good trade in market terms (as 'customers' on a labour market, they pay a great deal as resource and commodity, but also get quite a lot in 'products' such as income, titles, and status), while CCC employees think that they get a nice deal in community terms. In short, the two cases exemplify economic–rational versus community–intrinsic personnel concepts.

The two cases are probably typical. In many large PSFs the economic–rational model dominates (e.g. Covalski *et al.* 1998), while many smaller and middle-sized KIFs are more similar to CCC. But very large high tech companies such as the one studied by Kunda (1992) also share many of the traits of CCC, with a tendency to downplay financial rewards, and to emphasize informality and open communication.

Summary

In KIFs the use of human resources is crucial for results. These can be optimized by recruiting people who are as highly qualified as possible or through designing and putting into work certain human resource processes that lead to considerable synergy effects. One way of grasping this is by looking at what I refer to as the personnel concept of organizations. This is characterized by

- a model of (wo)man or an idea of desirable personnel based on the particular business and work of the firm as well as on cultural ideas of how people work and what is important in life;
- an idea of how to attract, retain, and motivate people by a certain mixture of rewards and other positive features of the workplace; and

- various ideas and practices for how to influence and shape people so that they develop or strengthen an orientation that matches the HRM policy of the company.

The personnel concept then functions as a starting point and framework for HRM strategies and tactics, but also influences organizational design and efforts by senior organizational members to shape values, beliefs, and meanings around how people see themselves in relationship to the organization and what it stands for in the interface between organization and individuals, and how the rewards and possibly more negative features of employment should be viewed. Personnel concepts are thus not limited to the HRM sector narrowly defined, but tend to be integrated into organizational culture and influence a variety of organizational practices.

The success of KIFs is directly contingent upon how they can create human capital or human process advantage. The former is a matter of recruiting and retaining 'the best and the brightest' or most hard-working. The latter can be accomplished through technocratic structures or cultures leading to synergy effects. Recruiting and adjusting people to the particular utilization of human resources that the firm is striving for call for careful consideration of the entire spectrum of HRM arrangements, but also of the cultural constructions around them (Alvesson and Kärreman 2001b, forthcoming).

It is crucial for KIFs to win loyalty, as the personnel are the most significant, sometimes the only really significant, resource for many firms. The loss of key personnel can lead to immediate or subsequent losses among clients. Loyalty can be achieved through instrumental or identification-based means.

There is a considerable variation among KIFs in terms of the rewards and sources of satisfaction emphasized by people in them. Sometimes wages, promotion, career, and ownership are emphasized, sometimes hierarchy and financial rewards are played down in favour of satisfying and development-facilitating work or close community and a positive workplace climate. This can to some extent be understood in terms of different organizations targeting different segments of the labour market (with different values and priorities in working life) and having different benefits to offer (e.g. high pay based on a strong market position or work that is interesting because it is carefully selected or operates in a beneficial niche). But it is also a matter of organizations being able to shape people's view of what is important in working life and how they see the pros and cons of their work situation. Motivation is, to some extent, an organizational accomplishment, at least in organizations in which rituals, talk, and artefacts comprise a layer in terms of meanings and symbolism around who employees are and what triggers their motivation and organizational commitment. I shall develop this theme further in Chapter 9, focusing on identity.

Chapter 8 Knowledge Management: Departures from Knowledge and/or Management

FAIRLY closely related to the management of 'human resources' in terms of significance and focus is knowledge management. Knowledge and human resources cannot be fully separated, although some authors reify knowledge. Knowledge management gives a particular perspective on how organizational resources—and especially the key one in the form of humans—are being managed, or at least how management tries to access and control them.

Although people have tried to utilize and improve knowledge throughout history, the term 'knowledge management' became popular in the 1990s. It is now an important area of organizational practice and a significant academic subdiscipline. Knowledge management (KM) is one of those rare fashionable ideas that have been celebrated by practitioners but also by academics across a broad range of disciplines.

KM certainly has a strong rhetorical appeal. It combines the characteristics of simplicity and ambiguity seen in other popular management ideas (Clark and Salaman 1996). Who could deny that 'the creation, acquisition, capture, sharing and use of knowledge, skills and expertise' (as Quintas et al. 1996 define KM) is important, especially in the so-called knowledge society? However, labels that attract a wide audience and have strong rhetorical appeal are often problematic in terms of coherence and invite accusations of faddishness. In this case, there are fundamental problems with the idea of the manageability of knowledge, at least in the strong, managerialist sense of a formal authority based on bureaucratic–hierarchical position being able to control the creation, sharing, and use of knowledge (Alvesson and Kärreman 2001a). Proponents of KM are well aware of the fads and fashion characteristics of management ideas, but are convinced that the phenomenon is 'not merely some passing fad, but is in the process of establishing itself as a new aspect of management and organization and as a new form of expertise' (Hull 2000: 49). KM is 'more than a sales pitch. It is an approach to adding or creating value by more actively leveraging the know-how, experience and judgment resident within, and in many cases, outside of an organization', according to Ruggles (1998: 80).

KM is certainly not restricted to being a preoccupation with KIFs. It is generally viewed as a field and function of broad and general relevance. Its significance, however, varies between companies and is often seen as of specific importance in KIFs. Examples of companies said to be very ambitious and successful with KM often come from the KIF sector (Hansen *et al.* 1999; Sarvary 1999).

This chapter is a somewhat sceptical review of the field of knowledge management. After a brief overview of various definitions of KM, I look more closely at how knowledge and management are addressed and illuminate some different perspectives within KM. Having unpacked these, I propose some ideas for the redefinition of KM by illuminating the metaphors used. Here it is argued that the concept of KM is inherently problematic: many uses tend to be either tension-ridden or trivial. In the chapter I identify some departures from 'knowledge' as well as from 'management' in KM. The idea is thus to explore some basic substitutes for foci on knowledge and management, respectively, as they appear in the literature framed as KM.

The Many Meanings of KM

As we saw in Chapter 3, 'knowledge' has many meanings. 'Management' has, in the context of organizational analysis, fewer. What about 'KM'? An investigation of how the term is used in the literature reveals that 'KM' is more like 'knowledge' than 'management' in this regard. 'KM' covers broad terrain indeed. It is 'a term which has now come to be used to describe anything from organizational learning to database management tools' (Ruggles 1998: 80). It can also be seen as encompassing the sourcing, mapping, and measuring of knowledge, as well as its creation and sharing (Storey and Quintas 2001). KM may either be about enhancing exploitation or exploration of knowledge. 'Exploitation' means the reuse of existing knowledge through capturing, transferring it, and encouraging its deployment in similar situations. 'Exploration' means the creation of new knowledge based on the sharing and synthesis of existing knowledge through in-depth interaction between knowledgeable people (Swan *et al.* 1999). In practice, many situations and activities are between the poles of replication of previous solutions and innovation.

KM is, like knowledge, not easy to delimit. Most aspects at least in KIFs can be seen as related to KM broadly defined. One extreme is to see the selection of assignments (in, for example, knowledge-intensive companies in the service sector) as a crucial part of KM, as this represents perhaps the most significant input to learning and development. It can be argued that KM calls for a broad conceptualization, at least in certain companies. McGrath (2000: 40) suggests that 'as KIF's primarily rely on the knowledge base of their employees ... then their knowledge management practices should effectively encapsulate the totality of management practices within these firms. All management activity ought to be ultimately directed at the acquisition, development, protection, sharing and exploitation of knowledge within these firms.'

KM can thus mean almost anything, in particular in KIFs. Focusing on knowledge issues does not necessarily limit the options very much. Moreover, the concept is broad and ambiguous enough to be appropriated in different ways by professional groups seeking to advance their own knowledge domains and claims to legitimacy. Thus the broader notion has been translated variously into: 'KM systems' among IT professionals; 'knowledge elicitation techniques' among artificial intelligence experts; 'the development of human and intellectual capital' among personnel management specialists; 'the measurement of intangible assets' among accountants; and so on (Swan *et al.* 2001). KM also has the capacity to get reinvented through time as different professional groups begin to increase their purchase on the term.

McDermott (1999: 116) identifies four challenges associated with KM: (1) a technical challenge of designing human and information systems that make information available and help people think together; (2) a social challenge of developing communities that share knowledge and maintain diversity; (3) a management challenge: to create an environment that truly values sharing knowledge; (4) a personal challenge of being open to the ideas of others and to share ideas. The managerial aspect is not too self-evident: creating an environment is not something that a management can do on its own, and it is definitely difficult to address in an instrumental way. Instead it is a much more dispersed and organic phenomenon dependent on the voluntary actions of a large number of people. Community and culture matter more than management, although the latter has some impact on the former.

The first of these challenges seems to dominate the concerns of practitioners, often mainly concentrating on IT solutions in order to improve knowledge-sharing and reuse. However, this tends mainly to concern explicit, easily codified knowledge, while the most important kinds of knowledge are not so easy to capture and package, but call for in-depth understanding and the use of theoretically informed judgement to be useful.

A Great Variety of Contacts

As all organizations are based on 'knowledge' in one form or another, KM could be seen as a function of utmost significance. The interest in KM as a specific function and area of attention varies, however, between different organizations, partly related to their organizational size and field of knowledge. Many science-based KIFs rely heavily on contacts with and capacity to absorb developments around the world in universities and in other R&D companies in the field, and these contacts cannot to any great degree be managed through a central agency or function.

The potential input to firms in, for example, the biotechnology industry is spread across very large numbers of scientists and science organizations worldwide. Connecting devices—conferences, journals, email lists—are not top-down driven or bureaucratically contained, but mainly self-organized. The overall challenge of the biotechnology firm is to maintain contact with as much of this continuously evolving knowledge area as possible. This calls for a great deal of internal flexibility and space for scientists to match the complexity of the environment (Miles *et al.* 1997). Powell (1998) argues that 'regardless of whether collaboration is driven by strategic motives, such as filling in missing pieces of the value chain, or by learning considerations to gain access to new knowledge, or by embeddedness in a community of practice, connectivity to an inter-organizational network and competence at managing collaborations have become key drivers of a new logic of organizing' (p. 231).

Specific KM arrangements can facilitate the search for contacts and collaborators, but the individual networks and scanning activities of researchers may matter more than what can be centrally administered and controlled. Scientists must act in flexible ways and be prepared to be open and to some extent willing to share their knowledge. In order to produce functioning working relationships and to get access to the knowledge of others, they must sometimes bend or even violate corporate rules for what can be revealed to outsiders in terms of projects and progress (Kreiner and Schultz 1993). Here trust, situated judgement, and identification with the organization one is employed by are crucial in order to carry out this work.

Many PSFs are less dependent on worldwide scientific development, but are eager either to reuse solutions or to create synergy effects by allowing different individuals and teams to benefit from contact with people with appropriate experience within the organization. This is partly accomplished in informal ways, through people organically, spontaneously, over time forming networks and communities. Many KIFs organize previously informal groups and networks into formal structures, with budgets for technology, knowledge coordinators, librarians, and other forms of administrative support. Some KIFs, in particular smaller ones, choose not to design formal organizational structures around knowledge-sharing issues, partly to avoid adding to overhead costs, and partly in order to avoid administrative arrangements that stifle spontaneity, informality, and engagement (Davenport and Prusak 1998).

All this can seldom be understood purely as a matter of getting access to, sharing, or exploiting knowledge. As pointed out in Chapter 4, there is also the image-enhancing aspect of belonging to the right knowledge networks, and competence-developing activities can sometimes be understood as rituals in which people re-create themselves as knowledge workers and signal to the external world the centrality of knowledge at work.

Information and Codification in KM

Many arrangements and activities labelled as KM involve exten-sive use of the available technology: databases, advanced search systems, sophisticated communication systems, and so on. IT initiatives and systems dominate the KM field in organizational practices. One definition of KM is that it 'involves blending a company's internal and external information and turning it into actionable knowledge via a technology platform' (DiMattia and Oder, cited in McInerney and LeFevre 2000: 1). In this approach KM is basically a process run by a particular central agency responsible for the compilation, synthesis, and integration of more or less idiosyncratic work and project experiences for the development of general knowledge. This knowledge is some-times expressed in the form of methodologies or solutions guiding further work. Such methodologies may be used more or less actively in the management of the company, i.e. by enforcing rules and prescriptions for working. This can take the form of blueprints for how to carry out assignments similar to previous ones. Sometimes, this comes rather close to what is normally referred to as bureaucracy. Motives for this may be quicker or better work or reinforced control, but may also underscore the coherence of the company, thus facilitating its image and identity.

But the effects of the KM system may also be a database or library accessible as support for those who need the information. Davenport and Prusak (1998) say that librarians frequently act as 'knowledge brokers'. They discover solutions in client firms, and can, after KM work, use knowledge about these in new ways to solve analogous problems in other companies.

However, a large amount of criticism has been directed against this view (McKinlay 2000; Swan *et al.* 1999). Critics say that the practice of KM is frequently reduced to the implementation of new IT systems for knowledge transfer. Knowledge is not easily transferred. The very idea of knowledge 'transfer'—indicating a kind of postal delivery—may be misleading and go against the view of knowledge proposed in Chapter 2. Knowledge is not a thing or thing-like object, and one cannot simply transfer the theoretically informed exercise of judgement or ability to make distinctions. Swan *et al.* (1999) argue that a strong emphasis on IT networks may actually lead to more formal relations, taking time and energy away from relationship-building. It may shape ideas, meanings, and expectations in a 'non-social' way. In particular, when it comes to more innovative work, KM initiatives that encourage active networking are key and 'an over-emphasis on building IT-based networks may ironically undermine rather than increase this' (p. 274). McKinlay (2000) is even harsher in his assessment when, referring to the case of a pharmaceutical company considering developing a comprehensive database of the experiences of key decision-makers, he writes that the key objection to such a technological approach to knowledge issues 'is not that it would fail but that it would succeed', arguing that 'the codification required would compromise the tacit knowledge it was designed to capture' (p. 108).

Despite all the criticism, this view of knowledge as thing-like comes through in many of the more popular ideas around knowledge and competence. As pointed out in Chapter 2, the idea of 'storing' knowledge is a popular metaphor, leading to an idea of knowledge as something that can be canned and the knowledge manager as a warehouse foreman.

Many view knowledge as an asset, which is to some extent reasonable but it tends to place knowledge on the same footing as physical objects that can be possessed and controlled by the owner. In more macro-oriented approaches such as the resource-based view (e.g. Prahalad and Hamel 1990), the shift is towards reifying organizational knowledge and treating 'it' as something (albeit intangible) the company simply owns and can use. 'Knowledge is presented not as a lived experience but as an objectified entity to be manipulated by top management' (Scarbrough 1999: 229). Here knowledge or core competence becomes an asset that is, at least to some extent, managed from the central control room of top management. Terms such as 'intellectual capital' and 'human capital' also signal a view of knowledge as a static essence with highly questionable claims to being able to put very diffuse constructions into numbers (Yakhlev and Salzer-Mörling 2000).

Codification

The idea of making tacit knowledge explicit through codification is a popular one. Companies are expected to become less vulnerable to people leaving, taking their knowledge with them. Knowledge can also be reused, leading to increased efficiency or improved quality. The problem is, of course, that knowledge may not readily lend itself to capture and codification. Newell *et al.* (2002) point to several reasons for this, including the difficulty of expressing knowledge in written form, the uncertainty of much knowledge, the preliminary, dynamic nature of knowledge, its context-dependency, the costs of trying to codify knowledge and the politics around sensitive knowledge, and the unwillingness of actors to share knowledge with 'everybody'. Practitioners in up-market fields frequently feel that the idea of codifying their knowledge signals a pejorative view on it: codification is seen as possible mainly for unsophisticated knowledge, a view in line with what is proposed in Chapter 2.

One example of codification is that of Microsoft, which used the employee rating process to build an on-line knowledge map that can be accessed company-wide. The system is then supposed to be able to inform senior people of, for example, candidates from a specific area who have leadership skills in 80 per cent of the knowledge competencies for a particular job (Davenport and Prusak 1998: 76). A major uncertainty is, of course, the relationship between what has gone into this system and people's de facto abilities. Ratings are very unreliable and are influenced by the idiosyncrasies of superiors, ambiguities in performance, and political issues. Ambitious assessment systems are dogged by uncertainties and tend in practice not to live up to the ideal (Alvesson and Kärreman 2001*b*). It is, of course, possible to go much further and also ask whether there exists anything like 'leadership skills' in any abstract sense, i.e. beyond a specific local construction and a specific social context. The codification may lead to a representation which one easily reifies and takes as given, while the representation may be totally unconnected to anything external to it.

Knowledge is Reduced to Information

In large parts of the talk about KM there is a departure or shift of emphasis from knowledge to information or to products of knowledge. Rhetorically, we have moved from the information society to the knowledge society, and as a consequence 'knowledge' tends to be the preferred term, although frequently 'information' seems to say more about what people are talking about, especially in KM contexts. For most people taking knowledge seriously there is, as discussed in Chapter 2, a clear difference: knowledge is more than contextually relevant data and refers to the exercise of judgement based on insight, experience, and/or theory (Davenport and Prusak 1998; Tsoukas and Vladimirou 2001). Of course, information in well-developed electronic libraries—and standard libraries for that matter—can be used in knowledge processes. Information can give some input to these, but familiarity with it and knowledge-able information carriers can also stimulate contact and knowledge-sharing between people. Nevertheless, knowledge is best understood as quite different from information.

Network, Community, and Culture in KM

Most executives seem to understand that knowledge is highly people-based, but 'they are stuck with an investment model that is geared primarily toward technology implementations' (Ruggles 1998: 86). KM is not seen as a matter of building a large electronic library, 'but by connecting people so they can think together' (McDermott 1999: 104). An electronic library can, however, facilitate such linking processes, although, as pointed out above, sometimes the outcome may counteract the intention. A large part of the literature presented under the heading of KM focuses on issues of networking rather than knowledge (or information) per se. Thus some argue for a community model that emphasizes dialogue and sense-making through active networking and the quality of social relations (Swan *et al.* 1999). From this perspective, knowledge-as-object is downplayed and wrapped into practices of sharing, networking, and developing social relations. The idea is that 'knowledge (unlike data) cannot simply be processed; rather it is continuously recreated and reconstituted through dynamic, interactive and social networking activity' (Newell *et al.* 2002: 107). It is emphasized that community is fundamental to shaping knowledge (Cohen 1998: 28; Leonard and Sensiper 1998: 121). A key element around knowledge in organizations becomes a matter of people supporting each other for altruistic or opportunistic reasons. Care is said to facilitate innovation, and the ideal is to develop high-care groups characterized by 'indwelling', looking *with* others at their task rather than *at* others. Knowledge-sharing involves an element of altruism (von Krogh 1998).

Swan *et al.* (1999) make a useful distinction between a cognitive network model, focusing on IT and information-processing, and a community networking model, emphasizing dialogue and sense-making through active networking. This reflects an interest in the exploitation of knowledge through technical means versus an interest in exploration, which focuses heavily on people and interaction, in which IT may or may not be enabling. 'Communities of practice' is a popular term referring to the existence of groups of people who develop shared orientations and mutual trust as a consequence of interaction around the same work process. Knowledge-sharing typically follows as a consequence of the norm of reciprocity: people help those who help them. Communities of practice are hard to create through managerial initiatives as they depend on bottom-up involvement and commitment.

'Communities of practice' has a positive ring to it, but it is important not to be blinded by its virtues. A community may imply exclusiveness and closure: it may make it difficult for people to enter and generate resistance to new impulses. Knowledge transfer between different groups after a merger between companies is often difficult (Empson 2001). Strongly (over)valuing one's own knowledge and denigrating the knowledge of the other camp is not uncommon. This may mean concentration of relations and collaboration within an internal group at the expense of broader but 'weaker' networks. As Granovetter (1973) has pointed out, the economic benefits of having a broader but 'thinner' network may be substantial as the potential resources that an actor can draw upon are large and flexible.

The term 'community' also indicates the significance of organizational culture, but culture goes somewhat beyond interaction between people around the same work process. 'Culture' means a certain degree of homogenization of the mindset of people in the absence of direct interaction around work. The development of shared meanings can be accomplished through indirect communication and by people going through similar experiences and socialization processes in different settings. According to Sarvary (1999) 'the few KM systems that act as benchmarks in the industry (e.g., those of McKinsey and Ernst and Young) evolved naturally from the firm's cultures and processes and it is not clear whether they can (or should) be replicated by others' (p. 106). The concept of culture can, however, be carried even further and be seen as the very core of social knowledge processes. The meanings, beliefs, and values around knowledge, support, collaboration, expectations of reciprocity, and a shared feeling of togetherness and a common identity associated with corporate belonging are crucial for the active sharing and offering of experiences and insights. The inclination to take time and make an effort to respond positively to requests for assistance or invitations to collaborate outside one's closest set of relations is an outcome of cultural orientation.

Two KM Strategies? Codification and Personalization

There are intensive debates between IT people—favouring what Swan *et al.* (1999) label a cognitive approach—and people focusing on the social part of work. Occasionally writers do not take a position, but argue that both approaches may be equally relevant for different work processes and corporate situations. Hansen *et al.* (1999) point to two contrasting strategies for KM: codification and personalization.

Codification puts more emphasis on behavioural aspects and attempts to exploit the promises of information technology. Here, 'the strategy centres on the computer. Knowledge is carefully codified and stored in databases, where it can be accessed and used easily by anyone in the company' (Hansen *et al.* 1999: 107). The idea is that organizational knowledge can be extracted from individuals and converted into databases. The stored knowledge provides templates for thinking as well as action, thus making relatively unskilled workers productive at a higher level of skill more or less instantaneously. As Hansen *et al.* point out, the idea of codification is typically motivated by an economics of reuse, where organizational members are encouraged or forced to reuse codified knowledge, rather than developing new solutions or knowledge. This means that organizations can gain leverage from relatively unskilled—and cheaper—workers.

The *personalization* strategy means that knowledge is closely tied to the person that developed it and is shared mainly through direct interaction. In the consultancy industry it is typically used by up-market companies that charge very high fees for the delivery of highly customized solutions to unique problems. It relies heavily on socialization—that knowledge can be 'managed' by selecting and orchestrating a mix of situations and individuals. The process of sharing deep knowledge is time-consuming and expensive.

The two strategies move the focus from knowledge and knowledge creation to management. KM seems to be a generic managerial tool. For example, what Hansen *et al.* (1999) label 'codification' is captured in the concept of formalization, which, of course, is a cornerstone of bureaucratic organization. 'Personalization', on the other hand, is another word for what most students of KIFs always claimed to be essential for that type of organization: reliance on the competence of highly qualified individuals. Whether personalization is a strategy or not can be debated. One could argue that personalization heavily downplays the role of senior people doing strategic work, as the employees are to a significant degree autonomous and take initiatives. This is not to say that strategic management is absent, but around issues of personalization there is not that much need for strategy.[1]

While personalization implies efforts to maximize human capital advantage mainly by prioritizing the recruitment and utilization of people who are as highly qualified as possible, codification is a means to accomplish synthesis through human process advantages. Human resources are utilized efficiently through systems and arrangements facilitating synergy effects.

Hansen *et al.* (1999) say that although some mixing of the two strategies is necessary, companies should go for an 80–20 per cent emphasis, i.e. choose and concentrate on one coherent KM strategy and complement this with limited elements from the other,

---

[1] At least not in the respect addressed by Hansen *et al*. (1999). Of course, in other fields there may be still be the scope and need for strategies in one sense or another.

spending not more than 20 per cent of the time and money on the 'wrong' one. Companies with a standardized, mature product relying on explicit knowledge should then concentrate on codification, while companies with a customized and innovative product in which people rely on tacit knowledge should go for the personalization version, according to these authors. Newell *et al.* (2002) point out some of the HRM implications, in terms of criteria for hiring, training, and reward systems. In the personalization version people need to be intellectually curious and creative; in the codification version people should preferably be adaptable, group-oriented, focused, and goal-directed.

Hansen *et al.* emphasize personalization and codification as corporate strategies that represent basic ways of dealing with KM issues in firms, reflecting the core characteristics of the type of work being done. But often choices around systematic gathering and storage of information about knowledge issues versus strengthening interpersonal contacts and informal knowledge-sharing is done in specific situations and with more medium-ranged implications. McKinlay (2000) reports a decision situation in a pharmaceutical company for KM initiatives. On the one hand, there was the question of developing a comprehensive database covering the experiences of key decision-makers accessible for all people in similar decision situations. On the other hand, a much more modest proposal suggested identifying the fora, organizational positions, and chronological moments at which individual and organizational learning is greatest in scope, depth, and intensity, which would then favour informal knowledge 'transfer'.

KM as Interactive Databases: Dialogue

Hansen *et al.*'s (1999) framework seems convincing, but a study of a large, successful management consultancy firm throws some doubt on it (Alvesson and Kärreman 2001*a*). In this company, Excellence (a pseudonym), KM has quite a high profile, and most consultants have a fairly elaborate conception of it. However, they tend to enlarge the meaning of KM and transcend Hansen *et al.*'s (1999) claim that successful companies concentrate on one of the two.

Knowledge management has three aspects. First, it makes me aware that there are enormous amounts of information that I know can be useful to me, stored in databases in a relatively structured way. Secondly, I am part of it and consciously contribute to extend this mass of knowledge. And you do that, not because you are forced to, but in a natural way through the processes that are constructed for it. Thirdly, I know that I can approach anyone in the company and ask a question without the risk of being denied help. Everybody is there for each other.

The conception of KM as codified experiences and information stored in databases and accessible for everyone is in some cases almost inverted, as when the term 'knowledge management' is used in a very broad way: 'There is not one single day here when you meet people, when you are not exchanging ideas. That's not codified [in databases] but it still involves the exchange of information and experiences.'

This broad conception of KM, while not dominant or typical, is not unusual. Here it is the informal, everyday exchange of ideas mainly among people who are physically close to each other that is important in KM. This general enlargement of the concept may have a technical explanation. People within the organization often find it difficult and messy to work with the databases. The databases were typically considered to contain a lot of useful information, but this information was also considered to be hard to extract. As one of our informants puts it, 'It is not difficult [to publish material in the KM system]. The problem is rather that the procedures for downloading information are weak. So when you search the databases you often get 1,000 hits with varying degree of relevance.'

The same informant also points out that the technology often is more helpful for communication than for information retrieval. In the end, the actual substance in the systems seems less significant, although in some cases it is perceived as very helpful. To a great degree it is rather their symbolic value that brings meaning to KM systems. The technology is important as a tool, but functions also as a powerful symbol for the cutting-edge quality of the company. It communicates significant cues about the workplace culture. KM tells me how to operate in this environment: I use what is already there. I contribute with what I know. And I am allowed to interject with questions, because we share. Davenport and Prusak (1998) point to large initiative in a US company producing a knowledge map, and indicate that the value was very much at the symbolic level: the initiative underscored the significance of knowledge and people useful to draw upon in this context. The way KM is implemented at Excellence may not be the only thing that provides such cultural cues, but it at the minimum operates as an integrative mechanism for cultural messages of this kind. KM is a technical system, but also a powerful organizational symbol. It stands for community—the expectation that people throughout this large international company belong to the same tribe, and that each supports the other. As one consultant says, 'knowledge management consists of tools to provide a common understanding'. In this company people used databases in order to make contact with knowledgeable people. The common experience was that the people they contacted typically were responsive and helpful, returned telephone calls, and were willing to share their insights (Alvesson and Kärreman 2001*a*). This case suggests that the distinction between different strategies for KM and work, as suggested by Hansen *et al.* (1999), is problematic: there is frequently a blurring of codification and personal elements in KM (see also Werr and Stjernberg 2003 for a similar observation).

From Hansen *et al.*'s (1999) point of view, this mixing of elements would be an ineffective way of dealing with KM themes, compared to systematically pushing for the 80–20 choice that is said to be the core of an effective KM strategy. Whether the organization referred to here is characterized by suboptimal KM or whether the strategy options proposed by Hansen *et al.* (1999) are mainly neat categories produced for busy *Harvard Business Review* readers wanting quick and simple recipes is hard to tell. Of course, there are two other possible interpretations: that Kärreman and I got it wrong in Alvesson and Kärreman (2001*a*) or that our example is an exception that does not undermine the general soundness of Hansen *et al.*'s (1999) ideas. Studies by Fosstenløkken *et al.* (2003) and Werr and Stjernberg (2003), however, also raise doubts regarding the fruitfulness of the strict separation between a personalization and a codification strategy.

One could here also point to the image- and marketing-supporting functions of KM systems. It can be used to support claims about being able to draw upon a broad set of experiences and knowledge worldwide. One consultant persuasively claimed that whatever the client wanted them to do, they can say that somewhere in the world they have done something similar and that they, through their KM system, could access and exploit this knowledge. Of course, it is often not so easy, but it is a persuasive argument.

Can Knowledge be Managed?

In KM there is considerable interest in saying something about knowledge, but few writers on KM make any serious attempt to theorize what management is about, and use the term rather loosely. Whether it is necessary or desirable to define it can be discussed, but when it comes to knowledge issues the tension between a formal, bureaucratically based position (management) and knowledge-based authority is important to consider. Over-lapping this is the formal organization and the profession (or, in many cases, the local community, to a great degree grounded in a profession—the term here broadly defined).

The term 'management' is probably most informative when it refers to an agency with considerable authority and discretion, grounded in a formal position, and with an asymmetrical relation to non-managers. By definition a manager calls for somebody, or something, to be managed. Of course, management is not om-nipotent, and power relations may be more or less asymmetrical or varied. But the idea of stressing the significance of knowledge means that it is the 'knowledge-able' who are in a superior pos-ition to deal with a particular issue, and in this context manage-ment, representing formally based power, as the controlling institution does not really function particularly well. Sometimes it becomes mainly a matter of administrative work, e.g. taking the initiative and creating electronic libraries and offering people the opportunity to use them. Here the kinship with 'full manage-ment'—where the hierarchical position puts a strong imprint on activities—is so remote that the 'management' label risks being stretched too far, and 'administration' is a better label. Neverthe-less, in codification projects, resource allocation and the creation and enforcement of a policy to reuse early solutions can be seen as a managerial task. Whether this is KM or not can be debated. It can perhaps also be described as Taylorism. In a sense all bureau-cracy and scientific management is based on somebody finding out how to do things and then formulating rules and instructions for others to go ahead. One might say that the first phase in this enterprise includes a version of KM, but then follows a great deal of managerial work to implement and reproduce the resulting rules and instructions, and there is not much KM here.

Within the 'people' camp in KM, authors—or passages in their texts—give an even more limited role to management than the weak one indicated above. The favoured vocabulary—of community, sharing, caring, nurturing social relations—is far from the conventional ideas of management as a bureaucratic phenomenon associated with hierarchy, formalization, control, and direction from above through 'rational' measures. In the context of knowledge creation, Nonaka (1994) claims that managers are best viewed as 'catalysts'. However, this idea of management remains vague, and ultimately seems to be strongly rooted in the rather commonsensical idea that a manager 'sets the direction, provides the field of interaction, selects the participants in the field, establishes the guidelines and deadlines for projects, and supports the innovation process' (Nonaka 1994: 31). This does not really relate to knowledge issues in any specific sense, and is so general that it may be valid for almost all forms of management.

As Tsoukas and Vladimirou (2001) put it, management of organizational knowledge implies rather 'the sensitive management of social relations and less the management of corporate digital information' (p. 991).

Managers may, of course, work with administrative support and financial resources, and control reward systems in ways that may facilitate knowledge-sharing, reuse, and synthesis. Most of the proposed means for managing knowledge are, however, more uncertain. To work with vision and corporate culture, to tell stories, and try to allocate time and provide physical place and space for knowledge-sharing or generating activities are (a) unpredictable and (b) not necessarily anything that management is more successful at than any other actors in the organization. The role of stories as carriers of rich and meaningful information is emphasized in parts of the KM literature (Davenport and Prusak 1998). Stories are mainly created, picked up, improved, and circulated in informal ways and can only to a small degree be controlled by management. Senior managers can, of course, use formal presentations and videos for subordinates in order to tell convincing stories. They may be good storytellers and be so experienced that they have good stories to tell and have a feeling for which stories may be read as intended and picked up for further circulation in the organization. But on the whole, other actors may be equally good, and when it comes to stories that communicate important knowledge messages—in opposition to stories illustrating values more broadly—people that are central in communities of practice may have more to say than managers. The role of managers in doing this culturally and communicatively based form of knowledge-influencing is thus not self-evident.

Some Doubts on KM

It is debatable to what extent various forms of KM are best represented—or even reasonably well represented—by the concepts of knowledge and management. In Chapter 2 I argued against the temptation to reduce the knowledge phenomenon to simple sets of distinctions, e.g. individual versus social, explicit versus tacit. As indicated above, some doubts about Hansen *et al.*'s (1999) distinction between strategies of codification and personalization are also motivated. Knowledge is a concept far too loose, ambiguous, and rich, and pointing in far too many directions simultaneously, to be neatly organized, coordinated, and controlled. Given the complexities, tacitness, and 'dispersed presence' of the knowledge phenomenon, there is a tension between knowledge and management. Given the problems of the objectivity and functionality of knowledge pointed out above, there is, for example, the need for constant discussion, reflection, questioning, and debate on what is 'valid' and how knowledge, as a resource, can be transformed into knowing in specific nonstandard situations. All this goes beyond what management as structural, behaviour, or normative control may deal with.

An illustrative example is that of Leonard and Sensiper (1998: 117), who say, in the context of divergence and innovation, that 'it is the tacit dimensions of their knowledge bases that make such individuals especially valuable contributors to group projects; perspectives based on such knowledge cannot be obtained any other way except through interaction'. They also talk about 'taken for granted collective tacit knowledge' and how communities of practice 'develop implicit ways of working and learning together' (p. 122). But when they move on to write about 'managerial implications', these insights tend to be less significant. Leonard and Sensiper suggest that managers 'can calibrate the level of divergent thinking that they can encourage by varying the number and disparity of tacit knowledge bases brought to bear on the task'. Managers can create collective tacit knowledge by constructing guiding visions and shared experiences such as trips to customer sites and apprenticeships. Guiding visions are typically very explicit—and simplistic—and very loosely related to tacit knowledge. Apart from encouraging apprenticeship, the content and outcome are mainly outside management control. Most management talk refers vaguely to culture-building. Davenport and Prusak (1998) emphasize the role of locations and, in particular, time for knowledge development and sharing practices. Many issues around knowledge transfer 'come down to finding effective ways to let people talk and listen to one another' (p. 88). Self-organization is presumably very important here, although management can assist with providing time and space, e.g. through encouraging time spent on non-production-oriented activities and encouraging conferences and workshops. Carefully thought-out architecture and office design can also make a difference.

A major problem from the management point of view is thus that it is difficult to penetrate and control knowledge. When management enters with a high profile, 'knowledge' tends to be turned into information or into social relations, at its best facilitating cooperative orientation, including knowledge-sharing. The first element is recognized in the literature. One author, for example, remarks that 'The great trap in knowledge management is using information management tools and concepts to design knowledge management systems' (McDermott 1999: 104).

One may well argue that another trap is that the design of 'knowledge *management* systems' falls short of the expectation of capturing 'knowledge'. The more management, at least in the strong sense of the term, the less knowledge. Furthermore, the term 'management' may carry unfortunate connotations and thus represent a trap for the development of the emergent social relationships seen as central to knowledge-sharing. At Unilever the company deliberately avoids using the term 'management' in this context, as it is seen as directing attention in the wrong way (von Krogh 1998). We can hardly talk about knowledge administration either, but administrative arrangements that facilitate knowledge work still make sense.

Conclusion

Knowledge management is a very broad field, and looks very different if one is focusing on IT or social interaction, databases or communities, 'knowledge' stored or the use of theoretical informed judgement in process, the exploitation or reuse of existing knowledge or the exploration of knowledge for the development of unique solutions. The label 'KM' may encourage a misleading impression of unity, coherence, and forcefulness in dealing with the complex, slippery, and ambiguous issues of knowledge. It is a persuasive label: by adding management to knowledge the latter seemingly becomes disciplined and put in a control context, promising that it will be used for valuable and predictable outcomes. The emphasis in this chapter, as in the rest of the book, is on knowledge in a social, interpretative context, which means that some downplaying of information, knowledge 'in the can', codification, etc. characterize my text.

Knowledge, defined as different from and more than information, is not easily accessed or controlled from a distance. The question is whether KM really focuses on knowledge. Davenport and Prusak (1998: 42) 'found that most successful initiatives addressed not the process of knowledge generation itself but rather the external circumstances of work, including location and team structure'. There are various synonyms for KM (of which some qualify as metaphors), all of which go beyond a strict focus on knowledge. KM is seen as information management, as architecture for spreading knowledge (Brown and Duguid 1998: 103), networking (Swan *et al.* 1999), as community-building, and as encouragement of care and altruism associated with knowledge-sharing (von Krogh 1998). A few studies relate these ideological and social dimensions of work more clearly to a focus on knowledge. Tsoukas and Vladimirou (2001), for example, view KM as 'primarily the dynamic process of turning an unreflective practice into a reflective one by elucidating the rules guiding the activities of the practice, by helping to give a particular shape to collective understandings, and by facilitating the emergence of heuristic knowledge' (p. 990). Here it becomes uncertain what management can really do.

In the KM literature 'management' frequently becomes translated into efforts to encourage social contacts, share ideas and experiences (e.g. storytelling), develop and sustain a spirit of community, encourage people to improvise and take initiatives, and maintain a sense of corporate mission. These ambitions are then somewhat loosely related to knowledge issues and are equally relevant for themes like creating a positive workplace atmosphere, corporate identity, organizational flexibility, job satisfaction, and motivation. KM may frequently be a matter of social or people management. As Kreiner and Mouritsen (2003) put it, 'although knowledge escapes management in a direct sense, its medium—the knowledge worker—does not' (p. 226). How knowledge workers relate to one another can, for example, be influenced by managers. Improved social relations may well have positive effects on knowledge issues, but the links may be rather indirect. And positive social relations do not necessarily focus around the intellectual dimensions of work that the idea of KM is supposed to highlight.

Much of this falls on the border or outside the formal remit of management (and managers). The literature is frequently ambivalent here. It partly emphasizes management as a vital source of moral, symbolic, and perhaps financial support, and partly emphasizes that the vital issues go beyond bureaucracy and top-down control. On the whole, it may be wise not to overemphasize the role of managers so much, but to recognize the significance of communities and professions.

Given the common, very broad definitions (e.g. Davenport and Prusak 1998; Blackler 1995; see also Chapter 2), knowledge is, of course, fundamental in organizations in general and in KIFs in particular, but something that captures almost everything is not necessarily very useful, either theoretically or practically. An interesting irony is that KM probably has a strong rhetorical appeal because of its promise to manage knowledge, at the same time as the point of using the term 'knowledge' is to indicate something that cannot really be managed. This irony prevails at least if management does not mean 'anything' but refers to the capacity to have influence based on a superior organizational position, and if knowledge partly draws attention to influence based on qualified judgement and insight associated with expertise. It is no coincidence that perhaps the most knowledge-intensive work, university research, is typically carried out with no or minimal interference from university management.

KM as a concept is thus under the threat of falling to pieces if the two ingredients are taken seriously (Alvesson and Kärreman 2001*a*). Most of the literature turns knowledge into information or social relations or turns management into administration, networking, or organizational culture. KM, however, is obviously an attractive label and it has some positive effects in rejuvenating constellations in fields such as expertise, organizational learning, information technology, and in inspiring rethinking aspects of organizations through the concept of knowledge. I am not averse to the use of the label, but sometimes I think it is overstretched and that it should be used with a greater sense of its drawbacks.

Knowledge is arguably important, but it is difficult to define or describe and its partly tacit nature makes it problematic to access and even more so to manage. For this reason, most researchers (and practitioners) are satisfied to signal an orientation towards knowledge, but then focus on something seen as highly relevant to, and facilitative of, knowledge work. It may be networks, organizational culture, supportive social relations, or accessibility to documents that may offer input to knowledge work. Paradoxically, then, 'knowledge management' appears to be a term that provides rhetorical appeal to a broad and differentiated field of theory and practice that on the whole deals specifically neither with knowledge nor with management, and even less with the two together.

Chapter 9   Identity: Uncertainties and Regulations

IDENTITY is broadly seen as crucial to understanding how people relate to their working world and how organizations function. Identity on a variety of levels, both individual and organizational, is at present very fashionable in management and organization theory. This chapter focuses mainly on the level of individual identity. This concerns how a person constructs a particular version of him- or herself and can be seen as the response to the question 'Who am I?' The answer to this question has consequences for the priorities and motivations, the thinking and acting, of the individual. Identity is not an exclusive individual issue, but is highly related to organizational context and social interactions. We form identities through social groups, and how others relate to us is crucial to how we see ourselves. Organizations are sources of identity of the employed. Identity is not fixed, but is to some extent an open question.

Identity is of particular relevance in the context of KIFs for a variety of reasons. It is important for management to influence in order to (*a*) achieve organizational control, (*b*) create an internal, organizational basis for image management, (*c*) secure loyalty and retention, and (*d*) counteract existential uncertainty and build self-confidence and self-esteem at work. As said in Chapter 7, HRM is partly about appealing to, as well as influencing, the identities of personnel.

This chapter starts with a brief theoretical review of the concept of identity and then moves on to analyse specific issues in KIFs that make identity an important subject. Some of these concern problems around identity, partly contingent upon the ambiguity of a lot of knowledge-intensive work, as explored in Chapter 3. The mutual definitions of identity and motivation are addressed. I briefly discuss gender and identity in KIFs. A large part of the chapter addresses how managers in knowledge-intensive companies try to produce the identities that they see as optimal from a corporate point of view.

The Concept of Identity

'Identity' is a term that can be used in many different ways referring to different levels and entities. We can talk about the identity of Europe, corporate identity, the identity of a profession, and about personal identity. Identity is sometimes viewed as a matter of the characteristics (essence), coherence, and distinctiveness of whatever one is referring to when identity is addressed (Albert and Whetten 1985). Frequently, when identity is addressed, it is in the context of some uncertainty, questionings, or unclarity about what may be coherent and distinct for, as well as the characteristics of, for example, an occupation, company, or person. In dynamic contexts, such as many parts of contemporary social and working life, identities change, making it more reasonable to talk about temporary forms of coherence rather than something fixed and stable (Gioia *et al.* 2000).

In this chapter I am mainly interested in identity issues relating to individuals, associated with their belonging to professions and organizations. Identity refers to subjective meaning and experience. 'Who am I and, by implication, how should I act?' These are questions answered by the construction of identity. A particular personal identity implies a certain form of subjectivity, and thereby 'ties' a person's feelings, thinking, and valuing in a particular direction. Decisions are often affected by the logic inherent in a specific self-image (Mitchell *et al.* 1986). If one defines oneself as primarily a professional working in a specific company or as an organizational member doing a particular job, this means rather different identities even though the 'objective' work situation is the same. The professional may be somewhat less inclined to follow the instructions of management, while the organizational member may be more inclined to take the firm's best interest into account.

'Role' and 'self' are sometimes used as synonymous with 'identity', which is a pity. 'Role' is perhaps better used to refer mainly to external expectations and the position taken in relationship to others. Roles are complementary. 'Identity' refers to a person's view of him- or herself; it is an experience and goes deeper than a role. A role is the position I take in interaction with others; identity is how I see myself. I may take a role and act smoothly in it but also feel that this is not me, just something I am temporarily doing, and distance myself from the role. It is not possible to distance oneself from one's own identity construction as against the efforts of others to define or regulate one's identity.

Identity is best understood as constructed, multiple, and varying, rather than something fixed, monolithic, and robust. Identity is, like social life in general, constructed; for example, it is not a reflection of a psychological or social 'objective reality'. Identity is about how individuals or groups of people understand and define themselves. Constructions involve an element of invention and the use of a vocabulary that creates a particular version of reality. Identity is constituted through comparisons and interactions with other people and groups. A person seeing herself as a consultant does so because there are clients and clients' personnel confirming the consultant's position. And she views herself as a particular kind of consultant partly contingent upon the negotiations of meaning around the relations and work involved. He or she is middle-aged owing to the presence of young or old people.

Within contemporary studies on identity it is thus increasingly common not to look for some essential traits or stable characteristics of self-definitions, but to acknowledge the processual nature of identity. People in organizations routinely engage in *identity work*, aiming to achieve the feeling of a coherent and strong self as well as a basis for social relations, which is necessary for coping with work tasks and social interactions (Alvesson 1994; Alvesson and Willmott 2002). Identities are constituted, negotiated, reproduced, and threatened in social interaction, in the form of narratives, and also in material practices. Identities are, at least partly, developed in the context of power relations (Foucault 1982; Knights and Willmott 1989). The exercise of power is then about the development of subjects tied to particular identities regarding how one should feel, think, and act. By defining who a person is—or what he or she should be like—and indicating deviations from the ideal, the person is regulated, and the thinking and feeling become effects of the exercise of power. This, of course, depends upon the person being regulated accepting the definition and the norms involved.

In the organizational and work context it is often social, rather than highly individualized, identities that are of greatest relevance. A social identity refers to the group category that the individual identifies with: company, division, occupation, gender, nationality, ethnicity, age (Ashforth and Mael 1989, 1996; Turner 1982, 1984). It is important to avoid confusing the concept of social identity with other issues such as internalization of values and norms and commitment to certain issues. 'Social identity' refers to self-categorizations as a point of departure for thinking and relating. It does not necessarily imply a set of sentiments, and should not be equated with corporate culture (or any other culture). One may feel like a corporate member, a woman, or a Frenchman without necessarily internalizing all or even most of the values and meanings assumed to be typical of the category. As experiments have shown, people may adopt a particular social identity without any distinctive ideas, values, or emotions being involved (Turner 1984). Two groups may have similar values and beliefs but still perceive differences and exaggerate their distinctiveness. Often, however, a specific social identity increases the likelihood that certain ideas, values, and norms associated with the group or company concerned are internalized. The opposite is also common: if the values of a group are appealing, one tends to identify with the group.

Identity in KIFs

Issues of identity are of general interest for management, organizations, and working life in general. They are, however, of special significance in many knowledge-intensive contexts for several reasons, including the significance of securing a base for control, image management, loyalty, and existential security.

The most significant issue, from a managerial point of view, is that identity is a central dimension of control in work that provides considerable space for employees to act based on their own understanding. Themes such as knowledge-sharing, client orientation in PSFs, and a focus on commercially useful work in science-based companies are highly contingent upon how the knowledge workers define themselves. When hierarchical and technical means cannot prescribe behaviour in detail owing to the complexity and organic nature of the work tasks, the self-image and social group(s) through which the worker defines himself or herself take on great significance. Construction and activation processes of identities are therefore themes of great relevance to understanding the management and working life of KIFs. This is somewhat connected to the theme of organizational culture or clan as it relates to the realm of how people think, feel, and value, and culture is an important aspect of what shapes identity. Identity, however, goes beyond culture, indicating how people define themselves, which also involves personal, individual issues, while 'culture' refers to socially shared meanings and ideas. Most aspects of culture have only indirect consequences for identity constructions, as they do not primarily refer to people's identities.

A second theme concerns the importance of backing up and living the image (or corporate brand) through a set of orientations that make people able to communicate the image both in specific, image-selling situations (presentations) and in everyday work situations. It is not necessary, nor perhaps profitable, to produce identities that perfectly match the aspired image, but if the discrepancy is too strong, the image may be undermined by much of the behaviour of employees.

A third theme is related to the presence of multiple, competing identities and the significant negative consequences of lack of loyalty to KIFs of employees. Issues of social identification are in general of great importance for the sentiments, thinking, and behaviour of people (Ashforth and Mael 1989; Turner 1984), but in much knowledge-intensive work, competition and ambiguities around this topic become even more significant than in many other workplace contexts. Client relationships are often long-term and complex, which makes the chance of identifying with the client—and possibly changing employment or giving priority to the client's interest—far from insignificant. Consultants in long-term projects sometimes say that they know the client's organization better than their own (Alvesson 1995). In an IT consultancy unit some people occasionally under-reported the (chargeable) time they worked for clients, e.g. when they felt that they had not worked particularly effectively, thus favouring the client at the expense of the employing organization (Deetz 1995). Certain versions of 'client orientation' can thus undermine loyalty to the employer, e.g. if the interest of the client in minimizing costs is taken too seriously. The profession or occupation is often a very strong source of social identity. Even though there is no necessary conflict between commitment to the organization and the profession or zero-sum relationship between organizational and professional social identities (as addressed in Chapter 7), managers of KIFs, in particular PSFs, may be wise to try to encourage strong identification with the company, even though there are other routes to loyalty than through identity.

A fourth theme follows from the significance of work identity for people in knowledge-intensive occupations in combination with the ambiguities of much knowledge-intensive work. In many other jobs, where people view the job mostly as a way of providing an income, work identity is less crucial for the self. But for most people in KIFs much is at stake. In many KIFs there is a blurring of boundaries between self and work, and sometimes organization. As Kunda (1992) observes in a large high tech company, 'members are expected to invest heavily not only their time and effort, but also their thoughts, feelings, and conceptions of themselves' (p. 91). In work and organizational contexts weak on 'substance' and where assessment of work quality is often difficult, some vital sources of the stabilization and reinforcement of identity that work well in other job contexts are only modestly helpful in KIFs. I am thinking of the practical mastery of physical objects, direct feedback from people receiving the service, and a stable social environment. The presence of alternative sources of identification and tensions related to loyalty as addressed in the previous paragraph also add to the ambiguities and vulnerabilities concerning identity in many KIFs.

For these reasons it is worth exploring in greater depth some of the problems that often make the development and securing of a positive and stable identity difficult.

Identity Problems

While rigid adherence to a particular construction of identity may lead to all sorts of problems in a society and working life that call for flexibility and change, some integration, coherence, and stability around identity are necessary for mental well-being and a sense of direction. For employees identity represents the securing of a sense of self and thus ontological security in a destabilized working world (Knights and Willmott 1989). Contemporary social life has many features that threaten a strong sense of self-identity, leading to uncertainty, anxiety, and low or fluctuating self-esteem (Lasch 1978; Sennett 1998). People in knowledge-intensive contexts are certainly not unique in experiencing difficulties in securing an identity, but some of the features addressed in previous chapters (Chapters 3–5) indicate more intensive efforts to regulate and secure a productive identity at work.

Compared to many other groups, knowledge-intensive workers have access to some powerful symbolic resources in the construction of a positive work identity. Education, status, high pay, and interesting work tasks facilitate identity work and represent definite advantages in developing and maintaining a positive work identity. At the same time the traditional mystique and exclusiveness of professional and other knowledge-intensive work is fading away as a consequence of the rapid increase in and inflationary tendencies of higher education of people in general and the expansion of occupations claiming expertise and status. In addition, people are increasingly aware of the broad critique of professions and expertise. There is growing scepticism and reflexivity about social institutions and claims of experts (Giddens 1991). Many professions thus face a loss of status. The centrality of work and thus work-related identities to people in KIFs means that much is at stake, and there is a strong sensitivity to lack of confirmation of the valued identity. Compared with people who have a negative work identity ('I only do this temporarily' or 'It pays the rent'), people in knowledge-intensive occupations invest more of themselves in work, and are thus vulnerable to frustrations and lowered status.

This heightened sensitivity to the contradictions and challenges of a positive and coherent work identity means that difficulties may have significant consequences. These difficulties concern instabilities and questioning.

Instabilities

Despite the comparatively high status of knowledge workers, their self-esteem is not always easy to safeguard in an ambiguous, fluid, and image-sensitive, 'substance-weak' world. As Robertson *et al.* (2003: 852) say, 'in a relatively instructured organizational context', typical for these workers, 'the usual organizational safety nets (such as hierarchical rank, formal role and so on) are largely absent—individual status is, therefore, always provisional and to some extent contested, being defined simply by individual performativity'. In comparison with workers whose competence and results are more materially grounded or based on the mastery of routines, and whose self-identity is less contingent upon success and confirmation at work, they must often struggle to achieve, maintain, and gradually improve self-identity.

A special feature for PSFs is the strong dependence upon the opinion of the client for assessments of performativity. There are always elements of randomness, arbitrariness, and politics involved here. In a study of a public relations company a vice-president spoke very favourably about a young man in the company, but when asked if he would be promoted, the interviewee responded: 'Well, just because he is great today does not mean he will be great tomorrow. Anything can happen. He has to keep his clients happy if he wants us to stay happy with him' (Jackall 1988: 172).

One advertising professional complained that the client might reject a proposal because 'his wife did not like it' (Alvesson 1994). A computer consultant said that in the worst case you could get an assignment where you didn't know what it was supposed to lead to, you didn't know the machine, the people you were supposed to work with didn't want you there because the project has been sold at the wrong level, etc. (Alvesson 1995). Of course, if such experiences become common they may erode self-esteem and a strong sense of work identity.

Oscillation between the ideal, glamorous, high status of professional and a less satisfying, more subservient positioning as an overpaid service worker with uncertain competence may threaten a sense of identity and stability in life. Sometimes individuals can act out their preferred identity, but sometimes they have to take a much more humble role positioning, threatening their self-esteem. As pointed out earlier, much KIF practice leaves limited space for what companies, professions, educational institutions, and the mass media promise in terms of advanced work. Grandiose ideals clash with an imperfect world, asking for a lot of mundane, sometimes routine work to be done. In much IT consultancy work, 'consultants' are employed as grey labour and are asked to do fairly routines jobs and not act as an independent adviser accredited expert status. One person in an administrative position in a large management consultancy company notes how people frequently are not allowed to take a profiled consultant role in assignments and that a particular sense of themselves needs to be developed in order to adapt to the demands of the job:

And I think that this self-view is damned important since otherwise they would not be able to do the job they are doing. At the same time I think that most people working here are so flexible that they can take a lower profile in the client relation. But I see them here at the office. And I think there is an enormous difference how they are here. For certain people it may be so that they are sitting in a closet and doing programming because that was the only space they got. And they are not at all allowed to walk around in suits and they are supposed to be seen and noticed as little as possible. They are not allowed to push the clients. But when they come in to the office then it is ... like 'the consultant is here'. I believe there are people that dress up when they come to the office and there are those that dress down. Because they find it nice to be more relaxed here. So the stereotype consultant says a lot—it definitively does.

The interviewee's observation suggests that a lot of the work tasks and client relations do not allow the employees to act out the valued identity. It is even actively disconfirmed, as when the expensive, highly qualified consultant gets a very humble, low-status workplace and is expected to take a very low profile and follow instructions. This identity is enacted at the company office instead: here the consultant identity is expressed and possibly confirmed by administrative personnel and colleagues. The clash between adapting to the client and to carefully orchestrated interaction, on the one hand, and acting out and confirming a socially and personally valued identity of being a management consultant means contradictions and confusions and puts burdens on identity work.

Another aspect that may destabilize identity is internal competition, which for some undermines a valued sense of self in particular in what are perceived as elite companies. In such organizations, which employ only a very small proportion of all job applicants, the competition may mean that many of those who have performed well above average in higher education or in previous jobs may feel that many of their colleagues are performing even better, and that they must work hard and be lucky in order to be perceived as average performers in the company. Working for a company with a very high status is thus for many a mixed blessing from the identity point of view. Corporate membership may fuel social identity and self-esteem (Ashforth and Mael 1989; Dutton *et al.* 1994), but working under conditions of stiff internal competition may undermine self-esteem and trigger intensive efforts to reconstruct and maintain a positive self-image. In some of the large management and accountancy firms, built upon comparisons of people in the same cohort, this work situation provokes strong motivational effects: the desire to perform as least as well as the others is a strong driving force. Sometimes forced distribution is used: superiors must place subordinates in different categories, and many people are thus assessed as below average.

The unpredictable, relationship-dependent, and fluctuating character of this kind of work can thus make it difficult to accomplish and sustain a stable, steady growing feeling of competence and respect. Self-esteem and a coherent sense of a self are vulnerable, calling for intensive identity work. As Deetz (1998) writes, 'the largely fluid nature of anything external to interactional accomplishments provides for very active symbolic labour' (p. 157).

Questioning

The market for many KIFs, e.g. management consultancy services, has increased rapidly and steadily over a number of years, and this may be seen as a sign of success and the high estimation of business life in the quality and value of these services. But the market is a very imperfect evaluator and clients have mixed feelings about the KIFs they are getting services and products from. More broadly, there is often considerable distrust, scepticism, or at least the absence of full confirmation of knowledge workers' claims to having a superior and effectively problem-solving knowledge base. Despite—or perhaps because of—the often high status and high fees of many knowledge workers, mixed impressions and sometimes bad reputations are widespread among these professions and companies. The combination of being both highly paid and questioned may be a source of confusion and bewilderment.

Management consultants are credited with giving important support to companies, but also with creating problems. The best-seller by O'Shea and Madigan (1998), for example, has the title *Dangerous Company: The Consulting Powerhouses and the Businesses they Save and Ruin*. The impression conveyed in the book is that very large, prestigious management consultancy companies cost their clients a lot of money and that their contributions are often of dubious, sometimes even negative value. Accusations of greediness, excessive salesmanship, and the uncritical embracing of fads and fashions are aimed at consultants. Many criticisms focus on large gaps between promises and results. The complexities of selling knowledge work mean that nurturing social relations and the emphasis on rhetoric become very important, which undermines consultants' claims to independence and integrity and to have a robust and rational competence base grounded in science and proven experience. The moral nature of the enterprise becomes open to doubt. Being viewed as agents of fashion bringing about ill-founded and expensive corporate changes makes consultants vulnerable to criticism concerning not only questionable cognitive rationality but also low moral integrity. Their strong dependence on the person who pays the fee also leads to scepticism on moral grounds. Consultants are sometimes referred to as prostitutes: 'whores in stripes', as some people in a client company studied by Jackall (1988) put it. Kunda (1992) quotes an employee commenting upon a session with a consultant:

We went to this off-site meeting. A consultant led a session on 'how we feel toward each other.' It's just an opportunity to see how you handle yourself in that kind of session. The only one who believed all that California bathtub crap was the consultant. I'd believe it too for fifteen hundred bucks a day. (p. 185)

Here we find two common opinions about consultancy work: it is not 'real' and it is overpaid. The prostitution analogy is implicit here as well—there is pretence, driven by the interest in the money.

The idea that consultancy work is not 'real' is also reflected in the remarks of a chief executive of a large US company, who expressed pejorative opinions about a range of professional service occupations:

What bothers me is that Ivy League schools are creating too many consultants and bankers. These professions don't add anything to the economy, or they don't do that much good or provide much satisfaction.... Humans are meant to build something. So I say, get students into management—don't become consultants, bankers, or lawyers. Go get a job. (Halpin 1999: 35)

Empson (2003) shows how people in PSFs during a merger expressed very negative remarks about the competence and knowledge base of the partner to the merger and were unwilling to be associated with them. One management consultant, for example, said that people in his company looked upon themselves as 'strategic architects' while the people from the merging partner were 'seen as more like plumbers'. From the latter's point of view, there was little confirmation of the self-understanding of the 'strategic architects'. Instead they were referred to as being like 'the emperor's new clothes': the work they were doing 'is just like a hologram. It is all smoke and mirrors.' Of course, during mergers people sometimes close ranks and ascribe negative qualities to the other in order to avoid contamination—or to legitimize their fear—but the opinions quoted still give evidence of negative views of the knowledge base and competence of many KIFs. In non-merger situations people also express negative views about many of their colleagues or competitors, e.g. in the advertising industry, where pejorative comments about other actors not being serious and cheating their clients are fairly common.

Young consultants often face scepticism. If a firm employs a large number of junior people, it will affect how other people perceive the firm as a whole and all its employees: 'These consulting companies, they've got very young people, they're not always that experienced and I'm not ready to pay £1000 a day to teach a G and G Consulting employee' (manager in client company).

Not only consultants, but other (semi-)professionals too, get their fair share of harsh assessment, indicating a misfit between their claims and self-image and the impression of others.

Advertising people are often sidestepped by clients who have limited faith in their ability to come up with excellent suggestions (Alvesson 1994; Svensson 2004). In addition, they often feel that a large section of the public is critical of their trade: some interviewees were reluctant to disclose their occupation at social events (Alvesson and Köping 1993). Knowledge workers in staff positions in non-PSFs often face similar verdicts. A study of marketing people in three UK companies indicated problems in being taken seriously by senior management and other groups in the company for their knowledge claims outside a rather narrow, technical work area (Chalmers 2001). Tensions around marketers' efforts to establish their breadwinning credentials are partly a matter of difficulty in convincing doubters 'that marketing is based not on superficial slickness but on entrepreneurial substance and that in difficult times it is marketers who deliver the goods' (p. 66). Personnel specialists are often seen as of limited use in many companies, apart from dealing with administrative matters (Legge 1994). They have problems in establishing the position and influence on personnel issues that they claim their professional knowledge warrants (Berglund 2002).

Knowledge workers in the 'harder', science-related, areas may have a less contested knowledge base and are less frequently questioned. I certainly would not suggest that all professional groups or companies face a similar degree of scepticism from their surroundings. Many, in particular perhaps doctors and scientists, probably have a good reputation and their authority is often respected. But there are also examples of questioning within the more technically oriented fields. In Chapter 3 I referred to a study of engineering consultants in the Eurotunnel project who were assessed fairly sceptically by people working more permanently on the project (Henriksson 1999). Interviews with managers in a large engineering company indicated that even though their knowledge base may be seen as more or less in order, the engineers in this company were considered to be narrow-minded, too focused on technical details, and asocial.[1]

---

[1] I shift focus slightly here into people's broader way of functioning, thus moving towards the border or even going outside a knowledge focus, although cognitive style and way of dealing with problems is not alien to such a focus. See my discussion of problems of delimiting knowledge in Ch. 2.

Optimally, people in working life should possess a respected and credible knowledge base and a morally sound orientation, and have a personal orientation and non-technical skills that facilitate good work outside the limited technical realm. Perceived failures in any of these respects invite questioning. Many traditional ideas on professionals and the rhetoric of professionals and their associations themselves emphasize their competence, morality, and general capacity to do good things for others (client orientation). They invite high expectations. These are often not met in the eyes of others, and more or less serious questioning becomes a part of the picture.

In a study of a very large international management consultancy firm with a generally good reputation employees sometimes felt that they were met with scepticism.

I think about it a lot because I had some trouble at the beginning of my career. I started on a project, feeling happy and thinking that 'here I am consulting' and it misfired. I am very cautious nowadays in a new company. I am cautious even in an old client company if there are people I haven't met. It's about dress code. No costumes and that stuff. It's all about blending with the crowd. Sometimes I don't even tell people that I am from Big. I tell them the project I am working on, but no more than that, because there is so much prejudice and it is just too much to handle. I remember a project a year ago on the computer. A guy from the project sat down beside me and started to bullshit about the Big consultants. Eventually I told him that I also belonged to Big. That put an end to that conversation. Sometimes it is a bit hard that the client's people are suspicious, which happens fairly often, and you don't know why. (manager)

The interviewee feels that he has to 'blend with the crowd', is unable to act according to his identity, and thus receives no confirmation of his sense of self associated with his work identity.

It is likely that consultants are frequently used as scapegoats. In assignments where consultants and the clients' personnel are intermingled and responsibilities are hard to sort out, it is always likely that the other will be blamed for what went wrong. Consultants coming in from the outside, being paid many times more than the client's personnel, run the risk of engendering bad feelings and blame. Sometimes they acknowledge that their role is to take some blame and to protect and nurture their relationship with the client, who is paying for the job. At the same time this scapegoating is probably only a minor part of the explanation for the questioning of consultants. Their knowledge base, their promised contributions, their strong sales orientations, and difficulties in measuring the results of their work often leave them open to doubt and criticism. My point here is not that the criticism is fair: it is probably not. And there are plenty of positive assessments about hardworking, focused, and bright consultants, as well as other knowledge workers. But there is widespread criticism, and this has consequences. The element of doubt and questioning from clients' personnel in combination with broad public scepticism and the instabilities of the work situation mean that a lot of identity work on creating, reconstructing, and repairing a positive and stable sense of self are sometimes needed.

Gender and Work

The identity issues mentioned may affect women more than men. It is not unlikely that stereotypical expectations increase negative assessments of people in ambiguous situations so that women face sceptical verdicts more frequently. One may also speculate on whether they will react more to them. In social settings traditionally dominated by men and characterized by a masculine image, women may feel less initial security and self-confidence so that the instabilities and questioning may have more impact on their self-esteem and work identity. Raising this point may reinforce the stereotype, so I would not emphasize it, but I think it is worth considering.

Another kind of gendered identity problem concerns the tension between working life and career, on the one hand, and family and leisure on the other. Traditionally such tensions have been most strongly experienced by career women, particularly when they have young children. Parenthood may reduce the significance of work as a source of identity, or even eliminate it when a person stops working in order to become a housewife or househusband.[2] Many KIFs are characterized by expectations

---

[2] Of course, one can, as some feminists do, argue that home work and child-rearing are also work and that there is a work identity based on that, but that is of less interest in this book, which focuses on organizations, and where work is defined as paid labour.

and norms of working long hours when needed. Project work often involves deadlines, and the idea of client orientation means there is strong pressure to adapt the life situation to the requests of the client. In order to become a partner, particularly in prestigious firms, employees must often work hard and show strong commitment to their work. All this sometimes fuels a masculine work orientation and a marginalization of values and priorities in life other than career-related ones. This is often seen as disadvantaging women. This is, of course, especially the case if they have primary responsibility for children. But a more general masculine notion of work and career may also disfavour women: it may foster stereotypical expectations that women will not fit in fully or that they may experience the work situation and organization as alien to their identity as women.

Such identities are not given, but are partly outcomes of social processes through which people become gendered or—in more progressive contexts—are not trapped in gender categories. According to several studies, the sex ratio at workplaces plays a role here (Blomqvist 1994; Kanter 1977). A study of US law firms showed that women working in firms with few women in senior positions (in comparison with women in firms with a higher proportion of senior women) characterized men as more masculine and evaluated attributes they associated with women less favourably in relationship to success criteria. They also rated themselves and women in general as more flirtatious at work and themselves as more attractively dressed (Ely 1995). This indicates that in male-dominated organizations women develop more stereotypical, sexualized gender roles and identities. To the extent that looks and appearance become central features not only of impression management, but also as sources of identity and self-esteem, success at work and professional identity may become less central for women. To some extent a sex-based identity competes with a profession-based one, even though it is not a zero-sum game.

However, KIFs are not only or mainly difficult settings for women to work in. Some firms are eager to retain people when they have small children and adjust to that situation in terms of work demands and career assessments. Even though project work, deadlines, and client orientation call for occasional extra work, many organizations expect people to put in extra hours only over short periods and do not calculate on a sixty-hour working week over time. This norm is sometimes more in operation for very young people in large PSFs—responding to a mixture of planned tight use of personnel and the desire of juniors to show that they can contribute and reduce their own uncertainty—and for people at senior levels (such as partners in PSFs). In many KIFs there is an emphasis on networks, relationships, client orientation, and social competence that is in line with the stereotypical expectations of women, leading to women experiencing a positive, open, and supportive work situation (Blomqvist 1994).[3]

Of course, there is enormous variation within KIFs, and one can point out endless numbers of instances that favour or disfavour women. In terms of identity constructions, the two aspects pointed up here capture some of the key themes for gender: the masculine work orientation associated with long working hours and the tendency to define KIF organizations and work in terms that are partly in line with steoretypical cultural meanings about feminine traits, values, and skills. The identity work of females in KIFs is consequently in some ways facilitated by, in some ways made more difficult through, the various gendered cultural ideas and social practices of various KIFs.

Identities and Motives

There are two ways in which identities and motives are closely related. The first is that identity can be a motive in itself. Securing a sense of self is an important motive. People want to perform well at work partly because the status and feeling of competence have positive effects on self-esteem and identity. We do things in order to confirm that we are particular kinds of people. I, for

[3] There is, however, no mechanical relationship between how work and organization are defined in terms of gendered meanings and the work situation of the two sexes. A study of an advertising agency showed that people ascribed feminine cultural meanings to the work and the organization (intuitive, emotional, relationship-sensitive, non-hierarchical, friendly), but that all professional positions were occupied by men while all the women had junior positions. Gender division of labour was interpreted as a means of supporting the masculinity of the dominant male organizational members, mainly employing younger and attractive females (Alvesson 1998).

example, write mainly books partly because this kind of project expresses and confirms me as a particular kind of academic—a more 'scholarly' one, not entirely happy with writing specialized papers and subordinating myself to too much formal review. Positive confirmation of identity as well as lack of it affect motivation. If others do not respond positively to one's claim to be an expert, one is motivated to try to change the situation and arrive at a correspondence between one's view of oneself and the view others are communicating. Questioning by others typically triggers efforts to reinforce a valued self-identity, and this can be accomplished through improved behaviour, triggering visible signs on validation. The continued lack of confirmation of identity may lead to a reduced investment of self in work and thus decreased motivation. People may, for example, emphasize their parenthood and reduce investment in their work identity as a response to limited confirmation in working life.

The other way in which identities and motives interact is through the way in which identity constructions affect the centrality or marginality of motives. What is perceived by employees as attractive and therefore motivating is frequently seen as given. It is typically assumed, for example, that 'employees bring their needs, aspirations, and hopes to their jobs, and become committed to employers that take concrete steps to help them develop their abilities' (Dessler 1999: 63). Conventional motivation thinking (e.g. Maslow's theory of needs) emphasizes a fairly stable and fixed set of needs or desires even though there may be movements between them. One key aspect of the personnel concept as addressed in Chapter 7 is this identification of a particular motivation configuration and the offering of a set of HRM and organizational arrangements (e.g. career steps or organizational community) that respond to it, thereby attracting, retaining, and motivating a suitable group of employees.

The other key aspect of the personnel concept is its dynamic features: how organizations do not simply respond to or work with fixed motivations but also actively shape them. It is not possible simply to establish needs and expectations and to rank different sources of satisfaction in a clear manner once and for all, nor is there a set of rewards to which people respond in a straightforward way. People's motives are contingent upon their self-construction—governed by various agents in the organizations they work in—and how they construct different advantages and frustrations in their work, and, in particular, how they construct their relationship between themselves and work in terms of fit, satisfactions, and frustrations. There is a relative openness (non-closure) in how most people, particularly perhaps relatively young people, relate to the world of work. Organizational cultures and social information processes gradually shape them by drawing attention to and valuing different features in different ways: pointing to certain needs and downplaying others, and constructing workplace and employment conditions in ways that can be linked to those needs and sources of satisfaction (Salancik and Pfeffer 1978).

One aspect of the interface between motivation and identity is how the inclination to maintain and enhance one's identity influences the appreciation of various driving forces. A person who, through education, training, and ongoing social relations, experiences herself strongly as a professional may as a result give priority to certain values and motivators at work—e.g. autonomy, knowledge development, specialization—as an outcome of the identity rather than an effect of the pure motivating power of instrumental and hedonistic sources of gratification. This person may not be very responsive to the idea of promotion involving managerial tasks as the tasks and the status context are somewhat alien to how this person sees herself ('I am not a bureaucrat', 'For me organizations are networks, not old-fashioned hierarchies').

'High-intensity' organizations based on strong images of the prototypical employee such as the two consultancies Big and CCC (addressed in Chapter 7, in particular) make heavy claims on their employees in terms of time and energy put into work. In such organizations and occupations the identities of the personnel are constructed and reconstructed in a more powerful way than in organizations and occupations that have lower profiles and express less distinctive claims on their employees. Of course, KIFs vary in terms of how heavy are the demands made on people's involvement with work and the centrality of work identities, but many clearly go beyond a nine-to-five view of work. The particular identity constructions and motivation configurations then mutually define each other. High pay and bonuses as well as strong community feelings fuel a norm of working when it is needed and an identity in which work and organizational membership are central. This means that strong material for identity work is offered, which can be used by individuals in struggling with the identity problems discussed above.

Management of Identities: Objectives

Having discussed the concept of identity and why it is critical for KIFs, in this and the next section I shall address this theme in a management context.

Management of Identity as Control

Management in general, but perhaps even more strongly so in many knowledge-intensive companies, is partly about trying to control people's identities (Alvesson and Willmott 2002). When complexity rules out, or reduces the efficiency of, direct control of employee behaviour or results, trying to control how people see themselves is one way of safeguarding what are deemed to be suitable priorities and efforts. People's modes of becoming and being in knowledge-intensive companies become targeted. In the rather extreme 'people-intensive' organizations that many knowledge-intensive companies may be said to be, systems, structures, technologies, and products matter much less than personnel do and, in particular, how they impress clients, partners, and others. Marketing and production are heavily sensitive to the identities of the personnel.

Identity thus becomes significant as an anchoring point for management control and regulation to create a 'subjectivity base' for the right kind of action, one that is in line with the appropriate image, rhetoric, and orchestration of social interaction.

Identity is obviously central to forms of control associated with corporate culture and clan, but also in other contexts where senior management tries to form or discipline professionals by other means than pushing for (what is claimed to be) a company-specific set of ideas, virtues, and ways of doing things. Hierarchical, bureaucratic, and technical control—including direct instructions and explicit monitoring from senior levels—also involve identity in one form or another. Even though these forms of control do not focus identity and are intended to work mechanically, to some degree they call for work identities supportive of—or at least not alien to—the control structures in order to work. Bureaucracies call for people who view themselves as rule-oriented and compliant.

The control of identity concerns not only present but also future identities. In KIFs it is common for junior people to define themselves through the prospect of making a career: they may even define themselves through a projected future position. This may make it easier for them, when asked to do routine work (e.g. 'bean-counting' in auditing), to rationalize their present situation. They may see it as an investment leading to a more positive position in the not too distant future (Grey 1994). Management can influence this through decisions about the ratio of partners to non-partners, through the design of career paths, through elaborated rituals around promotion, and through selective communication of the meaning of partnership.

Compliance and obedience also call for the right kind of subordinate identity. If people see themselves as professionals claiming a very high degree of autonomy and expertise, hierarchy and hierarchy-induced forms of control will meet with resistance. Client control may also meet with resistance, as the 'true professional' may insist on his or her expertise and be disinclined to accept that the customer knows best. A more commercial, service-minded version of 'professional identity' is called for. Rhetoric around client orientation, and persuasion that this should be understood as 'doing whatever is necessary to make the client happy', is often used here, which can be seen as the regulation of 'professional identity' so that 'professional' is defined in terms of flexibility rather than integrity.

Management of Identity as Support

Another reason for the centrality of identity as a theme and object in management control is that the ambiguous nature of most knowledge work calls for considerable efforts to secure a sense of a coherent self. As pointed out above, identity is also significant in order to support and strengthen self-esteem and existential security in a work context weak on substantive support and clear performances, and characterized by fluid images, demands for impression management, and a strong dependence on some-what arbitrary evaluations and opinions of others. Organizations risk their employees experiencing frustration and dissatisfaction. Uncertainty, low self-confidence, and reduced engagement in work are negative effects that can be painful for the employees and costly for the firm. Management sometimes has good reason to focus on identity issues in order to reduce these problems. Identity regulations here are motivated not so much by a desire to accomplish the right work orientation leading to 'correct' be-haviour, loyalty to the employer, and a base for image manage-ment as by a wish to provide 'positive' support. By various means, material and symbolic, firms can support identity con-structions at the individual level.

Corporate identity—constructions of what the company stands for and in what respects it is more or less unique—is important here. The experience of being part of a distinct and high-quality organization can compensate for a variety of fragmented work tasks and work experiences. Appearing confident may also lead clients and others to assess work performance more positively. Coherence of internal communication of who one is and stands for can balance the incoherences and randomness of what exter-nal actors may signal. Management here has an important role to play.

Now it is time to address how management works more spe-cifically with the identity theme.

Three Modes of Identity-Focused Control

I shall draw attention here to three modes of identity-focusing control common in many KIFs (as well as in some other organiza-tions): identification with the company as an institution (organ-izational identity), cultural control, and subjectification.

Organizational Identity and the Institutionalization of the Company

The identification of employees with the organization is some-thing that management in all kinds of companies wants to en-courage, except in situations of down-sizing and in individual cases where people are asked to leave as they have not been chosen for promotion (in getting-up-or-out systems). In some companies the possibilities and value of being successful in nurturing identification with the organization are better than in others. The high status of many large knowledge-intensive organizations facilitates identification with them (Alvesson *et al.* 2001).

Identification then works via a combination of internal corporate pride and perceived status of being affiliated with a prestigious organization. For the employee there is great value attached to being a successful member of this specific institution, perceived as representing a value in itself (Selznick 1957). The more distinctive, well known, and well respected the organization, the more likely it is that the employee will define him- or herself as a member of the organization (Ashforth and Mael 1989; Dutton *et al.* 1994). In less fortunate companies, managers may engage in great efforts to construct an appealing corporate identity and support identification with it. Efforts include elaborated rhetoric and image management regarding the claimed unique characteristics and excellence of the company. Robertson (1999) describes a small law consultancy firm that signalled quality and success through the use of exclusive status symbolism in the form of the location and quality of its office, its choice of bank, the use of a company limousine for local and regional travelling, etc. Another case is a small advertising agency whose weekend 'conference trip' in a ski resort strongly underscored the close social spirit of the company for the employees as well as to outsiders: at the start of the trip the employees received green jackets with the corporate logo on the back, which they wore during the entire 'conference', participated in the same activities, drank the same drink, ordered and consumed the same wine, and thus consistently utilized the event to emphasize strongly belonging to the community and the company (Alvesson and Köping 1993).

Organizational identification is facilitated through the recruitment of a similar kind of people with similar class background, education, and personal attributes and orientations. Often the development and employment of a distinct personnel concept also lead to a certain homogenization of employees in terms of values and work orientation. The creation of fairly homogeneous groups associated with the firm strengthens the organization as a source of identification and identity: being a member of the organization seems to stand for something specific. Belonging to a collective gives strong symbolic support for self-definition and may counteract the fragmentation and mixed messages that the rest of the world produces.

The personnel policy of PSFs with a partnership system that revolves around people being promoted or they are out (and far from everybody can become senior manager or partner) means a contradictory mix of various elements. This is particularly pronounced in large and prestigious PSFs, which dominate, for example, the management consultancy and accountancy fields. The employees, the core of the firm's success, are regularly presented with the idea that they are replaceable, and that they may sooner or later be forced to resign because of restricted possibilities and high demands for promotion. This creates an uncertainty between feeling important and proud and being forced to develop and move on in order to avoid feedback that one is not up to standard and may be replaced (Bergström 1998; Kärreman and Alvesson 2004). Given the value attached to being employed by this company and the impossibility of relaxing and being satisfied with the status quo, there is often strong motivation to be career-oriented. You must improve in order to continue in the company. It is either up or out.

The attraction of large, well-known companies to some extent contingent more upon name and image than the work conditions offered means that management does not have to be too concerned about personnel issues below partner level. According to a case study of a large management consultancy firm, there is 'never a shortage of hopefuls eager to join the ranks, so the partners have over the years developed a callous and cavalier attitude to personnel management' (Akehurst 1994: 192). The status and self-esteem associated with working for this kind of organization carry far and may be a contributing factor to the continuing success and steady growth of many of these firms, leading to a few large organizations dominating the market. The significance of the image on the personnel as well as customer markets is, as pointed out in Chapter 4, very great.

More generally the very notion of being (constructed as) knowledge-intensive or professional has strong rhetorical value and can be exploited by managers and employees for identity regulation. The rhetorical value of knowledge was emphasized in Chapter 4 in the external organizational context, but it is also mobilized for internal identity reasons. A strong case for sophisticated knowledge as a core characteristic of an organization increases the chance of people letting their identities be formed and constrained through organizational membership. Creating— or at least making credible claims to—knowledge-intensiveness provides a platform for positive identity constructions. Here, of course, management can try to move into a certain niche or work actively with high-profile knowledge themes, employing people with degrees from leading universities, investing in training, launching KM initiatives, and drawing attention to particularly advanced work, etc. But in addition to this, and perhaps sometimes independently of it, the rhetoric of knowledge can be one important field of management, for internal identity reasons as well.

Cultural Control

As mentioned above, most KIFs rely on a corporate culture (ideology)—a set of guiding ideas, beliefs, emotions, and values often more influential than formal structures in controlling people. The specific control accomplished—providing guidelines how to think, feel, value, and act—is typically de-centred and exercised by a myriad of sources. 'Everybody'—or at least broader groups—is involved in the reproduction of ideas, values, and meanings guiding thinking, feeling, and acting. Kunda (1992), for example, observed in his study of a large high tech company 'a decentralization of power. Symbolic power, as one might expect, is clearly possessed by those invested with formal authority and high status' but also in much more distributed ways, including that

in Tech's open and shifting environment, reputation, status and real rewards are in the hands of numerous, often unknown, others; and, if nothing else, a fluency in the language, mode of thinking and style of ideological discourse. In short, from the point of view of the individual participant, agents of control are everywhere; one is surrounded and constantly observed by members (including oneself) who, in order to further their own interests, act as spokespersons and enforcers of the organizational ideology. (p. 155)

The computer consultancy company CCC, mentioned earlier, mobilized a wide set of resources in order to develop and maintain a set of beliefs, values, and perceptions among managers and personnel, including slogans ('fun and profit', 'treat everybody as a friend'), activities (conference and other activities with a strong social, community-building content), and material arrangements (including locating top management on the ground floor close to reception in order to signal accessibility, rapid communication, and equality) (Alvesson 1995).

Cultural control overlaps and informs identity-focused control. Cultural material—symbolic management behaviour, rites, rituals, stories, jargon, material artefacts—not only provides guidelines for orientation in a social landscape but gives clues for how individuals working there should see themselves. Of course, cultural control reaches well beyond identity control, but it carries effects on the identity construction projects of individuals.

These cultural clues and the richness of cultural symbols offer material for people in their definitions of themselves, providing a mixture of guidance, control, and support.

Subjectification

The concept of subjectification, drawing upon Foucault (1976), refers to a process tying the individual to a particular model of self-knowledge, i.e. the individual creates him- or herself as a distinct kind of subject. The openness and ambiguity of how an individual can define him- or herself is replaced by formation around a specific self-definition. It is the idea of what kind of person I am that is at stake here. The individual is central, but managers and other social institutions can be actively involved, e.g. through providing psychological tests, communicating explicit criteria for jobs, providing feedback, and providing certain forms of training. The crucial element is the extent to which the individual accepts certain templates and definitions of him- or herself and lets them structure and guide existence.

One example of this phenomenon, orchestrated by some companies, is 'cultural matching', i.e. encouraging a fit between candidate and job through 'realistic' job description and giving the candidate the chance to choose whether he or she fully matches the job and the organization. This means that the emphasis is moved from surveillance of individual abilities, knowledge, and traits to surveillance of the job candidate's own self-understanding and subjectification. Cultural matching exemplifies a kind of control focusing on how the individual experiences work as a result of his or her autonomous and well-informed choice (Bergström 1998: 200). The employee is encouraged to define him- or herself as the kind of person who has chosen this kind of work; this definition then produces a model to which the subject becomes committed.

Sometimes the norms to be followed are internalized to the point where people fully adopt the orientations deemed to be best for the company. As one partner in an accounting firm expressed it, 'I do what I want, but the things I want are likely to help the firm because that is the way I have been trained. At one level we are completely independent, but we all march to the same tune without even thinking about it' (Morris and Empson 1998: 618). Here a variety of organizational regulations seem to have resulted in people having been formed or forming themselves in a similar way.

In the study of the computer consultancy company CCC people responding to a job advertisement were given the following response from a manager in an initial telephone contact: 'if you are interested in a job here, write a page, say who you are, what you can and what you want to do, but don't send us any certificates. We are not interested in those.' Here, an image of the company as being informal, having trust in people, paying more attention to people's way of being than their formal qualifications, is signalled. People responding to this invitation then define themselves—project a future self—according to the workplace scenario implied by the manager's statement and similar subsequent signals (Alvesson 1995).

Deetz (1995) observed the consequences of relabelling a computer professional service unit an 'internal consultant group' and a 'profit centre'. This immediately changed the identity of employees and meant new control processes:

Conceptions of self-value changed from pleasing a client and doing a good job as goods in themselves to the instrumentalisation of these in the service of making money. Most worked harder for the same pay.

Employees defined themselves as being of value based on feeling more important if someone was paying the company for their services, rather than based on work quality or the level of their own pay. (p. 149)

Subjectification here refers to the arena being defined in a particular way, thus constituting a 'regime' calling for a certain kind of subject. When individuals decide to enter and comply with this, they subject themselves to this regime.

Key Themes in Identity Constructions

In terms of the constructions and regulations of identity in knowledge-intensive organizations, two very different versions, mentioned in Chapter 4, seem to be common and can be seen as offering prototypes for identity constructions. One is indicated by key words such as 'innovative', 'informal', 'creative', 'intuitive', 'non-hierarchical', 'ad hoc', espousing feelings and cultural values typical of some high tech, 'creative' (e.g. advertising agencies), and computer consultancy companies (e.g. Alvesson 1994, 1995; Grugulis *et al.* 2000; Kunda 1992). Another is based on notions such as 'professional', 'rational', 'reliable', 'strict', 'controlled', 'career steps or career hierarchy', 'result-oriented', and seems to be typical of a large professional organization such as accountancy and management consultancy firms (e.g. Covaleski *et al.* 1998; Grey 1994; Morris and Empson 1998). A third emphasizes moral virtues such as integrity, but is probably less salient in internal communications of identity. The two major prototypes offer powerful input to identity control and the self-construction of employees, although in many cases the identity regulations are less distinctive and combinations of these and other elements are common. Identity constructions are typically partly a matter of using broadly available discourses, and partly a matter of highly local and situational construction processes.

The Pressure for Flexibility: Difficulties in Managerial Regulations

Since corporate life—and even more so, client interactions—is often fluid and contradictory, the identities are seldom simple, straightforward, and monolithic. In corporate contexts constructed as, for example, creative, non-hierarchical, and flexible, client expectations and management priorities sometimes call for people to be prepared to adapt to positions applying available knowledge, to adapt to hierarchies, and to do routine work and flow with these demands without feeling too strongly 'this is not me' and experience the alienation, frustration, and propensity to resist. Identity control is not just a matter of fixing people in one coherent self-definition; it is also about accomplishing a pragmatic, flexible orientation. Management control targeted at identities is not a simple affair. Apart from constructing a positive and appealing story suitable for use in various promotional and pride-, and self-esteem-boosting situations, identity regulations need to consider the imperfections and frequently less flattering aspects of business and working life.

Part of the complexity and difficulties comes from the tension, in professional service work, between the knowledgeable, autonomous expert versus the client-centred, adaptable service worker. In product-oriented KIFs, such as pharmaceutical companies, there is sometimes a similar tension between the self-governing scientist and the constrained component worker in a large R&D machinery where everybody is supposed to do their limited part in the chain. Sometimes overlapping this is a tension between developing knowledge of interest from a scientific point of view and doing something perceived as commercially more optimal.

On the one hand, managerial identity regulations are very much about trying to produce a particular appealing version of the individual—creating a corporate person that defines him- or herself in a fairly standardized and positive way—that gives support for organizational work and builds up an identity capable of taking some of the blows against self-esteem following from the instabilities, questioning, and pressure to comply with organizational hierarchy and even elements of machine bureaucracy. On the other hand, the constructed identity can be a source of rigidity against demands and expectations to be adjustable. 'Positive' identity constructions may also clash with a social world that does not live up to expectations, leading to confusion and frustration—as when the consultant is asked to do programming rather than give strategic advice. Some identity constructions are more in line with such demands for adaptability and service-mindedness—e.g. the client-centred person viewing the client as king—but it is difficult to build identity solely around responsiveness, and any work relationship calls for some grounding and a base for establishing confidence and authority. The very idea of identity is to some extent by definition antithetical to drifting flexibly between all the contingencies in complex social life. Identity is a source of inertia and a force against extreme adaptability. An identity as a compliant service provider is not experienced as very appealing and is not supportive of the high level of commitment and investment of energy in the job through transcending the boundaries between job or organization and self typical of KIF employees. Knowledge work is broadly seen as different from more simple service work, both in terms of adaptiveness to the wishes of the customer and in the ways identity is constructed and defined.

Summary

Identity is a key theme in contemporary management and organization studies. Although academics, and practitioners working in all kinds of organizations, in general may have good reasons to take an interest in organizational identities as well as identities of the employees, there are particular reasons for those interested in or engaged in KIFs to do so. These include the centrality of identity to organizational control, loyalty, and image management, and its importance in countering the existential and psychological problems that follow from working in an ambiguous and fragmented world.

For management, it is particularly important to regulate identity in the absence of reliable bureaucratic–hierarchical control mechanisms. Since management can only monitor and control work behaviour and results to a limited degree, it is important that personnel have internalized the 'right' orientation, which is partly a matter of their work identity to the extent that it includes identification with the organization. It is also, however, important for management to address the issue of identity in order to secure the functioning of bureaucratic–hierarchical control forms, particularly in contexts where these are not self-evidently expected, as in large KIFs. An alignment between orientations based on knowledge work and professionalism and elements of bureaucratic–hierarchical control is called for. Managers have an interest in 'moulding' people so that they don't find a large apparatus of systems, rules, and procedures too frustrating or alienating. The employment of young graduates directly from college facilitates such a development (Alvesson and Kärreman forthcoming; Grey 1994). In KIFs it is also important that systems and procedures are not adopted in any mechanical way, and that employees use these selectively and rely on their own judgement. A combination of the compliant organizational person and the more independent professional is the kind of identity that management often tries to nurture.

A second vital theme is commitment and loyalty. As mentioned in Chapter 6, it is possible to secure loyalty by instrumental means, but making employees identify with the firm and seeing themselves partly through being connected with the organization means a much deeper, genuine, and less financially costly form of loyalty. By constructing the organization in a particular way and influencing individuals' self-understanding so that a fit between this and the constructed organizational characteristics is achieved, an element of identification and sense of belonging is created and reinforced.

A third vital theme is the connection between identity and image, making it important for managers in KIFs to regulate identities so that they are in harmony with the projected organizational image. Image work and the effective use of corporate rhetoric call for people to have an anchored view of the company and what it stands for in their own ways of being. An effective corporate brand—particularly in people-intensive businesses—calls for employees to express the brand voluntarily in their work and in encounters with others. Image management without back-up in corporate identity and individual work identities may not be very credible (Cheney and Christensen 2001; Hatch and Schultz 2003).

Identity support is also important for the well-being and existential security of the employees. In society today, characterized as it is by complexities, ambiguities, and a multitude of floating images, identities tend to be uncertain and vulnerable, calling for more or less intensive construction work in order to build up, retain, reinforce, develop, and repair a positive and not too disjointed self-identity.

Many people in KIFs have prestigious jobs and are generally viewed with respect. The material rewards are often substantial. Educational background and corporate and professional rhetoric are also vital resources in identity work. But they often face scepticism and questioning. This is the case in public, where, for example, management consultants often are castigated by critics, as well as in specific work contexts. Since these jobs are frequently highly complex and ambiguous, and are carried out in various work contexts with different groups of people, it is often difficult to develop and maintain a stable sense of self. The work situation is rather mixed in terms of both identity-strengthening and -undermining elements. Self-esteem may fluctuate. Heavy investment in a job-related identity, blurring the boundaries between self, job, and organization, means that a lot is at stake. Organizations that mobilize considerable symbolic and material support for people's identity construction are likely to produce more confident and satisfied employees as well as a workforce that in certain ways is more effective. Identity work is, however, carried out in the context of various significant others and in a variety of social relations. If the identity regulations produced by corporate management are contradicted by the experience and communications of other groups, such as clients, the public, the media, and co-workers, then people may become caught up in difficult situations, with contradictory, confusing, and fragmentary experiences.

Organizationally influenced work identities are partly an effect of organizational cultures and management actions creating certain templates for the prototypical employee in the company by embracing a specific personnel concept and consequent arrangements. Management often works with

- the construction of an organizational identity and encouragement of employees to identify themselves with the organization;
- the communication of ideals and values (organizational culture) with special reference to employees' self-understanding;
- specifying the demand and characteristics of the 'normal' organizational member who is seen as fitting in, e.g. through job descriptions and feedback.

Psychological mechanisms are also involved, interacting with specific management tactics for identity regulations. The tendency for people to self-select and self-eject in particular organizations and work environments is, for example, partly affected by what management communicates about the organization to the labour market and potential job applicants and what behaviour is rewarded and discouraged. The negotiation of identities in everyday interaction, and the tendency to use social categories, such as the organization, in self-classification and thus identity, are mechanisms of identity work that may be more difficult for management to affect. The degree of managerial impact varies, but typically there is an interplay between managerial regulations and other organizational forces so that the collection of individuals is far from a random collection of identities. Nor is it just a matter of the importation of people with fixed and similar identities. KIFs, and in particular PSFs, are, more than most other organizations, characterized by the active shaping and homogenization of identity constructions. There are thus two steps: recruiting and retaining people whose 'initial' identity constructions are roughly in line with the identity constructions valued in the organization, and an ongoing shaping and regulation of the identities of employees.

Identities cannot be directly controlled, but various means of management can provide input to and guide identity constructions. In this chapter corporate identity, cultural control, normalization, and subjectification have been addressed. These are not exclusive to KIFs, but tend to play a more significant role in KIFs than in many other organizations.

As the material core of most KIFs is weak or unclear, questions of the type 'Who are we?' become important to raise, and it is often difficult to come up with a coherent and clear answer that is useful over time and context. The processual nature of efforts to regulate identity and identity constructions must therefore be emphasized.

Chapter 10 Conclusions: Rethinking Knowledge-Intensive Organizations and Work

In this final chapter I summarize and draw out some of the conclusions of the book, and discuss the limits of the ideas suggested here. One provocative question is whether knowledge is the solution or a dead end as an approach to understanding organizations and to improving their functioning.

I start, however, with discussion of a version of the key theme of tension between knowledge work as a cognitively and possibly ethically rational activity versus knowledge work as a more uncertain, pragmatic, politically sensitive, and otherwise 'non-rational' social phenomenon. I do so by discussing professionalism and the efforts of some firms that do not belong to the certified branches to mimic certain key themes of professionalism, thus introducing an idea of the quasi-professional firm. Some key themes of the book are addressed here from a somewhat different perspective than in previous chapters.

I then move over to a discussion of contingencies of the key themes for understanding KIFs, and raise the question of the extent to which they are central or critical to all KIFs, or whether the variety of KIFs means that they are less relevant to different firms within this broad and in many respects heterogeneous category.

My next move is to reintroduce the discussions in Chapters 3 and 8 and ask whether knowledge is an analytically productive way into organizational analysis and theory-guided management practice. Perhaps knowledge, as commonly used, scores better at the level of rhetoric than in relation to analytical and interpretative criteria. In other words, it is perhaps more valuable in drawing attention to an area and convincing people of its importance than helpful in analysing phenomena and guiding practice. Some problems with the concept of knowledge—or perhaps with how it tends to be used—are debated.

Then follows a discussion of the need for a moderate degree of scepticism in understanding knowledge work and KIFs. I end the book with a summary of its key messages in terms of non-functional metaphors for KIFs, emphasizing the symbolism of knowledge at a variety of levels.

Professionalization as a Mixed Blessing: Resource and Constraint

At the heart of much knowledge work—or at least of academic and practitioner claims about such work—is the use of knowledge for achieving a high level of rationality in situations of complexity. As emphasized in Chapter 5, institutional back-up for this knowledge is then crucial. This back-up consists of scientific and other form of legitimized knowledge, as well as ceremonial arrangements and activities around it. The certified 'full' professions score strongest in this regard, not necessarily in guaranteeing that superior rationality is achieved, but in giving those certified by the profession formal recognition and more or less exclusive access to a particular market.

For the 'new' knowledge workers, such as management consultants, who are greater in number and probably play a larger economic role than the traditional (liberal) professionals in business life (as distinct from public sector), professionalization in a formal sense is of limited relevance. They rely mainly on the market, and are not dependent on the state or a professional association for authorization and legitimization (Poulfeldt 1999; Reed 1996). For management consultants the prospect of formal professionalization, associated with state-regulated certification and strict regulation of entry to the area, is not particularly important. One could imagine a situation where the title 'consultant' was reserved for people with an MBA in business, five years as a manager, and/or five years as a junior in a consultancy firm, plus additional formal education and the passing of formal examinations controlled by the association of certified consultants; and where those without the resulting certification would not be allowed to do consultancy work. This situation seems unlikely to materialize within the foreseeable future and would probably be seen by most consultants and their clients as missing what is vital in this kind of work. In addition, there are so many types of consultancy and so many routes to it that any effort to establish a set of fixed criteria for qualification would be misleading.

Nevertheless, the great variety and unpredictability of characteristics of those active in the consultancy market are sources of frustration. Even if the market wants the services and products, it does not necessarily mean that customers are free from worries, distrust, and ambivalence. For individual actors it is very important to produce evidence of competence and rationality. Fear of arbitrariness, unpredictability, and amateurism as well as opportunism among players in the field are salient. There is also a fear that all this may lead to deep scepticism among clients and the public. PSFs, like many other KIFs, need trust and faith from those who pay highly for something where they don't know what it is until too late—or where they may never know, since after delivery the quality and value of the service may be hard to assess. This 'unknowability' matters, in particular, in marketing to new clients, but also in relationship to the labour market and the public in general.

The very large management consultancy companies in particular clearly exhibit features of what can be described as 'quasi-professionalism'. In terms of the homogeneous educational background of the employees, standardization of knowledge in training, emphasis on a formalized knowledge base that appears to be rational, reliable, and predictable, strictly controlled career prospects, the extended use of methods and tools and documentation of completed cases, as well as documented assignment reports, etc., they match many key features of the (recognized) professions. All this can partly be explained by the need to improve image and strengthen socio-political skills, but it would be unfair to deny all this as a sign of the value of consultants' shared experiences and competence. Symbolism is important, and it is seldom possible to separate it from substance, but it is not my aim to reduce all these arrangements to ones that only or mainly fulfil a ceremonial function (as indicated by, for example, institutional theory; Meyer and Rowan 1977). We have here internal efforts to mimic the logic of professionalization, as a rationality-facilitating as well as symbolic–ceremonial project. When a consultancy firm grants an employee the title of manager, it may be said to correspond to the status of a certified professional, primarily internally (where the meaning and symbolism are most obvious) but also to some extent externally.

The point of this is, of course, not only to influence the relationship of consultancies with the environment; it can also be understood as an identity project, primarily with internal consequences. At the organizational level, the rationality and reliability of a firm are communicated. At the individual level, employees participate in identity-reinforcing rites. Training, development, promotion, and 'quasi-certification' inform the person that he or she is a competent and quality-secured professional. The apparent self-confidence and coherence of the firm's personnel that this may lead to may also affect external actors, possibly decreasing their doubt and uncertainty. Consequently there are possible image effects on two levels: through the image-communicating arrangements and through the effects of these on the employees encountered by external groups.

Professionalism, as well as quasi-professionalism constructed by large management consultancy firms, is a resource, but it is also a constraint. Optimally, from the professional's point of view, the benefits can be maximized while the drawbacks may be circumscribed or minimized. One may imagine situations where the legitimization aspect of professionalism and quasi-professionalism is played out at the surface level, while productive work is mainly disconnected from and undisturbed by it (Meyer and Rowan 1977). Successful professionalization does, however, to some extent prevent free and flexible manoeuvring. Certain claims and acts undermine the project in the eyes of clients and the public, but may also be at odds with the identity of the thoroughly socialized professional (or quasi-professional). Professionalization involves the nurturing of an occupational identity of 'sober conservatism' that is not fully compatible with the wilder versions of management fashions or adaptation to the political interests of top management in politically charged situations in client organizations. Professionalism, if taken too seriously, may thus be a commercial liability.

In this book I have argued that professionalization and knowledge-intensity are not traits or accomplishments, but are better understood as claims that are more or less successful in terms of social confirmation, and that there are ongoing struggles to reproduce and reinforce these confirmations. In this sense KIFs and professions are perhaps better described as knowledge-claims-intensive. The claim is not validated once and for all, but is invoked in various situations and may be considered more or less seriously by those involved. As such it is sometimes present and sometimes put aside in consultancy relationships. Consultancy projects are affected by claims and strategies by consultants, but also by clients. They are also affected by structural conditions and by management discourses that define what is normal, rational, progressive, and leading-edge, thereby offering input for the constitution of consultants as well as clients. These conditions blend with consultants' ambitions and claims to appear as professionals and the expectations and confirmation or rejection of clients. Despite the muscularity ascribed to consultants by both themselves and their critics, consultancy is a relationship, and the willingness and capacity of clients to resist consultant-driven discourses on management-change projects, as well as to define the role and professional status of consultants, are often significant.

The relationship between PSFs and their clients is frequently, like so much in business and working life, characterized by tensions. To some extent overlapping these are 'internal' tensions and subject positioning around being a full-scale professional and being a commercially oriented, client-centred service provider. To the extent that the latter tension is not experienced so clearly, it may indicate that claims of professionalism and quasi-professionalism, apart from providing some standardized technical knowledge, mainly follow a ceremonial–symbolic logic, and elements such as integrity, superior expert status, and autonomy are not very central. Of course, from the client's point of view, the latter qualities can mainly be a source of irritation and conflict and may be in opposition to the compliant service-mindedness sometimes sought for, depending upon the desire of clients to use consultants for their own specific and predefined purposes.

Knowledge Work and the Matter of Substance: The Contingency of Ambiguity, Impressions, and Image

In this book I have emphasized—and I hope not unfairly over-emphasized—the notorious ambiguity of organizations, work, and activities, together with the need for the actors involved to attend to image, social interaction, and rhetoric as well as to identity themes at both organizational and individual levels. All these are seen as elements in the social construction of knowledge-intensiveness. Although I have emphasized my theses at a general level, it may be worth asking whether the relevance of these ideas might vary. Some apparently knowledge-intensive firms and occupations may bother less about the environment's perceptions of their knowledge-intensiveness and choose instead to rely on the results of their knowledge work to speak for themselves. As mentioned, many sociologists of science disagree with this and emphasize the socially constructed nature of even the most sophisticated experiment-based science (Knorr-Cetina 1994). Even here, the negotiation of meaning and social construction of the truth characterize knowledge, leaving the impression of knowledge as being better understood as a matter of social agreement than as unquestionable, objective truth.

Nevertheless, one may consider the possibility that there is strong variation among knowledge-intensive sectors in terms of possibilities of demonstrating knowledge or accomplishing a high level of consensus among stakeholders about problem-solving capacity. Professional service work may then be more ambiguous and dependent on rhetoric than high tech or science-based work, which results in a product that lends itself better to inspection. Those engaged in 'internal activities'—i.e. who do not regularly face clients—may not directly bother very much about how they appear since it hardly affects how the environment perceives the product. Market- and environment-oriented rhetorical and image work in high tech companies that offer a physical product may to some extent be centralized and much activity carried out 'internally', protected from the gaze of customers. Many product companies within, for example, the high tech and pharmaceutical industries do not have to bother about adapting to the wishes of individual clients as they typically operate in a mass market. On the other hand, the knowledge-intensive work of professionals, groups, and units *within* such companies does not lend itself directly to monitoring by the qualities of an end product, which may take several years to develop and produce, and where specific strengths and weaknesses—themselves an outcome of social judgement processes—may be difficult to ascribe to particular workers or units. Clan or cultural control is often proposed as the best or only realistic mode of management of work that is long-term, and difficult to monitor or evaluate owing to its complex character (Alvesson and Lindkvist 1993; Wilkins and Ouchi 1983). More or less relevant or reliable indicators of, or surrogates for, knowledge qualities become central to the construction of the knowledge-intensiveness at stake. Rhetoric, image manipulation, coping with shifting social relations, and the formation and maintenance of social and political networks thus become significant here.

It makes sense to emphasize ambiguity as a general feature, but also to note that it may be salient in different ways and at different stages of the work process and development of service- and product-oriented knowledge-intensive work. Consultants' performances can, in the short term, be measured by the amount of time they can debit to clients, while their work and outcomes are frequently ambiguous. In pharmaceutical companies, for example, the quality of the work outcomes in the form of product can, in the long run, be assessed with a fairly high degree of inter-evaluator reliability. Does a particular drug produce better effects than competing products, and what is its market share? Of course, tests are sometimes uncertain and market share is not a simple measure of product quality, but these outcomes still reduce some of the experienced ambiguity involved. However, during the R&D work, which may last for years, there is considerable uncertainty about what people are doing and the extent to which progress is being made. Also in the end products that are highly successful in market and profit terms have sometimes been threatened by decisions to discontinue the project.

It is thus not self-evident whether some knowledge work or organizations may be much less well understood through emphasizing ambiguity, rhetoric, image, and interaction than others. The question 'Does it work (well) or not?' may, however, bring disagreement among experts to varying degrees, and the demonstration of technical competence may be more or less important. Also, within a specific professional service organization there may be considerable variation in this respect. Based on a study of a large accountancy firm, Grey (1998) talks of a 'technical-behavioural' spectrum. In some areas, such as tax work, considerable command of technical issues was required, while in other areas, such as insolvency, behavioural–symbolic issues were much more central.

It makes sense to assume that KIFs and knowledge-intensive work, while typically dealing with complex, mainly intangible phenomena, are generally well conceptualized through the key concepts and frameworks presented here. This should, however, be balanced against the insight that the category of the KIF is neither unitary nor unique. Ambiguity, image, rhetoric, social interactions, and struggles with organizational and individual worker identities are certainly important aspects of most, if not all, organizations. My point is, however, that they are even more significant in most or perhaps virtually all KIFs.

A sensitivity to variation within this rather broad category is important, and an openness to the productivity of other vocabularies and dimensions must be borne in mind. Not only KIFs but also PSFs differ considerably. Where technical skills are significant and companies take great pains to standardize their products, attention to ambiguity, image, rhetoric, and the symbolism of social and business relations may have somewhat less prominent interpretative capacity. In some such cases the concept of knowledge-intensive work or a knowledge-intensive organization may become less valuable: knowledge-intensity, as understood in this book, to some extent runs against technical skills and product standardization. Consequently, where knowledge-intensity is central, often ambiguity is as well, and, contingent upon it, issues of image, rhetoric, and orchestrating social relations and processes.

Knowledge as Dead End

An interesting question concerns the value of addressing knowledge in organization theory and management practice. There is currently a wealth of literature that emphasizes knowledge as a key to the success of contemporary organizations. In this book I have taken a sceptical position and expressed reluctance to follow this enthusiasm. Contrary ideas and challenges seem called for. Could one argue that knowledge is not important? Such an argument would appear strange. But it is not self-evident that knowledge is necessarily the best concept or label to unfold complex and multifaceted issues.

My approach in this book is partly a response to all this uncritical enthusiasm and fashion for highlighting knowledge. To summarize my position, I see two traps: the 'everything-and-nothing' and 'knowledge-is-just-good' errors. Since everything can be seen as knowledge in one way or another, the term easily leads to rather vague and all-embracing statements. It is odd to read texts that avoid defining what knowledge actually refers to but still confidently claim that this unknown quality or ill-defined phenomenon accomplishes all sorts of good things. The problem with knowledge covering everything and nothing is hardly solved by mainstream efforts to unpack it: common distinctions such as codified (explicit) and uncodified (tacit) knowledge and individual and organizational knowledge are not particularly helpful. As argued in Chapter 2, most knowledge is better understood as transcending these questionable popular distinctions.

If we distinguish between information, knowledge outcomes, and knowledge, the latter term is perhaps best used to include personal meaning and the exercise of judgement based on a framework and a set of fine-tuned distinctions, a combination of theory (broadly defined) and experiences of occupational and organizational practice. This means that issues of thinking, the use of judgement, motivation, cultural meanings, and beliefs enter the picture. As knowledge, particularly in work and business contexts, always exists within a social context, it is difficult and misleading to abstract and isolate knowledge from social and rhetorical processes around claims to knowledge, validation, and rejection of these claims. For these reasons it is not self-evident that the current focus on knowledge and knowledge management is a productive way of dealing with issues around the development, mobilization, and support of people's accumulated experiences, judgements, insights, and problem-solving. As explored in Chapter 8 (and in Alvesson and Kärreman 2001*a*), in practice most talk about knowledge in organizations and most efforts to manage knowledge become less about knowledge per se than about knowledge workers, social relations, and technical systems that are supposed to aid people in using each other and information to do more effective or high-quality work.

Geertz's (1973) recommendation to students of culture is worth repeating and its relevance for knowledge students should be underscored: trim the concept so that it covers less and reveals more. I cannot claim to have followed Geertz's advice completely. Knowledge (too) easily leads to efforts to cover broad terrain, unless one is doing in-depth empirical studies. But I take a narrower approach than most authors producing conceptual work on this point. A disadvantage of this is, of course, that many forms of what could be labelled as 'knowledge' are not treated.

The second problem, which is partly related to the broadness and vagueness of the concept of knowledge, are its rhetorical qualities. There is a risk with the term that it is too strongly rhetorically loaded. As with quality, development, learning, and equal opportunity, you can only be for it. Knowledge is good. You easily buy into a whole set of assumptions and associations around value creation, rationality, truth, functionality, etc. It is difficult to accomplish analytical sharpness in relationship to themes framed in a rhetorically seductive way.

This book has tried to avoid these two traps by drawing attention to (*a*) the claims of knowledge put forward by various actors and (*b*) the difficulties of establishing what is 'knowledge' in the sense of something that has got it right and leads, if correctly used, to positive outcomes (from the point of view of the knowledge user)—at least in the great majority of all cases. If these knowledge qualities cannot be established by the researcher—and it is often tricky to do so—then a more agnostic position is appropriate. There are organizations and occupations in which knowledge is strongly emphasized and these call for careful investigation. Knowledge is thus an important social phenomenon. But we do not have to approach it by accepting the claims of the knowledgeable and those that they serve as necessarily valid and unproblematic, nor to focus our attention on knowledge per se. As this book has tried to show, knowledge themes can be approached from other angles.

Most authors writing on knowledge seem to treat it as a six-lane highway. There is no denying that traffic jams create problems, but knowledge is such a broad and effective way of going forward that an enormous amount of trafficking of support, creativity, productivity, and profit-making can be accomplished through societies, firms, and individuals taking the knowledge route. A counter-metaphor could be knowledge as a dead end. It may be difficult to go forward using this focus.

Without denying the enormous significance of knowledge in one sense or another, knowledge may be too difficult and vague a concept to be very helpful in precise theoretical work and informed organizational practice. I am *not* proposing the 'dead end' metaphor as a superior way of approaching—or rather avoiding—the theme of knowledge in organizations. I am just raising the warning flag. Of course, 'knowledge' has no essential meaning, and people use the term in an infinite number of ways. Undoubtedly, for many people the term is inspirational and it can trigger thinking and action that may be positive for business as well as quality of working life. And many people have a carefully thought-out idea of how to think about knowledge issues, although, as I have said, many frame these partly in other terms such as community of practice, supportive culture, or information management. Minimally, a productive way of using 'knowledge' as an analytical term, as opposed to a term used to signal interest in a particular area, calls for awareness of the traps that the knowledge enthusiast can fall into. Such an awareness may reduce the risk of 'knowledge' diverting people into a dead end.

The Need for Moderate Scepticism

As I and many others see it, the very idea of research and academic knowledge in the social sciences is that it should be built on and contribute to critical reflection. This book has taken this idea fairly seriously, without locating itself firmly within a tradition of critical theory. Knowledge easily invites a set of very positive associations and the same is the case, although less so, with concepts such as knowledge work, the KIF, and the profession. The opposites of 'knowledge' and 'professional'—'ignorance' and 'unprofessional'—sound very bad. Knowledge work and KIFs indicate something grandiose, intelligent, cutting-edge, and, almost by definition, leading to a positive impact. Even many more critically minded researchers tend to follow somewhat idealistic notions of the basis and nature of the work. Reed (1996), while drawing attention to the political issues, writes that ' "knowledge workers" depend on a highly esoteric and intangible knowledge base' and 'rely on a sophisticated combination of theoretical knowledge, analytical tools and tacit or judgmental

skills that are very difficult, but not impossible to standardize'
(p. 585). I do not disagree, but find this focus and framing somewhat tricky as it overemphasizes a rational knowledge base as the
key characteristic. This book's possible tendency to underempha-
size such a base is understandable in that it balances current
positions and debate.

As briefly mentioned in Chapter 2, Foucault (1980) puts forward powerful opposition to this positive view of knowledge, but
is seldom invoked in talk about the knowledge society, KIFs,
PSFs, and knowledge management. In studies of PSFs references
to Foucault do not often refer to the knowledge PSFs claim to
have and contribute to the marketplace, but refer rather to HRM
and other forms of organizational control (Covaleski *et al.* 1998;
Grey 1994). Foucault's emphasis on knowledge as linked to
power and as dangerous also tends to give a somewhat one-
dimensionally negative or hyper-sceptical view to everybody
who is in the knowledge business. Since much of this knowledge
is about highly technical issues, Foucault's concept of knowledge,
which works best on social and human topics, is not always
productive here. It still, however, offers a valuable alternative
picture.

In this book I have tried to be open to the understanding that
knowledge is frequently much more uncertain, contested, and
problematic than indicated by dominant discourses—academic,
mass media, and practitioner-driven ways of talking and thinking. I have also raised doubts about the significance of knowledge: perhaps highly esoteric expertise is not always at the centre
of what KIFs are doing.

This book does not, of course, suggest that knowledge is unim-
portant or that knowledge-intensive companies lack 'substance',
and I am concerned that my position may be read as too sceptical.
I am not denying that technical skills, theoretical knowledge,
practical experience, etc. are often vital and that outcomes seen
as valuable are produced. My emphasis on the ambiguity of the
results of knowledge work does *not* mean that I am claiming that
these results are typically weak or absent or just a matter of loose
belief or deceiving stakeholders. I have no reason to doubt that
many KIFs often contribute to the social good through ambitious,
well-intended, intelligent, and productive work, which their
clients and customers often benefit from. But nor do I think that

we benefit from an unquestioned assumption that all these good intentions, capacities, and outcomes necessarily characterize what KIFs typically do. It is important to be agnostic rather than religious or atheistic about the competence base and contributions of knowledge workers and KIFs. This can seldom be reduced just to social opinions and ill-founded myths, nor to objective capacities existing beyond ambiguity: the exercise of uncertain judgement and negotiations of meaning. What these workers and firms actually do and accomplish calls for more, and more open, research. This is especially the case in the professional service sector.

We need to be more sceptical about the popular broad-brush view that knowledge is increasingly significant and is the key feature of many organizations and workers. This view is too often expressed with strong ideological overtones. Arguably, knowledge is better understood as a social process than as a functional resource, as socially constructed rather than an objective fact, or as a factor replacing capital and labour as the most significant in the economy and in companies.

We can thus take seriously not only that knowledge 'in itself'— or at least many forms of it—is ambiguous, but also that it is highly ambiguous what role this factor plays in (and for) most knowledge-intensive—and presumably in many other—organizations and workers. This move is quite different from traditional views on professions and contemporary functionalist writings about knowledge-intensive organizations. Abbott (cited by Sharma 1997), for example, states that abstract knowledge is the key distinguishing characteristic of professions. Advocates of the professions have stressed that these practitioners 'are applying knowledge, acting rationally, deploying trained and specialized competence' (Fores *et al.* 1991: 97). But this is misleading, since 'All this serves to take the sting out of the disorderly, threateningly ambiguous character of social experience' (p. 97). By placing ambiguity as a key element of companies and work of this kind, the entire field is reframed. Such a reframing is much needed within management and organization studies. Instead of being perceived as agents of superior cognitive rationality effectively dealing with indeterminacy, the latter characterizes the entirety of the social processes in which knowledge-intensive organizations are engaged. The shift of focus from what is to the claims that are made, and how these are confirmed, rejected, or met with uncertainty demands an acceptance of the need to take the ambiguities more seriously.

The view proposed here inspires a broader and more questioning understanding of what knowledge-intensive organizations and workers (including the so-called professionals) do. It is then in line with some recent work on the sociology of professions (e.g. Brante 1988; Collins 1990; Fores *et al.* 1991; Jamous and Peloille 1970) more than with mainstream management studies on knowledge-intensive organizations. Without denying that knowledge may sometimes be a functional resource that is directly applied in work, other functions and aspects of knowledge and knowledge talk may be more central. Knowledge plays other roles, such as

- a means for creating community and social identity through offering organizational members a shared language and a common way of relating to themselves and their world;
- a resource for persuasion in marketing and interaction with customers;
- a means of creating legitimacy and good faith with regard to actions and outcomes; and
- a means of obscuring uncertainty and counteracting doubt and reflection through 'knowledge' imposing a definite, supposedly cognitively and functionally superior meaning on a phenomenon.

This last point indicates that 'knowledge' and 'knowledge work' may lead to the opposite of what they claim: to limited reflection and uncritical attitudes. In all these roles knowledge may be seen as helpful in the construction of the identity of knowledge workers. Producing knowledge claims can thus also be seen as identity work.[1]

The ambiguities involved in the notion of knowledge, what knowledge workers do, and the difficulties in evaluating work results mean that a potential (experienced) instability, arbitrariness, and vulnerability often characterize knowledge-intensive work and organizations. Difficulties in 'grounding' lead easily to problems with securing organizational identity as well as worker identities. However, the opportunities to construct

---

[1] This is, of course, one aspect of my own activity when producing this text.

imaginatively the organization, the work, and the workers in various ways are great, as interpretations of material circumstances are less likely to protest against constructions proposed. In 'ambiguity-intensive' organizations rhetoric, image management, and ongoing negotiations become necessary and are offered a large arena (Alvesson 1990; Cheney and Christensen 2001). Since clients and customers often have problems in establishing the value of the product or service offered, establishing close social links between the KIF and the client becomes vital. In the absence of functioning competition based on quality (which is difficult to establish) and price (but price-sensitivity is relatively low in many markets for knowledge-intensive work), social relations and image become central. Professionalization and quasi-professionalization can be used here to offer some image support, but the market is not always persuaded by this alone. Interactions must be carefully orchestrated and efforts to strengthen ties given priority. Rhetoric, image production, and the fine-tuning of social bonds rely upon supportive work identities. Successful talk, appearance, and interaction call for the right kind of subjectivity. There is a close and complex relationship between these qualities; identity constructions are backed up by rhetoric and images at the same time as the fluid and fluctuating nature of persuasive talk, appearance, and adapting to the whims of clients undermines the prospect, as well as the usefulness, of fixed identity constructions.

Management is not, then, only or even mainly about attracting, maintaining, and developing subjects who possess knowledge and use this resource in optimal ways, but also a matter of influencing employees on a broader scale, including developing, controlling, and securing worker and organizational identities. It is often crucial here to make people believe in the knowledge claims of the firm and to develop and maintain a supportive cultural orientation.

In the case of R&D based organizations, culture and identity are of special relevance, less as providing a subjectivity base for making knowledge claims and more in the context of providing a flexible long-term direction as well as loyalty to the organization. This is particularly important in highly ambiguous development work and complex network interactions, in which university-based socialization may encourage other commitments and

priorities than those deemed to be commercially optimal by corporate management.

Perhaps needless to say, the theoretical approach offered here
as a way of understanding KIFs is partial, and aims to give some
insights at the expense of other ways of understanding. Knowledge and theory in social science are never about presenting the
absolute truth or an objective picture in any abstract or neutral
way. We always proceed from our pre-understanding, based on
conscious and unconscious assumptions and expectations. This is
the case for the researcher as well as the reader. Good research
builds upon received ideas and wisdom, but also challenges it
and adds something. In order to make sense of a complex, ambiguous world, we need access to alternative vocabularies and to
make multiple readings (Morgan 1997). Research makes a contribution less by proceeding from dominant assumptions and
repeating conventional wisdom and more by breaking with
these and adding something different. This book then challenges
but also complements other approaches that are less sceptical and
more functionally oriented. It does so with an ironic twist in two
senses. One is the conventional one of trying to counteract serious
and pretentious claims by looking at things from a different
perspective, sometimes expressing mild irony. Another is
through an awareness that there is always more than one way to
understand something: other vocabularies and ways of reasoning
may offer as good or perhaps even better ways of addressing
issues to the one I favour. Awareness of this in academic
writing—or in other forms of intellectual activity—is what Rorty
(1989) refers to as irony and Alvesson and Sköldberg (2000) as one
element in reflexivity. This book to a small degree tries to live up
to this idea.

This means that there are indeed contingencies relating to
the value and relevance of the framework suggested here
(*a*) in the empirical sense of different organizations and work
situations being more or less productively understood in this
way, and (*b*) in relationship to alternative understandings of the
subject matter: the idea of emphasizing ambiguity and social
constructions in light of it is not so much a matter of 'objective'
qualities of KIFs as of what additional and enriched understanding this offers in combination to other, established ways of
seeing things.

KIFs: A Summary

Let us briefly return to some of the key characteristics of KIFs as understood by the majority of the researchers in the field, addressed in Chapter 2. These include:

1. highly qualified individuals doing knowledge-based work, using intellectual and symbolic skills in work;
2. a fairly high degree of autonomy and the downplaying of organizational hierarchy;
3. the use of adaptable, ad hoc organizational forms;
4. the need for extensive communication for coordination and problem-solving;
5. idiosyncratic client services;
6. information and power asymmetry (often favouring the professional over the client);
7. subjective and uncertain quality assessment.

    I should like to qualify the first point by drawing attention to how 'non-knowledge' issues, such as committed labour, and political, social, and rhetorical skills, are crucial in KIFs. Of course, people need to be qualified, but perhaps in ways other than are commonly believed. On the whole I find these seven characteristics still very relevant to an understanding of the work and organizations targeted in this book.

    But I should like to add four additional features:

8. Knowledge work is characterized by a high level of ambiguity in input, process, and output: knowledge may play a more limited and less robust role in work and for results. This means that we view the knowledge-intensive as *ambiguity-intensive*.
9. In ideational work with symbols (plans, blueprints, ideas, concepts, etc.) issues around persuasive talk and the management of image are vital in dealing with external relations as well as in internal work. KIFs then can be conceptualized as *systems of persuasion*.
10. Knowledge work is frequently carried out in a macro and micro context of high-flying, rhetorically appealing talk and an imperfect material world, where 'reality' in the form of everyday life experiences and client expectations

sometimes break with the 'ideologies' expressed in public and corporate discourses. KIFs are then frequently caught in the contradiction-ridden social universe of *grandiose discourse at odds with social practice* (in which less grandiose, more mundane discourse is activated).

11. Knowledge work KIFs are sites of high-intensive identity regulation and work. Management is involved here, trying to regulate identities, but the acceptance of prescribed identities is not sufficient, and intensive symbolic labour to develop, maintain, and modify identity is a vital part of working life. Knowledge workers then become understood as *identity workers*, and management becomes to some extent *identity regulation*.

KIFs can thus be understood as high-ambiguity, image, and rhetoric-focused identity regulators existing in a world where ideologically appealing constructions (profession, knowledge, consultancy, expertise, autonomy, strategy) risk clashing with everyday work experiences.

This understanding can also be framed as a move towards taking seriously the symbolism of knowledge and of work, occupations, and firms that is claimed to revolve around knowledge seriously (in the sense of the word used here). This symbolism can be addressed on several levels.

On an overall level knowledge work is *about* symbols: words, ideas, plans, maps, formulas, etc. Sometimes knowledge workers are referred to as symbol analysts. They do not produce or distribute physical objects or tangible services, although sometimes the outcome of the symbolic objects that knowledge workers deal with influences or changes material practices and physical objects. But the knowledge work itself is mainly confined to conducting symbolic work.

On another level it can be argued that 'knowledge' is *itself* a strongly symbolically loaded term. 'Knowledge' has very positive connotations for most people. It stands for rationality, progress, problem-solving capacity, superiority. The opposite of knowledge is ignorance. With knowledge follows status, respect, and often power and financial rewards. The more firms, occupations, and people can associate themselves with knowledge, and the more that they can make it credible that they score more highly in this respect than others, the more they will benefit in terms of money and reputation.

On a third level we find the symbolism *indicating* knowledge, e.g. how knowledge is not just a matter of being measurable in terms of essence or easily assessable through the monitoring of the outcomes of knowledge. We cannot observe knowledge, but must rely on various indicators. There are seldom any pure outcomes of knowledge in operation—typically many other issues also matter. Owing to the ambiguity and inaccessibility of knowledge, various indicators or symbols pointing towards knowledge become central. Given that so much is at stake, and given this high level of ambiguity, typically a wealth of arrangements and rhetoric are put into action to persuade not only various external audiences, but also the knowledge people themselves, of the existence and productive powers of knowledge. Without denying the technical and substantive role of knowledge management initiatives and knowledge-focused HRM policies and acts, the persuasive aspects of a range of acts, policies, structures, and vocabularies are worth emphasizing. The existence and significance of knowledge are signalled through KM arrangements and practices like intranets, knowledge maps, policies to employ people from leading, high-profile universities, collaboration with other actors with a reputation for being 'knowledge-able', or extensive use of verbal symbols such as 'knowledge-sharing culture', 'professionalism', and 'community of practice'.

In sum, then, a symbolism approach to knowledge would then emphasize

- the basically symbolic nature of knowledge,
- the value-loaded symbolism of knowledge, and
- how rituals, actions, arrangements, and vocabularies are used in order symbolically to express and persuade various groups about knowledge.

All this means a change of focus from the knowledge-intensive to the knowledge-*claim*-intensive.[2] In a sense I see the latter term as slightly more illuminating and novel, and perhaps a more productive focus for understanding the situation and success elements

---

[2] This is not just relevant at the levels of the firm and the workers ('professionals'). We could also refer to the present society as 'knowledge-claiming'. I don't know how much 'knowledge' there is, but there is definitely much fuss about it.

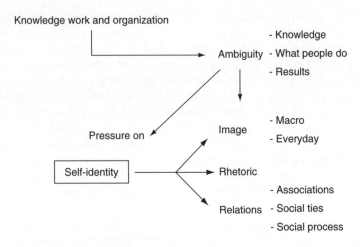

FIG. 1 Some connections between ambiguity, image, rhetoric, and identity in knowledge work and organizations.

of the organizations belonging to the category of KIFs. In a society where traditional sources of elitism and status are losing ground, the competition for position is heightened and knowledge is enlisted as an important strategic resource.

All this means a radically different understanding than the dominant one revolving around esoteric expertise, sophisticated problem-solving, cognitive rationality, and professional autonomy, and stable, positive identities, capacity to cope with uncertainty, and added value for clients and the common good. I am not claiming that this different understanding is necessarily better than the one expressed in dominant traditions, but I suggest that it is worth taking seriously.

Let me summarize this in Figure 1, which should be understood as follows: knowledge-intensive work tends to be ambiguity-intensive, which makes abilities to deal with rhetoric, regulate images, and manage relationships and interactions with clients central. All these circumstances put some strain on, as well lead to the centrality of, the securing and regulation of identity. Ambiguity leads to space for innovative constructions of identity at both organizational and personal levels, but also puts pressure on activities to develop and validate these constructions. Ambiguity, in other words, allows an open arena for positive action, but represents a tension that calls for defensive measures. Consequently, intensiveness includes not only knowledge, but also these other issues that are crucial for any claim to knowledge to be successful. The knowledge-intensive means intensified work with issues of rhetoric, image, interaction, and identity regulation.

References

ABBOTT, A. (1991), 'The Future of Professions: Occupation and Expertise in the Age of Organization', in S. Bacharach *et al.* (eds.), *Research in the Sociology of Organizations* (Greenwich, Conn.: JAI Press).

AKEHURST, G. (1994), 'Brownloaf-MacTaggart—Control and Power in a Management Consultancy', in D. Adam-Smith and A. Peacock (eds.), *Cases in Organisational Behaviour* (London: Pitman).

ALBERT, S., and WHETTEN, D. (1985), 'Organizational Identity', in L. L. Cummings and B. M. Staw (eds.), *Research in Organizational Behaviour*, vii (Greenwich Conn.: JAI Press).

ALVESSON, M. (1990), 'Organization: From Substance to Image?', *Organization Studies*, 11: 373–94.

—— (1993*a*), 'Organization as Rhetoric. Knowledge-Intensive Companies and the Struggle with Ambiguity', *Journal of Management Studies*, 30/6: 997–1015.

—— (1993*b*), 'Cultural–Ideological Modes of Management Control', in S. Deetz (ed.), *Communication Yearbook* (Newbury Park, Calif.: Sage).

—— (1994), 'Talking in Organizations: Managing Identity and Image in an Advertising Agency', *Organization Studies*, 15: 535–63.

—— (1995), *Management of Knowledge-Intensive Companies* (Berlin: de Gruyter).

—— (1998), 'Gender Relations and Identity at Work: A Case Study of Masculinities and Femininities in an Advertising Agency', *Human Relations*, 51/8: 969–1005.

—— (2000*a*), 'Social Identity and the Problem of Loyalty in Knowledge-Intensive Companies', *Journal of Management Studies*, 37/8: 1101–23.

—— (2000*b*), *Ledning av kunskapsföretag* (Stockholm: Norstedts 2000, 3. Uppl).

—— (2002*a*), *Understanding Organizational Culture* (London: Sage).

—— (2002*b*), 'Up-or-Out vs. Fun-and-Profit: A Study of Two Management/IT Consultancy Companies', Lund Institute of Economic Research, Working Paper 2002/2.

—— and DEETZ, S. (2000), *Doing Critical Management Research* (London: Sage).

—— and JOHANSSON, A. (2001) 'Professionalism and Politics in Management Consultancy Work', in T. Clark and R. Fincham (eds.), *Critical Consulting* (London: Blackwell).

—— and KÄRREMAN, D. (2001*a*), 'Odd Couple: Making Sense of the Curious Concept of Knowledge Management', *Journal of Management Studies*, 38/7: 995–1018.

—— —— (2001*b*), 'Perfection of Meritocracy or Ritual of Bureaucracy? HRM in a Management Consultancy Firm', Paper presented at the 2nd International Conference on Critical Management Studies, Manchester, July.

—— —— (forthcoming), 'Interfaces of Control: Technocratic and Socio-ideological Control in a Global Management Consultancy Firm', *Accounting, Organization & Society*.

—— and KÖPING, A. S. (1993), *Med känslan som ledstjärna* (Lund: Studentlitteratur).

—— and LINDKVIST, L. (1993), 'Transaction Costs, Clans and Corporate Culture', *Journal of Management Studies*, 30: 427–52.

—— and SKÖLDBERG, K. (2000), *Reflexive Methodology* (London: Sage).

—— and SVENINGSSON, S. (2002), 'Stop Fooling Around: Managers Putting Scientists in Line', Paper presented at the Euram Conference, Stockholm, May.

—— —— (2003), *Praise and Blame: Assessments of a Consultancy Project*, Working Paper, Department of Business Administration, Lund University.

—— —— (2003), 'The Good Visions, the Bad Micro-Management and the Ugly Ambiguity: Contradictions of (Non-)Leadership in a Knowledge-Intensive Company', *Organization Studies*.

—— and WILLMOTT, H. (1995), 'Strategic Management as Domination and Emancipation: From Planning and Process to Communication and Praxis', in P. Shrivastava and C. Stubbart (eds.), *Advances in Strategic Management* (Greenwood, Conn.: JAI Press).

—— —— (2002), 'Producing the Appropriate Individual: Identity Regulation as Organizational Control', *Journal of Management Studies*, 39/5: 619–44.

—— ROBERTSON, M., and SWAN, J. (2001), 'The Best and the Brightest: Construction of Elite Identities in Knowledge-Intensive Companies', Paper presented at the 2nd International Conference on Critical Management Studies, Manchester, July.

ANDERSON-GOUGH, F., GREY, C., and ROBSON, K. (2000), 'In the Name of the Client: The Service Ethic in Two Professional Service Firms', *Human Relations*, 53/9: 1151–73.

ASHFORTH, B., and MAEL, F. (1989), 'Social Identity Theory and the Organization', *Academy of Management Review*, 14: 20–39.

ASHFORTH, B., and MAEL, F. (1996), 'Organizational Identity and Strategy as a Context for the Individual', *Advances in Strategic Management*, 13: 19–64.

BACHARACH, S., BAMBURGER, P., and CONLEY, S. (1989), 'Between Bureau-cracies and Professionals', Paper presented at the 49th Annual Meeting of the National Academy of Management, Washington, DC, Aug.

BECKMAN, S. (1989), 'Professionerna och kampen om auktoritet', in S. Selander (ed.), *Kampen om yrkesutövning, status och kunskap* (Lund: Studentlitteratur).

BÉDARD, J., and CHI, M. (1993), 'Expertise in Auditing', *Auditing: A Journal of Practice and Theory*, 12, suppl., 12–45.

BENDERS, J., and VAN KEEN, K. (2001), 'What's in a Fashion? Interpretive Viability and Management Fashions', *Organization*, 8/1: 33–53.

BERGLUND, J. (2002), 'De otillräckliga', Ph.D. thesis, Stockholm: School of Economics.

BERGSTRÖM, O. (1998), *Att passa in*, Ph.D. thesis, BAS, Gothenburg.

BERNSTEIN, D. (1984), *Company Image and Reality: A Critique of Corporate Communication* (Eastbourne: Holt, Rhinehart & Winston).

BLACKLER, F. (1993), 'Knowledge and the Theory of Organizations: Organizations as Activity Systems and the Reframing of Management', *Journal of Management Studies*, 30/4: 863–83.

—— (1995), 'Knowledge, Knowledge Work and Organizations', *Organization Studies*, 16/6: 1021–46.

BLOMQVIST, M. (1994), *Könshierarkier i gungning. Kvinnor i kunskapsföretag*, Studia Sociologica Upsaliensia 39 (Uppsala: Acta Universitatis Upsaliensis).

BONORA, E., and REVANG, Ø. (1993), 'A Framework for Analysing the Storage and Protection of Knowledge in Organizations', in P. Lorange *et al.* (eds.), *Implementing Strategic Processes* (Oxford: Blackwell).

BOORSTIN, D. (1961), *The Image: A Guide to Pseudo-Events in America* (New York: Atheneum).

BOXALL, P., and STEENEVELD, M. (1999), 'Human Resource Strategy and Competitive Advantage: A Longitudinal Study of Engineering Con-sultants', *Journal of Management Studies*, 36: 443–63.

BRANTE, T. (1988), 'Sociological Approaches to the Professions', *Acta Sociologica*, 31: 119–42.

—— (1989), 'Professioners identitet och samhälleliga villkor', in S. Selan-der (ed.), *Kampen om yrkesutövning, status och kunskap* (Lund: Student-litteratur).

BRAVERMAN, H. (1974), *Labor and Monopoly Capital* (New York: Monthly Review Press).

BROMS, H., and GAHMBERG, H. (1983), 'Communication to Self in Organ-izations and Cultures', *Administrative Science Quarterly*, 28/3: 482–95.

BROSHAK, J. (2001), 'Do the Actors Make the Play? Individual Mobility and the Dissolution of Interorganizational Relationships', Paper pre-sented at the 2001 Academy of Management Annual Meeting.

BROWN, J., and DUGUID, P. (1998), 'Organizing Knowledge', *California Management Review*, 40/3: 90–111.

BRUNSSON, N. (1985), *The Irrational Organization* (Chichester: Wiley).

BURRIS, B. (1993), *Technocratic Organization and Ideology* (Albany: State University of New York Press).

CALÁS, M., and SMIRCICH, L. (1988), 'Reading Leadership as a Form of Cultural Analysis', in J. G. Hunt *et al.* (eds.), *Emerging Leadership Vistas* (Lexington, Mass.: Lexington Books).

CHALMERS, L. (2001), *Marketing Masculinities* (Westport, Conn.: Greenwood Press).

CHENEY, G., and CHRISTENSEN, L. T. (2001), 'Organizational Identity: Linkages between Internal and External Communication', in F. Jablin and L. Putnam (eds.), *The New Handbook of Organizational Communication* (Thousand Oaks, Calif.: Sage).

CLARK, T. (1995), *Managing Consultants* (Milton Keynes: Open University Press).

—— and SALAMAN, G. (1996), 'The Management Guru as Organizational Witch Doctor', *Organization*, 3: 85–108.

CLEGG, S. (1990), *Modern Organizations: Organization Studies in the Postmodern World* (London: Sage).

—— *et al.* (1996), 'Management Knowledge for the Future: Innovation, Embryos and New Paradigms', in S. Clegg and G. Palmer (eds.), *The Politics of Management Knowledge* (London: Sage).

COHEN, D. (1998), 'Toward a Knowledge Context', Report on the First Annual University of California at Berkeley Forum on Delivering Knowledge and the Firm, *California Management Review*, 40/3: 22–39.

COLLINS, R. (1990), 'Changing Conceptions in the Sociology of Professions', in R. Torstendahl and M. Burrage (eds.), *The Formation of Professions* (London: Sage).

COOK, S., and BROWN, J. S. (1999), 'Bridging Epistemologies: The Generative Dance between Organizational Knowledge and Organizational Knowing', *Organization Science*, 2/1: 40–57.

—— and YANOW, D. (1993), 'Culture and Organizational Learning', *Journal of Management Inquiry*, 2: 373–90.

COOPER, D., HININGS, C. R., GREENWOOD, R., and BROWN, J. (1996), 'Sedimentation and Transformation in Organizational Change: The Case of Canadian Law Firms', *Organization Studies*, 17/4: 623–47.

COVALESKI, M., DIRSMITH, M., HELAN, J., and SAMUEL, S. (1998), 'The Calculated and the Avowed: Techniques of Discipline and Struggles over Identity in Big Six Public Accounting Firms', *Administrative Science Quarterly*, 43: 293–327.

CZARNIAWSKA-JOERGES, B. (1988), *Att handla med ord* (Stockholm: Carlssons).

—— (1990), 'Merchants of Meaning: Management Consulting in the Swedish Public Sector', in B. Turner (ed.), *Organizational Symbolism* (Berlin: de Gruyter).

DAVENPORT, T., and PRUSAK, L. (1998), *Working Knowledge* (Cambridge, Mass.: Harvard Business School Press).

DEETZ, S. (1995), *Transforming Communication, Transforming Business: Building Responsive and Responsible Workplaces* (Cresskill, NJ: Hampton Press).

—— (1997), 'The Business Concept and Managerial Control in Knowledge-Intensive Work: A Case Study of Discursive Power', in B. Sypher (ed.), *Case Studies in Organizational Communication* (New York: Guilford).

—— (1998), 'Discursive Formations, Strategized Subordination, and Self-Surveillance', in A. McKinley and K. Starkey (eds.), *Foucault, Management and Organization Theory* (London: Sage).

DESSLER, G. (1999), 'How to Earn your Employees' Commitment', *Academy of Management Executive*, 13/2: 58–67.

DOUGHERTY, D. (1996), 'Organizing for Innovation', in S. Clegg *et al.* (eds.), *Handbook of Organization Studies* (London: Sage).

DU GAY, P., and SALAMAN, G. (1992), 'The Cult(ure) of the Customer', *Journal of Management Studies*, 29/5: 615–33.

DUTTON, J., DUKERICH, J., and HARQUAIL, C. (1994), 'Organizational Images and Member Identification', *Administrative Science Quarterly*, 39: 239–63.

—— ASHFORD, S., O'NEILL, R., and LAWRENCE, K. (2001), 'Moves that Matter: Issue Selling and Organizational Change', *Academy of Management Journal*, 44/4: 716–36.

EKSTEDT, E. (1990), 'Knowledge Renewal and Knowledge Companies', in L. Lindmark (ed.), *Kunskap som kritisk resurs* (Umeå: Umeå Universitet).

ELY, R. (1995), 'The Power in Demography: Women's Social Construction of Gender Identity at Work', *Academy of Management Journal*, 38/3: 589–634.

EMPSON, L. (1998), 'Mergers between Professional Service Firms: How the Distinctive Organizational Characteristics Influence the Process of Value Creation', Ph.D. thesis, London Business School.

—— (2001), 'Fear of Exploitation and Fear of Contamination: Impediments to Knowledge Transfer in the Professional Service Firm', *Human Relations*, 54/7: 839–62.

—— (2003), 'Organizational Identity Change: Managerial Regulation and Member Identification in an Accounting Firm Acquisition', Paper presented at the EGOs Conference, Copenhagen, July.

ETZIONI, A. (1964), *Modern Organizations* (Englewood Cliffs, NJ: Prentice-Hall).

FELDMAN, M. (1991), 'The Meaning of Ambiguity: Learning from Stories and Metaphors', in P. J. Frost *et al.* (eds.), *Reframing Organizational Culture* (Newbury Park, Calif.: Sage).

—— and MARCH, J. (1981), 'Information in Organizations as Signal and Symbol', *Administrative Science Quarterly*, 26: 171–86.

FICHMAN, M., and LEVINTHAL, D. (1991), 'History Dependence in Professional Relationships: Ties that Bind', in S. Bacharach *et al.* (eds.), *Research in the Sociology of Organizations* (Greenwich, Conn.: JAI Press).

FINCHAM, R. (1999), 'Extruded Management: Contradictions and Ambivalences in the Consultancy Process', Paper presented at the 1st Critical Management Studies Conference, Manchester, July.

FORES, M., GLOVER, I., and LAWRENCE, P. (1991), 'Professionalism and Rationality: A Study in Misapprehension', *Sociology*, 25: 79–100.

FOSSTENLØKKEN, S., LØWENDAHL, B., and REVANG, Ø. (2003), 'Knowledge Development through Client Interaction: A Comparative Study', *Organization Studies*, 24/6: 859–79.

FOUCAULT, M. (1976), *The History of Sexuality* (New York: Pantheon).

—— (1980), *Power/Knowledge* (New York: Pantheon).

—— (1982), 'The Subject and Power', *Critical Inquiry*, 8: 777–95.

GEERTZ, C. (1973), *The Interpretation of Cultures*, (New York: Basic Books).

GIDDENS, A. (1991), *Modernity and Self-Identity* (Cambridge: Polity Press).

GIOIA, D., SCHULTZ, M., and CORLEY, K. (2000), 'Organizational Identity, Image and Adaptive Instability', *Academy of Management Review*, 25/1: 63–81.

GOULDNER, A. (1957), 'Cosmopolitans and Locals: Toward an Analysis of Latent Social Roles—I', *Administrative Science Quarterly*, 2: 281–306.

GRANOVETTER, M. (1973), 'Economic Action and Social Structure: The Problem of Embeddedness', *American Journal of Sociology*, 91: 481–510.

GRANT, R. (1996), 'Toward a Knowledge-Based Theory of the Firm', *Strategic Management Journal*, 17: 109–22.

GREEN, S. (1975), 'Professional/Bureaucracy Conflict: The Case of the Medical Profession in the National Health Service', *Sociological Review*, 23: 121–38.

GREENWOOD, R., and EMPSON, L. (2003), 'The Professional Partnership: Relic or Exemplary Form of Governance?', *Organization Studies*, 24/6: 909–33.

—— HININGS, C. R., and BROWN, J. (1990), 'P2-Form Strategic Management: Corporate Practices in Professional Partnerships', *Academy of Management Journal*, 33/4: 725–55.

GREENWOOD, R., SUDDABY, R., and HININGS, C. R. (2002), 'Theorizing Change: The Role of Professional Associations in the Transformation of Institutionalized Fields', *Academy of Management Journal*, 45/1: 58–81.

—— *et al.* (2003), 'Leveraging Invisible Assets: Determinants of Performance in Professional Service Firms', Paper, Centre for Professional Service Firm Management, University of Alberta.

GREY, C. (1994), 'Career as a Project of the Self and Labour Process Discipline', *Sociology*, 28: 479–97.

—— (1998), 'Homogeneity to Heterogeneity: Being a Professional in a "Big Six" Firm', *Accounting, Organizations and Society*, 23/5–6: 569–87.

GRÖNROOS, C. (1984), *Strategic Management and Marketing in the Service Sector* (Lund: Studentlitteratur).

GRUGULIS, I., DUNDON, T., and WILKINSON, A. (2000), 'Cultural Control and the "Culture Manager": Employment Practices in a Consultancy', *Work, Employment and Society*, 14/1: 97–116.

HABERMAS, J. (1984), *The Theory of Communicative Action*, vol. i (Boston: Beacon Press).

HÅKANSSON, H., and SNEHOTA, I. (1989), 'No Business is an Island: The Network Concept of Business Strategy', *Scandinavian Journal of Management*, 5: 187–200.

HALPIN, J. (1999), 'CompUSA's CEO James Halpin on Technology, Rewards, and Commitment', Interviewed by S. Puffer, *Academy of Management Executive*, 13/2: 29–36.

HANSEN, M. T., NORHIA, N., and TIERNEY, T. (1999), 'What's your Strategy for Managing Knowledge?', *Harvard Business Review* (Mar.–Apr.), 106–16.

HATCH, M. J., and SCHULTZ, M. (2003), 'Bringing the Corporation into Corporate Branding', *European Journal of Marketing* 37: 1041–64.

HEDBERG, B. (1990), *Exit, Voice, and Loyalty in Knowledge-Intensive Firms*, Book presented at the 10th Annual International Conference of the Strategic Management Society, Stockholm, Sept.

HENRIKSSON, K. (1999), *The Collective Dynamics of Organizational Learning: On Plurality and Multi-Social Structuring* (Lund: Lund University Press).

HERRIOT, P., and PEMBERTON, C. (1995), *Competitive Advantage through Diversity* (London: Sage).

HININGS, C. R., BROWN, J., and GREENWOOD, R. (1991), 'Change in an Autonomous Professional Organization', *Journal of Management Studies*, 28: 375–89.

HOWARD, J. (1991), 'Leadership, Management and Change in the Professional Service Firm', *Business Quarterly* (Spring).

HULL, R. (2000), 'Knowledge Management and the Conduct of Expert Labour', in C. Pritchard *et al.* (eds.), *Managing Knowledge* (Basingstoke: Macmillan).

JACKALL, R. (1988), *Moral Mazes* (New York: Oxford University Press).
JAMOUS, H., and PELOILLE, B. (1970), 'Professions or Self-Perpetuating Systems? Changes in the French University-Hospital System', in J. Jackson (ed.), *Professions and Professionals* (Cambridge: Cambridge University Press).
JONES, C., HESTERLY, W., FLADMOE-LINDQVIST, K., and BORGATTI, S. (1998), 'Professional Service Firm Constellations: How Strategies and Capabilities Influence Collaborative Stability and Change', *Organization Science*, 3: 396–410.
Journal of Management Studies, 30/6 (1993).
KANTER, R. M. (1977), *Men and Women of the Corporation* (New York: Basic Books).
—— (1983), *The Change Masters* (New York: Simon & Schuster).
KÄRREMAN, D., and ALVESSON, M. (2004) 'Cages in Tandem: Management Control, Social Identity, and Identification in a Knowledge-Intensive Firm', *Organization*, 11/1: 149–75.
—— SVENINGSSON, S., and ALVESSON, M. (2002), 'The Return of the Machine Bureaucracy? Management Control and Knowledge Work', *International Studies of Management and Organizations*, 32/2: 70–92.
KNIGHTS, D., and MORGAN, G. (1991), 'Corporate Strategy, Organizations and Subjectivity: A Critique and Illustration from the Financial Service Industries', *Organization Studies*, 12: 251–73.
—— and WILLMOTT, H. (1989), 'Power and Subjectivity at Work', *Sociology*, 23/4: 535–58.
—— MURRAY, F., and WILLMOTT, H. (1993), 'Networking as Knowledge Work: A Study of Strategic Interorganizational Development in the Financial Services Industry', *Journal of Management Studies*, 30/6: 975–95.
KNORR-CETINA, K. (1994), 'Primitive Classification and Postmodernity: Towards a Notion of Fiction', *Theory, Culture & Society*, 11: 1–22.
KREINER, K., and MOURITSEN, J. (2003), 'Knowledge Management as Technology: Making Knowledge Manageable', in B. Czarniawska and G. Sevon (eds.), *The Northern Lights* (Malmö: Liber; Oslo: Abstrakt; Copenhagen: Copenhagen Business School Press).
—— and SCHULTZ, M. (1993), 'Informal Collaboration in R & D: The Formation of Networks across Organizations', *Organization Studies*, 14/2: 189–210.
KUHN, T. S. (1970), *The Structure of Scientific Revolutions*, (Chicago: University of Chicago Press).
KUNDA, G. (1992), *Engineering Culture: Control and Commitment in a High-Tech Corporation* (Philadelphia: Temple University Press).
LACHMAN, R., and ARANYA, N. (1986), 'Job Satisfaction and Turnover Intentions among Professionals in Different Work Settings', *Organization Studies*, 7: 279–93.

LANGER, S. (1957), *Philosophy in a New Key* (Cambridge, Mass.: Harvard University Press).

LASCH, C. (1978), *The Culture of Narcissism* (New York: Norton).

LEE, N., and HASSARD, J. (1999), 'Organization Unbound: Actor-Network Theory, Research Strategy and Institutional Flexibility', *Organization*, 6/3: 391–404.

LEGGE, K. (1999), 'Representing People at Work', *Organization*, 6/2: 247–64.

—— (2001), 'On Knowledge, Business Consultants and the Selling of TQM', in T. Clark and R. Fincham (eds.), *Critical Consulting* (London: Blackwell).

LEONARD, D., and SENSIPER, S. (1998), 'The Role of Tacit Knowledge in Group Innovation', *California Management Review*, 40/3: 112–32.

LEVITT, H. (1981), 'Marketing Intangible Products and Product Intangibles', *Harvard Business Review* (May–June): 94–102.

LINCOLN, J., and KALLEBERG, A. (1985), 'Work Organization and Workforce Commitment: A Study of Plants and Employees in the US and Japan', *American Sociological Review*. 50: 738–60.

LINDMARK, L. (ed.), (1990), *Kunskap som kritisk resurs* (Umeå: Umeå Universitet).

LØWENDAHL, B. (1997), *Strategic Management in Professional Service Firms* (Copenhagen: Copenhagen Business School Press).

McDERMOTT, R. (1999), 'Why Information Technology Inspired but Cannot Deliver Knowledge Management', *California Management Review*, 414: 103–17.

McGRATH, P. (2000), 'Knowledge-Intensive Firms: Configuration or Community?', Ph.D. thesis, University of Warwick.

McINERNEY, C., and LeFEVRE, D. (2000), 'Knowledge Managers: History and Challenges', in C. Pritchard *et al* (eds.), *Managing Knowledge* (Basingstoke: Macmillan).

McKINLAY, A. (2000), 'The Bearable Lightness of Control: Organizational Reflexivity and the Politics of Management', in C. Prichard *et al.* (eds.), *Managing Knowledge* (Basingstoke: Macmillan).

MAISTER, D. (1982), 'Balancing the Professional Service Firm', *Sloan Management Review* (Fall): 15–29.

—— (1993), *Managing the Professional Service Firm* (New York: Free Press).

MARTIN, J., and MEYERSON, D. (1988), 'Organizational Cultures and the Denial, Channeling and Acknowledgement of Ambiguity', in L. Pondy *et al.* (eds.), *Managing Ambiguity and Change* (New York: Wiley).

MEYER, J. W., and ROWAN, B. (1977), 'Institutionalized Organizations: Formal Structure as Myth and Ceremony', in M. Zey-Ferrell and M. Aiken (eds.), *Complex Organizations: Critical Perspectives* (Glenview, Ill.: Scott, Foreman).

MEYERSON, D. (1991), 'Normal Ambiguity? A Glimpse of an Occupational Culture', in P. Frost *et al.* (eds.), *Reframing Organizational Culture* (Newbury Park, Calif.: Sage).

MILES, R., *et al.* (1997), 'Organizing in the Knowledge Age: Anticipating the Cellular Form', *Academy of Management Executive*, 114: 7–19.

MINTZBERG, H. (1983), *Structure in Fives: Designing Effective Organizations* (Englewood Cliffs, NJ: Prentice-Hall).

—— (1990), 'The Design School Reconsidering the Basic Premises of Strategic Management', *Strategic Management Journal*, 11: 171–95.

—— and McHUGH, A. (1985), 'Strategy Formation in an Adhocracy', *Administrative Science Quarterly*, 30: 160–97.

—— and WATERS, J. (1985), 'Of Strategies, Deliberate and Emergent', *Strategic Management Journal*, 63: 257–72.

MITCHELL, T., REDIKER, K., and BEACH, L. R. (1986), 'Image Theory and Organizational Decision Making', in H. Sims and D. Gioia (eds.), *The Thinking Organization* (San Francisco: Jossey Bass).

MOLANDER, B. (1993), *Kunskap i handling* (Göteborg: Daidalos).

MORGAN, G. (1997), *Images of Organisation* (Thousand Oaks, Calif.: Sage).

MORRIS, T., and EMPSON, L. (1998), 'Organisation and Expertise: An Exploration of Knowledge Bases and the Management of Accounting and Consulting Firms', *Accounting, Organizations and Society*, 23/5–6: 609–24.

—— and MALHOTRA, N. (2002), 'Towards Managerialism: Analysing the Process of Change in Professional Service Organisations', Paper presented at the 4th Biennial Workshop on Professional Service Firms, Alberta, Aug.

MOZIER, P. (1992), *The Response of UK Auditing Firms to a Changing Environment*, Book presented at the Workshop on the Organization and Management of Professional Service Firms, University of Alberta, May.

NEWELL, S., ROBERTSON, M., SCARBROUGH, H., and SWAN, J. (2002), *Managing Knowledge Work* (London: Palgrave).

NEWTON, T. (1998), 'Theorizing Subjectivity in Organizations: The Failure of Foucauldian Studies', *Organization Studies*, 19: 415–47.

NONAKA, I. (1994), 'A Dynamic Theory of Organizational Knowledge Creation', *Organization Science*. 5: 14–37.

NORMANN, R. (1983), *Service Management* (Chichester: Wiley).

O'SHEA, J., and MADIGAN, C. (1998), *Dangerous Company: The Consulting Powerhouses and the Businesses They Save and Ruin* (London: Nicholas Brealey).

OUCHI, W. G. (1979), 'A Conceptual Framework for the Design of Organizational Control Mechanisms', *Management Science*, 25: 833–48.

OUCHI, W. G. (1980), 'Markets, Bureaucracies and Clans', *Administrative Science Quarterly*, 25: 129–41.

252   *References*

PARKER, M. (1992), 'Postmodern Organizations or Postmodern Organization Theory?', *Organization Studies*, 13: 1–17.

PERROW, C. (1979), *Organization Theory: A Critical Perspective*, 2nd edn. (Glenview, Ill.: Scott, Foreman).

PETERS, J. D., and ROTHENBUHLER, E. (1989), 'The Reality of Construction', in H. Simons (ed.), *Rhetoric in the Human Sciences* (London: Sage).

PFEFFER, J. (1981), *Power in Organizations* (Boston: Pitman).

—— (1994), *Competitive Advantage through People* (Boston: Harvard Business Press).

PODOLNY, J. (1993), 'Market Uncertainty and the Social Character of Economic Exchange', *Administrative Science Quarterly*, 39: 458–83.

POLANYI, M. (1975), 'Personal Knowledge', in M. Polanyi and H. Prosch (eds.), *Meaning* (Chicago: University of Chicago Press).

POULFELDT, F. (1999), 'Konsulentrollens anatomi', *Nordiske Organisasjons Studier*, 1/1: 25–48.

POWELL, W. W. (1998), 'Learning from Collaboration: Knowledge and Networks in the Biotechnology and Pharmaceutical Industries', *California Management Review*, 40/3: 228–40.

PRAHALAD, C. K., and HAMEL, G. (1990), 'The Core Competence of the Corporation', *Harvard Business Review* (May–June), 79–91.

QUINTAS, P., DEMAID, A., and MILLAR, J. (1996), 'Knowledge Management in Design and Innovation Networks', Paper presented at the Design Council Research Workshop, London.

RAMFELT, L. (1993), 'Näringspolitiska samverkansprojekt i organisationsteoretisk belysning', Ph.D. diss., Dept of Business Administration, Stockholm University.

RAMSAY, H. (1996), 'Managing Sceptically: A Critique of Organizational Fashion', in S. Clegg and G. Palmer (eds.), *The Politics of Management Knowledge* (London: Sage).

REED, M. (1996), 'Expert Power and Control in Late Modernity: An Empirical Review and Theoretical Synthesis', *Organization Studies*, 17/4: 573–97.

RITZER, G. (1996), *The McDonaldization of Society* (Thousand Oaks, Calif.: Sage).

ROBERTSON, M. (1999), 'Sustaining Knowledge Creation within Knowledge-Intensive Firms', diss., Warwick Business School.

—— and SWAN, J. (1998), 'Modes of Organizing in an Expert Consultancy: A Case Study of Knowledge', *Organization*, 5/4: 543–64.

ROBERTSON, M., SCARBROUGH, H., and SWAN, J. (2003), 'Knowledge Creation in Professional Service Firm: Institutional Effects', *Organization Studies*, 24/6: 831–57.

RORTY, R. (1989), *Contingency, Irony and Solidarity* (Cambridge: Cambridge University Press).

—— (1992), 'Cosmopolitanism without Emancipation: A Response to Lyotard', in. S. Lash and J. Friedman (eds.), *Modernity & Identity* (Oxford: Blackwell).

RUGGLES, R. (1998), 'The State of the Notion: Knowledge Management in Practice', *California Management Review*, 40/3: 80–8.

SALANCIK, G. R., and PFEFFER, J. (1978), 'A Social Information Processing Approach to Job Attitudes and Task Design', *Administrative Science Quarterly*, 23: 224–53.

SANDBERG, J. (1994), *Human Competence at Work* (Gothenburg: BAS).

SARVARY, M. (1999), 'Knowledge Management and Competition in the Consulting Industry', *California Management Review*, 41/2: 95–107.

SCARBROUGH, H. (1995), 'Blackboxes, Hostages and Prisoners', *Organization Studies*, 16: 991–1020.

—— (1998), 'Path(ological) Dependency? Core Competence from an Organizational Perspective', *British Journal of Management*, 9: 219–32.

—— and BURRELL, G. (1996), 'The Axeman Cometh: The Changing Roles and Knowledges of Middle Managers', in S. Clegg and G. Palmer (eds.), *The Politics of Management Knowledge* (London: Sage).

—— and SWAN, J. (2001), 'Explaining the Diffusion of Knowledge Management', *British Journal of Management*, 12: 3–12.

SCOTT, W. R. (1987), 'The Adolescence of Institutional Theory', *Administrative Science Quarterly*, 32: 493–511.

—— (1995), *Institutions and Organizations* (Thousand Oaks, Calif.: Sage).

SELANDER, S. (ed.) (1989), *Kampen om yrkesutövning, status och kunskap* (Lund: Studentlitteratur).

SELZNICK, P. (1957), *Leadership in Administration: A Sociological Interpretation* (New York: Harper & Row).

SENNETT, R. (1998), *The Corrosion of Character* (New York: Norton).

SHARMA, A. (1997), 'Professional as Agent: Knowledge Asymmetry in Agency Exchange', *Academy of Management Review*, 22: 758–98.

SPENDER, J.-C. (1996), 'Workplace Knowledge as a Competitive Target', in A. Malm (ed.), *Does Management Matter?* (Lund: Lund University Press).

STARBUCK, W. (1992), 'Learning by Knowledge-Intensive Firms', *Journal of Management Studies*, 29/6: 713–40.

STARBUCK, W. (1993), 'Keeping a Butterfly and an Elephant in a House of Cards: The Elements of Exceptional Success', *Journal of Management Studies*, 30/6: 885–921.

STEIER, F. (ed.) (1991), *Research and Reflexivity* (London: Sage).

STOREY, J., and QUINTAS, P. (2001), 'Knowledge Management and HRM', in J. Storey (ed.), *Human Resource Management* (London: Thomson).

STURDY, A. (1997), 'The Consultancy Process: An Insecure Business', *Journal of Management Studies*, 34/3: 389–414.

SUDDABY, R., and GREENWOOD, R. (2001), 'Colonizing Knowledge: Com-modification as a Dynamic of Jurisdictional Expansion in Professional Service Firms', *Human Relations*, 54/7: 933–53.

SVEIBY, K.-E., and RISLING, A. (1986), *Kunskapsföretaget* (Malmö: Liber).

SVENINGSSON, S. (1999), *Strategisk förändring, makt och kunskap* (Lund: Lund University Press).

SVENSSON, L. (1990), 'Knowledge as a Professional Resource: Case Stud-ies of Architects and Psychologists at Work', in R. Torstendahl and M. Burrage (eds.), *The Formation of Professions* (London: Sage).

SVENSSON, P. (2004) *Setting the Marketing Scene. Reality Production in Everyday Marketing Work*. Ph.D. Diss., Dept. of Business Administra-tion, Lund University.

SWAN, J., NEWELL, S., SCARBROUGH, H., and HISLOP, D. (1999), 'Know-ledge Management and Innovation: Networks and Networking', *Jour-nal of Knowledge Management*, 3/4: 262–75.

—— BRESNEN, M., and ROBERTSON, M. (2001), 'Professional Networks and the Fashionization of Knowledge Management', *EGOS Colloquium* (Lyons).

SWIDLER, A. (1986), 'Culture in Action: Symbols and Strategies', *American Sociological Review*, 51: 273–86.

TEECE, D. (1998), 'Capturing Value from Knowledge Assets: The New Economy, Markets for Know-how, and Intangible Assets', *California Management Review*, 40/3: 55–79.

THOMPSON, P., WARHURST, C., and CALLAGHAN, G. (2001), 'Ignorant Theory and Knowledgeable Workers: Interrogating the Connections between Knowledge Skills and Services', *Journal of Management Studies*, 38/7: 923–42.

TORSTENDAHL, R. (1989), 'Professionalism, stat och kunskapsbas. Förut-sättningar för en teooribildning', in S. Selander (ed.), *Kampen om yrke-sutövning, status och kunskap* (Lund: Studentlitteratur).

TOWNLEY, B. (1994), *Reframing Human Resource Management* (London: Sage).

TREVELYAN, R. (2001), 'The Paradox of Autonomy: A Case of Academic Research Scientists', *Human Relations*, 54: 495–525.

TSOUKAS, H., and VLADIMIROU, E. (2001), 'What is Organizational Know-ledge?', *Journal of Management Studies*, 38/7: 973–93.

TURNER, J. (1982), 'Towards a Cognitive Redefinition of the Social Group', in H. Tajfel (ed.), *Social Identity and Intergroup Relations* (Cam-bridge: Cambridge University Press).

—— (1984), 'Social Identification and Psychological Group Formation', in H. Tajfel (ed.), *The Social Dimension* (Cambridge: Cambridge Univer-sity Press).

VAN MAANEN, J., and KUNDA, G. (1989), 'Real Feelings: Emotional Ex-pression and Organizational Culture', in B. M. Staw and L. L. Cummings (eds.), *Research in Organizational Behaviour* (Greenwich, Conn.: JAI Press).

VON KROGH, G. (1998), 'Care in Knowledge Creation', *California Management Review*, 40/3: 133–52.

WALLACE, J. (1995), 'Organizational and Professional Commitment in Professional and Nonprofessional Organizations', *Administrative Science Quarterly*, 40: 228–55.

WALLANDER, J. (2002), *Med den mänskliga naturen—inte emot!* (Stockholm: SNS).

WATSON, T. (1995), 'Rhetoric, Discourse and Argument in Organizational Sense Making: A Reflexive Tale', *Organization Studies*, 16: 805–21.

WERR, A., and STJERNBERG, T. (2003), 'Exploring Management Consulting Firms as Knowledge Systems', *Organization Studies*, 24/6: 881–908.

—— —— and DOCHERTY, P. (1997), 'The Functions of Methods of Change in Management Consulting', *Journal of Organizational Change Management*, 10/4: 288–307.

WHITTINGTON, R. (2002), *What is Strategy—and Does it Matter?*, 2nd edn. (London: Routledge).

WIKSTRÖM, S., NORMANN, R., *et al.* (1993), *Knowledge and Value* (London: Routledge).

WILKINS, A., and OUCHI, W. (1983), 'Efficient Cultures: Exploring the Relationship between Culture and Organizational Performance', *Administrative Science Quarterly*, 28: 468–81.

WINROTH, K. (1999), *När management kom till advokatbyrån*, diss., Dept. of Business Administration, Gothenburg University.

YAKHLEF, A., and SALZER-MÖRLING, M. (2000), 'Intellectual Capital: Managing by Numbers', in C. Prichard *et al.* (eds.), *Managing Knowledge* (Basingstoke: Macmillan).

YUKL, G. (1989), 'Managerial Leadership: A Review of Theory and Research', *Journal of Management*, 15: 215–89.

Index